Praise

The Big Mo pulls together lots of strands of varied thinking from many fields. It will make people think and reflect.

Paul Marsh, Emeritus Professor of Finance,
London Business School

Speed and size define the events of our age. As news travels ever faster, its impact increases. The strength of [Roeder's] book is the idea that momentum's effects can be felt right across society, including in the media, where 15 minutes of fame is possible on a scale unimaginable a decade ago.

Steven Matcham, *The Australian Review of Books*

Mark Roeder has produced a fascinating history of the concept of momentum, and a clear explanation of the role it has played in producing the recent global financial crisis. *The Big Mo* is a unique history and analysis of a force which drives a great deal of human behavior. The author's command of his material, infused with an inspiring, enlightening theme, is an entirely fresh approach to the human science of economics.

David Hale, Global Economist, Chicago USA

Roeder's book is a revelation. In our personal, political and economic lives we seem to be swept along by circumstances. Our attempts to change direction are doomed. *The Big Mo* explains why. It is a fascinating read.

Phillip Adams, broadcaster, writer and film producer

We all talk about the 'pace' we now work at . . . how everything seems to happen instantly. *The Big Mo* helps explain this phenomenon and provides thoughtful insights into how the power of momentum can both help and hinder modern business and social structures.

Kim McKay, AO, National Geographic Consultant and
founder of UN sponsored Clean Up the World program

Momentum is like the air around us. Everybody can feel its effects, the good, the ridiculous and the catastrophic. Almost nobody understands it. Mark Roeder does. In quiet, thoughtful prose at times reminiscent of Thomas Merton, he makes it starkly clear why it can never be 'business as usual' if we are to address the grave threat posed by the 'Big Mo' in all its guises. This book is a brilliant wake-up call.

Joe Bageant, author of *Deer Hunting with Jesus*
and American social commentator

Mark Roeder is an author, cultural commentator and corporate executive. He was global head of advertising at UBS, one of the largest banks in the world, and previously held senior positions at Zurich Financial Services and Westpac Banking Group. He has lived and worked in New York, London, Sydney and Zurich.

The Big Mo

Why Momentum
Now Rules Our World

Mark Roeder

2 4 6 8 10 9 7 5 3 1

Published in 2011 by Virgin Books, an imprint of Ebury Publishing
A Random House Group Company

First published in Australia by ABC Books in 2010

The Random House Group Limited Reg. No. 954009

Addresses for companies within the Random House Group can be found at
www.randomhouse.co.uk

A CIP catalogue record for this book is available from the British Library

The Random House Group Limited supports The Forest Stewardship Council [FSC],
the leading international forest certification organisation. All our titles that are
printed on Greenpeace-approved FSC-certified paper carry the FSC logo.
Our paper procurement policy can be found at www.rbooks.co.uk/environment

Typeset by Palimpsest Book Production Limited, Falkirk, Stirlingshire
Printed in the UK by Mackays

ISBN 9780753539378

To buy books by your favourite authors and register for offers visit
www.rbooks.co.uk

For Orlando

CONTENTS

CONTENTS

Introduction:
A Mystery

In February 2008, about a year before the global financial crisis reached its peak, some intriguing research was published by three London Business School academics: Elroy Dimson, Paul Marsh and Mike Staunton.[1] They were trying to understand why share prices tended to continue in the same direction and why, in the short run, you could make money simply by backing winners and selling losers. This should not happen according to the 'efficient markets' theory, which says that in a highly competitive environment like the stock market, there should be no easy formula for beating the market.

The researchers had reviewed the 1900 to 2007 stock prices in the UK, together with evidence from sixteen other countries, in what was the most exhaustive analysis of its kind. They soon discovered something quite odd. Once a stock gained positive traction (momentum) over a certain time period, it would continue to outperform well into the next time period. There was a similar pattern for negative momentum, or 'losers'. In other words, you could make money by trading on these momentum patterns. One of the researchers, Professor Paul Marsh confessed to being mystified by the findings. 'We remain puzzled and we are not the only ones; most academics are vaguely embarrassed by this.' The financial markets are not supposed to work this way. They are supposed to be self-correcting. They are certainly not supposed to be so heavily influenced by something as abstract as 'momentum'.

Another team of researchers, Eugene Fama and Ken French, the world's leading experts on stock returns, had earlier come to a similar conclusion: momentum seemed to have a disproportionate impact on the investment markets that could not be readily explained. They went as far as to describe the momentum phenomenon as the premier anomaly of the financial markets.[2]

Following the global financial crisis of 2008–9, there has been intensive post-mortem analysis of what went wrong. Why did the financial system spiral out of control to such an extent that it brought the global economy to the brink of collapse? Trillions of dollars* in value were wiped from the global stock markets, thousands of businesses failed, including major banks, property markets crashed and unemployment soared. It was the greatest financial upheaval since the Great Depression in the 1930s. Such were the scale and impact of the global financial crisis that it raised questions about the viability of the capitalist system which has underpinned the Western world for hundreds of years.

The most common explanation for this calamity is that it was another speculative bubble gone bust, albeit on a grand scale. This bubble was caused by the perennial forces of greed, ignorance and ambition, which were exacerbated in the debt-fuelled, deregulated environment of the twenty-first century. But was this crisis really so straightforward? Was it really, in essence, just another financial crisis like others before it?

It would be somewhat comforting to see it in these terms. Then we could ignore the clamour for reforms and go back to business as usual when things settled down, with only a few relatively painless adjustments to the financial system. The reality is, however, that the global financial crisis was far more mysterious than many would have us believe. Despite all the exhaustive analysis and commentary, there is still no consensus on why

*All references to dollars are to US dollars unless otherwise stated.

it happened in the first place or why it was so destabilising to the established order. Paul Krugman, the 2008 Nobel Laureate in Economics, wrote: 'This time, the market players seem truly horrified because they've suddenly realised that they don't understand the complex financial system they have created.'[3] Moreover, we have little understanding of what drove this complex financial system off the cliff.

But we do have an important clue. With their research on momentum, the three London Business School academics may have stumbled upon something that could help unlock the mystery. Their groundbreaking work suggests that momentum has a bigger influence on share prices than previously thought. But what if this influence extends beyond share prices? What if it also affects other aspects of the financial system in ways we are not aware of?

Before we delve into this possibility, however, let's reacquaint ourselves with what we know about momentum. Most of us would be aware that momentum has something to do with the power of a moving object. Some may recall that Sir Isaac Newton defined momentum as being the product of an object's mass times its velocity. The bigger the mass and the faster it is moving, the more momentum is generated. But the momentum concept is not confined to physics; it is also relevant to other aspects of our world. The world of competitive sports, for example, has long recognised the impact momentum can have on performance and refers to this phenomenon as 'the Big Mo'. Every football or basketball player knows what a positive difference momentum can make to the outcome of a game. Similarly, in the fields of business, politics, science and the arts, we tend to think of momentum as being a 'good' thing, a constructive force that can work for us.

There are many indicators, however, that the influence of momentum in our world has not only grown exponentially in recent years, but that its influence is not always for the better. The rapid and unprecedented integration of technology, media, communications and markets has greatly accelerated and magnified the impact of events. Things tend to happen faster, with bigger consequences. We saw recently how a deterioration in one part of the US housing market reverberated throughout the global financial system with devastating results. We also know that, given our highly interconnected global transport system, it would be impossible to quarantine a rapidly spreading lethal flu virus or avoid the kind of mass disruption caused by Iceland's Eyjafjallajökull volcano in 2010. And when a major Internet service provider breaks down, entire regions of the world experience a communications blackout. 'We don't understand how interconnected we are until we can't do it any more,' observed Peter Westaway, chief economist for Europe at the Nomura investment bank.[4] Our world has never been more interconnected and interdependent.

In terms of Newtonian physics, we are dealing with bigger issues (mass) moving at greater speed (velocity), which generates more momentum. As our globalised world becomes more efficient and automated, there is less 'friction' to slow this momentum, particularly in highly deregulated, freewheeling industries such as financial services. We are far more likely to be swept up in forces that propel us forward in a particular direction, like leaves in a fast-flowing stream heading for a waterfall.

I was one of those leaves. As a senior executive of one of the world's largest banks, the Swiss-based UBS,* I experienced the exhilaration of being swept up in the market euphoria that preceded the crash, followed by the sudden freefall as the financial world imploded. I was not alone. All around me the best and brightest of my colleagues had succumbed to the thrills of going with the flow. UBS was, up until this time, the largest private bank in the world and the tenth-largest company.[5] Nearly one-third of the world's billionaires were its customers, and it

---

*UBS was formed by the merger of the Union Bank of Switzerland and the Swiss Bank Corporation and is now known as UBS.

managed nearly $3 trillion of clients' money, which is about the same amount as the US government's annual budget. Yet, within a period of just eighteen months, it lost $50 billion, was bailed out by the Swiss government and almost brought the revered Swiss banking system to its knees.

Of course, UBS was not the only big bank to be devastated by the crisis, but its story is perhaps the most instructive. For UBS, like most Swiss financial institutions, was regarded as financially astute and conservative. It had highly sophisticated systems to manage risks; brilliant, experienced executives; and enormous global resources. It epitomised the power and presumed stability of the global banking system.

Like many people directly caught up in the global financial crisis I was shocked and curious as to why it happened in the first place. One of my jobs at UBS was to help develop a communications strategy to explain what was going on to the bank's clients and stakeholders and to hopefully reassure them. But this was difficult do without first understanding what had caused the crisis. Although I had worked at a senior level in big banks and financial companies for many years in various countries and had experienced a number of booms and busts, I sensed, like many of my colleagues, that there was something different about this crisis. And not just in terms of its sheer scale. I read countless reports about what had gone wrong and why the banks had failed so spectacularly, particularly my own. Most of what I read made sense, yet I felt there was something missing.

Then I read the report by the three London Business School researchers about the strange impact of 'momentum' on financial markets, and the jigsaw pieces started to form a picture. I started to see that momentum was not only more influential than I had realised, but that this influence might actually be negative, rather than positive. Although, like my peers, I had been conditioned to believe that the crisis was the result of a 'subprime-induced exponential credit bubble' or a 'stochastic volatility implosion' or some such highly technical explanation, I began to suspect that something as simple as momentum could explain the most complex financial crisis on record. I grappled with this thought for some time because it ran so counter to the prevailing view.

Then I recalled a meeting I had attended some years earlier, with some bankers and high-powered business consultants to discuss a corporate restructure. At one point the lead consultant uttered a string of phrases of such magnificent prolixity that the whole room fell silent in awe of this woman's obvious mastery of the subject matter. I felt out of my depth. During the coffee break, I asked her for further clarification of what she meant. She said, 'Nothing really. I was just stalling for time until I could think of something meaningful to say.' She then added, 'You see, you financial guys feed on complexity. If we give you a simple solution, you don't trust it.'

The recollection of her words was a revelation to me. Although they were uttered half in jest, they revealed one of the great unspoken truths of the financial world. That is, it really does prefer complexity to simplicity, not only because it offers more intellectual stimulation for its high-priced executives, but because banks can charge more for complex, sophisticated products. I decided then that I would explore this seemingly simple concept of momentum in more depth. I set about it by interviewing people who were in a position to experience the momentum effect first-hand. I also spoke with people outside the financial industry whose work brought them in touch with the phenomenon. The interviews were conducted in England, the United States, Australia and Switzerland, and supported by extensive follow-up research.

It soon became apparent to me that the influence of momentum has not only grown in recent years but that it extends beyond the financial markets and affects many other dimensions of our lives, such as the media, climate change, war, religion and business. It also became clear just how little we really know about momentum, and particularly its 'dark side', which can influence human behaviour in negative ways that cannot be explained by traditional concepts like the 'herd mentality' or 'group dynamics'. This influence is likely to increase as our world becomes more efficient and automated, because there is less 'friction' to slow the momentum.

Paradoxically, in this new environment, a large, integrated organisation can be just as vulnerable to negative momentum as a weaker one, perhaps even more so. This is because momentum feeds on an organisation's internal efficiency and integration to accelerate and magnify its power, until it pushes it beyond a state of equilibrium. Consider how it was the biggest, most sophisticated banks that were most affected by the global financial crisis rather than the smaller regional banks that had not updated their computer systems for years.

More broadly, the influence of momentum is exacerbated by the modern media, which create a perceptual environment in which the world around us seems to be moving faster and in which every news story is a big story. We become conditioned to see the world as a series of rapidly escalating events, which we experience voyeuristically and vicariously. The sheer volume of information we are exposed to encourages us to 'skim' the surface of the media in order to cope with so much data from so many sources. But by dwelling in the shallows of the Information Age, we are devolving into what the playwright Richard Foreman calls 'pancake people' – individuals who spread their attention wide and thin – at hyper-link speed.

Moreover, this obsession with speed and efficiency is undermining our capacity as a civilisation to reflect on, and confront, the more pressing issues of our time. It blinds us to the true nature of the problems we face. For example, we have just been through the second-worst financial crisis in the history of the world, yet in its aftermath there has been no significant overhaul of the way the global financial system works. Some countries, such as the US, have made progress, but the key global problems remain. Speculative capital flows just as freely and rapidly between markets. Trading in derivatives and other potentially explosive assets continues largely unabated. Stock markets remain vulnerable to high-frequency computer-driven trading programs. Bank executives are still encouraged to take excessive risks through extremely generous bonus payments that bear little relation to their company's long-term performance, let alone their contribution to society. The system is still dominated by – and dependent on – a handful of financial institutions that are so big they represent an unacceptable 'systemic risk' – in other words, they're too big to fail. In fact, the banking oligopoly is even more concentrated now than it was before the crash, following shotgun takeovers like Bank of America's acquisition of Merrill Lynch, Wells Fargo's takeover of Wachovia and the JPMorgan Chase purchase of Bear Stearns, to name just a few. Moreover, the financial industry is still too large relative to the rest of the economy, particularly in advanced countries like the US and the UK. And the global regulatory environment continues to resemble a global 'lubrication' system, with no braking capacity. It is as if the debacle that brought the world economy to its knees never happened.

Such inaction, in the face of a threat of this magnitude, demonstrates how far we have devolved into a momentum-driven society, a society that worships speed and efficiency above all else and would prefer to keep moving forward – no matter in which direction.

Momentum is the new zeitgeist.

The aim of this book is to put this mysterious and powerful phenomenon under the microscope. I want to show you how easy it is for individuals and organisations to become swept up in momentum, to surrender to the flow, often with devastating consequences. In the process, I will challenge some widely held assumptions that underpin our understanding of how the world works. The book shakes up the kaleidoscope a little. Although I often focus on the global financial system, this is not a 'finance' or 'economics' book in the traditional sense. Rather, the financial system is used as a metaphor for the kind of world we are building – that is, a lightning fast, highly interconnected one that is increasingly propelled by its own dynamic. More broadly, I have drawn on numerous disciplines such as sociology, technology, politics, physics, philosophy and the media, to illustrate how momentum influences our world. For, as we shall see, Big Mo has many faces. It should be stressed, however, that the book does not attempt to create a 'unified theory' for social behaviour, nor is it being suggested that momentum is the only factor involved. Rather, my intention is to highlight a particular phenomenon that has become more predominant in our world today, often with far-reaching consequences, as demonstrated by the recent global financial crisis. The concept provides a prism through which we can better understand the dynamics that are reshaping our world and how various societal forces interact with each other.

The book comprises four main sections. Part 1: 'The Flow' explores the history of the momentum concept from its discovery over a thousand years ago, and why it has recently become such a powerful force in our world. It highlights examples from the global banking system, where a 'surrender to the flow' ethos brought the system to its knees. Part 2: 'Behavioural Momentum' looks at why momentum exerts such a powerful influence over people and organisations and the consequences that result from it. Part 3: 'The Faces of Big Mo' explores some of the many ways in which momentum manifests in our world, ranging from 'Corporate Mo' to 'Techno Mo' to 'Geopolitical Mo'. Part 4: 'Changing Lanes' looks at some practical steps we can take to avoid or minimise the negative impact of momentum and perhaps even harness its power for more constructive purposes.

I hope this book will be of interest to anyone who is curious about the dynamics that now drive and shape our society in the early twenty-first century. It is really an invitation to step out of the fast-flowing stream for a while, sit on the riverbank and contemplate the consequences of surrendering to the flow.

Part 1

The Flow

Chapter 1

The Thrills and Perils of the Flow

The global headquarters of UBS, the largest private bank in the world, is not an imposing building. It is just five storeys high and blends in unobtrusively with the other low-key buildings that line Bahnhofstrasse, the main boulevard of Zurich, Switzerland. At street level, elegantly dressed shoppers stroll in and out of the exclusive boutiques toting bags embossed with names like Cartier, Chanel, Ermenegildo Zegna and Hugo Boss. They provide a sharp contrast to the dark-suited bankers who walk purposefully between meetings while glancing at their BlackBerrys and fine watches. The whole effect is one of quiet, understated wealth. It is very Swiss.

Behind this reassuring façade, however, an altogether different scenario was unfolding during the first half of 2007. Some senior executives at UBS were becoming concerned about a segment of the US housing market that was deteriorating rapidly. Increasingly large numbers of Americans with low incomes were defaulting on their home loans. It had been assumed that this low end of the housing market, or 'subprime' as it is known, would be quarantined and not affect the wider financial markets.

Peter Wuffli, the CEO of UBS, certainly hoped that this was the case. Despite his low-key, cerebral demeanour, he had led an aggressive strategy to penetrate the lucrative US market and become the first foreign bank to break into the elite 'bulge bracket' of US superbanks that have dominated Wall Street for decades. Integral to this strategy was the use of mortgage-backed securities and sophisticated financial instruments called 'derivatives', which offered the potential for high returns for the bank and its customers. A large proportion of these derivatives were tied to the deteriorating subprime markets. More troubling for Wuffli was the fact that no one within UBS seemed to know the bank's level of exposure to these markets. The deals were so complex they were difficult to calculate.

One thing was clear though: UBS had gone into the subprime markets harder and faster than anyone else. Between 2004 and the first quarter of 2007, its aggressive push into these markets had helped increase UBS's balance sheet by 41 per cent to $2.2 trillion, which was about 2.5 times the size of Goldman Sachs or Merrill Lynch. The investment-banking division of UBS had grown particularly quickly and now processed one out of every seven stocks traded in the world.[1] The gleaming new UBS trading floor in Stamford, Connecticut, was the size of two American football fields and exemplified UBS's meteoric rise. It seemed UBS was on the brink of achieving its long-sought-after status as 'bulge bracket' player in the United States.

Then the financial world turned upside down. In mid-2007 the subprime markets collapsed and the global financial system went into meltdown. Over the next year, UBS lost almost $50 billion, its share price fell by 75 per cent, and Peter Wuffli and a host of UBS executives were forced to resign, including the bank's revered chairman, Marcel Ospel, the most powerful businessman in Switzerland. Of all the world's megabanks UBS was one of the hardest hit. Hans Jurgen Schmolke, managing director of Metrinomics, a company that tracks customer perceptions of financial organisations, made the observation to me that, particularly in Europe, 'UBS has been the face of the crisis, largely because it fell from such a great height.'[2]

In retrospect, it is puzzling that despite some serious warning signs about the dangers of the subprime markets some years earlier, UBS had continued to push forward with its aggressive strategies. When one of the bank's most respected economists, Dr Klaus Wellershoff, raised concerns about the growing instability of the US real-estate markets in October 2005, his warnings fell on deaf ears.[3] Even after the subprime markets collapsed in mid-2007 and the writing was on the wall, UBS still maintained large positions. When asked to explain the reasons for the debacle, Marcel Rohner, who succeeded Peter Wuffli as CEO, said that UBS had been afflicted by a 'me-too strategy' designed to 'close gaps with our competitors'.[4] In other words, because the rest of the market had been moving in a certain direction, UBS had followed suit.

What causes intelligent, independently minded people to ignore their better judgement and support an idea or direction they know or suspect is wrong?

History is filled with stories about people who were swept along by the events of their day and paid the price in blood or treasure. Since the earliest days of the Phoenician traders in around 1000 BC, there have been periodic market upheavals, from the Dutch tulip-bulb collapse of the 1600s to the South Sea Bubble of 1720 – in which Sir Isaac Newton himself lost money – to the 1929 stock-market crash, and the more recent collapses of 1987 and the bursting of the 'dot.com' bubble in 2001. The tendency of markets to behave erratically has been well documented in books such as *Extraordinary Delusions and the Madness of Crowds*, written by Charles Mackay in the nineteenth century, and more recently by Charles Kindleberger in his classic book *Manias, Panics and Crashes*. In all these cases, one of the prime suspects for the bubble and subsequent crash has been what is known as 'herd behaviour', whereby people blindly and irrationally follow those around them and work themselves up into a frenzied panic.

But what we saw recently with the global financial crisis was something quite different. It was hardly the frenzied and chaotic situation that preceded previous crashes. There was no great stampeding herd running amok. Certainly the subprime real-estate market in the United States was overheated, but overall the global financial system appeared to be humming along quite nicely, albeit at a high velocity. Even the International Monetary Fund, right up until the eve of the crash, predicted rosy economic conditions for 2007 and 2008.[5] Everything appeared to be quite in order.

Also, unlike previous collapses, it is hard to point to a particular stimulus, or metaphorical 'gunshot', that would have prompted the herd to move en masse and accelerate. There was no significant event – no regulatory change, no shortage, no sudden geopolitical upheaval – of the kind that played a role in triggering previous events. Rather, what happened was a gradual build-up of pace, and an alignment of forces, which gathered steam over time and began to permeate large banks such as UBS and eventually the entire financial system. It was a drawn-out, incremental process.

There was also little of the fear factor that one normally associates with herd-like behaviour. Most UBS executives with whom I worked were thoroughly enjoying the ride, especially around bonus time, when the expensive bars near our office in London's Broadgate Circle filled to overflowing. Every so often, towards the end of a long evening, you would hear mutterings about the sustainability of the boom, but these concerns would dissipate with the next round of drinks and be forgotten by the following morning. Such is the selective nature of banker's amnesia.

The most important difference, however, between the recent financial crisis and previous ones has to do with a subtle change in the perception of accountability. With previous crises there was a sense that they were caused primarily by people's behaviour – whether spurred on by greed, fear, panic or the herding tendency. This time there was an eerie feeling that the crash was somehow caused by the financial system itself, and that the 'herd' was no longer driving things. As one equities trader at a major investment bank in London told me, 'The financial system has become so complex and technologically sophisticated that it runs itself now. We are just along for the ride. It's like in the film

2001 Space Odyssey when HAL [the spaceship's onboard computer] takes over and starts calling the shots. You have no choice but to go with it.'[6] This scenario is not as far-fetched as it seems. Up to 60 per cent of all trading in the stock market is now driven by computer programs based on complex algorithms that automatically decide when and how much to trade in response to market data. Such programs were blamed for the biggest single drop in the history of the Dow Jones index, when, on 6 May 2010, it fell by almost 1,000 points in a matter of minutes – wiping out almost $1 trillion in equity values – before bouncing back. At the time no-one could explain what had happened. It was a trillion-dollar mystery. Robert L D Colby, former deputy director of trading and markets at the Securities Exchange Commission, lamented, 'This is the sort of situation that has been a worry for a long time, but the markets have changed in a way that has made things more difficult.'[7]

In other words, it seems that the global financial system has reached a historic inflection point where the influence of human behaviour has become less important than the workings of the machine itself. This should not be surprising. All complex man-made systems tend to eventually reach this point. The first inklings of this transformation occurred during the 1987 stock-market crash when many observers blamed computer-based trading programs for exacerbating the scale of the crisis. But the market in those days was relatively primitive compared to the ultra-hi-tech, fully integrated financial system that we have today. It would be like comparing a 1980s car to a modern one.

In fact, the automobile provides us with a useful analogy to understand this evolution. Up until a few decades ago it was still possible to tinker around with your car and change the way it operates. You could be your own mechanic and have a direct influence over how it ran. You were in charge of the system. But these days cars are so technically complex, integrated and auto-mated that their inner workings are like a black box and deeply mysterious. They can also be more unpredictable, as evidenced by a recent spate of incidents in the United States where some hi-tech Toyota cars have appeared to accelerate of their own accord and caused crashes.

The point is that as a system becomes more complex, hi-tech and interdependent, as the global financial system has in recent years, it begins to be driven more by its own internal dynamics rather than by external factors. And as we shall see, one of the most important of these dynamics is momentum.

The combination of a gradual build-up and a feeling of buoyancy that we saw in the lead-up to the financial crisis is highly indicative of how momentum works. It emerges stealthily rather than arriving suddenly. It creeps up and envelops us, and we are often not aware of it until it has already made an impact. Momentum often feels good, at least in the initial phases. It is seductive. There is a feeling of moving forward, of getting somewhere. It can be thrilling to go with the flow.

Momentum is also experienced in different ways in different circumstances. Often, it can feel like being on a river journey, which starts off flowing gently past sloping riverbanks. But with each bend in the river the current moves more swiftly, until you find yourself clinging tightly to the boat as it lunges back and forth over swirling rapids, racing towards the falls ahead.

It is the gradual onset and immersive quality of momentum that make it so difficult to detect and guard against. You may be barely aware that you are being drawn into a situation, a venture, a relationship or a particular course of action. Initially, it may feel like the right thing to do for whatever reason. You feel comfortable about the direction and so let yourself become more committed to it. After a while, however, you notice that it may not be so easy to change course or exit the journey. You are no longer puttering along on a scooter; you are now on a long-haul flight with your seatbelt tightly fastened. Only after the directional momentum is firmly set do you become aware that something is not quite right. And when you get an inkling of trouble, you'll probably repress your concerns or deny them. Before long, though, the evidence mounts and it becomes clear that the danger is real and imminent.

At this point, you have a stark choice: do everything possible to avert the danger by changing course and cutting your losses or ignore the dangers and press on. A rational person would be expected to choose the first option and do everything possible to escape the situation or reduce its impact. But momentum makes this more difficult than it seems. The nature of momentum is that it tends to galvanise a range of forces towards a particular direction and generate a powerful self-reinforcing mechanism which resists interference, even from within. It was a lesson that the equities trader in London and his colleagues found out the hard way.

Momentum is hardly a new concept. It was first recognised and documented over a thousand years ago by an Islamic scholar named Ibn Sina, who was also known by his Latinised name Avicenna (c. AD 980–1037). Ibn Sina was one of the great intellects of Islam's golden age, which flourished from about 800 to 1100 and which was dominated by the spirit of reason and enquiry. This era also gave rise to classic literature, such as *The Thousand and One Nights* (i.e. *The Arabian Nights*), *The Tales of Aladdin*, *Ali Baba* and *Sindbad the Sailor*, which went on to become part of global folklore.[8] Like many scholars of the time, Ibn Sina was a polymath, or hakim, a man of such vast learning that he was conversant with numerous disciplines and master of many. He was a physician, philosopher, astronomer, chemist, geologist, logician, palaeontologist, mathematician, physicist, poet, psychologist, scientist and teacher. Indeed, Ibn Sina, who was a scholar with a prodigious output – he wrote almost 450 treatises on a wide range of subjects – was one of the main interpreters of Aristotle; revolutionised many scientific methods, and created a comprehensive medical encyclopaedia, *The Canon of Medicine*, which continued to be used as a standard text at the universities of Montpellier and Louvain as late as 1650.

Remarkably, while juggling all these roles, Ibn Sina was also able to develop an elaborate theory on motion, in which he referred to a force called 'impetus' or *mayl*. He determined that this force was proportional to a body's weight and velocity and that such a moving body would eventually be slowed down by the air resistance around it (which was consistent with the theory of inertia). These groundbreaking insights provided the first theoretical basis for understanding the concept of momentum, and established Ibn Sina as the 'father' of momentum theory. His work would pave the way for generations of other scientists, such as Galileo and René Descartes, who would develop their own theories about momentum.

Newton's gift

It wasn't really until the seventeenth century, however, that the idea of momentum began to seep into the public consciousness. This was when Sir Isaac Newton developed a way of explaining the concept that could be readily understood by a more general audience. In his classic work *Philosophiae Naturalis Principia Mathematica* in 1687 he defined *quantitas motus* (momentum) as 'arising from the velocity and quantity of matter conjointly', which is neatly expressed in the formula we know today: momentum = mass × velocity. Newton's laws of motion clearly articulated important aspects of how the physical universe works. The French mathematical physicist Alexis Clairant said that Newton's work 'marked the epoch of a great revolution in physics. The method followed by its illustrious author Mr Newton . . . spread the light of mathematics on a science which up to then had remained in the darkness of conjectures and hypotheses.'[9] In other words, Newton enabled physics to go mainstream.

The work of Newton and other early physicists prompted some philosophers to ponder whether the laws of physics could also be applied to human behaviour. This gave rise to the field of 'social physics', which seeks to understand how society works by relating it to our scientific knowledge of the wider universe. Social physics has a long and rich history, dating back to pioneers such as Thomas Hobbes and his bold attempt to construct a 'calculus of society', and social theorists such as Jeremy Bentham,

John Locke, Adam Smith, Auguste Comte and John Stuart Mill, all of whom applied some of the laws of the physical universe to better understand the forces that drive society.[10]

Social physics didn't simply make society more comprehensible; it also helped to shape it. Up until the seventeenth-century, Western society (and most other societies) was largely governed by rules which emanated from a religious, philosophical and political perspective. Science had no role to play in such matters. But the new physics encouraged people to see that their lives might also be influenced by concepts like 'cause and effect', 'trajectories' and 'impetus', rather than simply being at the mercy of God or the capricious whims of fate. In this more rational view of the world, people saw that they might be able to chart their own 'trajectory'. It may seem odd to us that people would need to be encouraged to take responsibility for their own destiny, but in those days people had a much more restrictive view of what they could do. They were more accepting of their 'place'. Social physics, and the ideas that flowed from it, began to shift this static view of society into one which more closely emulated the dynamic reality of the universe. Of course, social physics wasn't the only factor challenging the rigid social order at that time, but it was certainly influential and somewhat empowering to many people keen to get ahead.

By the nineteenth century, the influence of social physics extended to areas like economics, where its principles were applied by early economists such as Léon Walras and William Stanley to develop their theories. At the turn of the twentieth century, Irving Fisher, who was to become a great neoclassical economist, even wrote his doctoral thesis under the supervision of a physicist.

Social physics eventually fell out of favour for many years because sociologists began to believe, somewhat justifiably, that the scientific models available at the time were too limited to explain the complex, organic nature of society. They began to look towards the emerging disciplines of psychology, psychiatry, anthropology and the biological sciences (including genetics) to explain and predict human behaviour. Each new discipline spawned its own behavioural models, which exerted a growing influence on our perception of society and the policies that govern it. More recently, however, the rise of quantum theory has revived interest in the field of social physics by providing fresh perspectives on the physical laws and their application to everyday life. This renewed interest has been reflected in a number of popular books, such as *The Wisdom of Crowds* by James Surowiecki, *The Tipping Point* by Malcolm Gladwell, *Nudge* by Richard Thaler and Cass Sunstein, and *Critical Mass* by Philip Ball, all of which serve to remind us of how useful physical and organic concepts can be in helping us to understand human behaviour.[11] Philip Ball's *Critical Mass*, for example, shows how the movement of atomic particles provides insights into the way people behave en masse which can be applied to designing traffic-management systems and urban centres. Malcolm Gladwell's *The Tipping Point* draws on epidemiological studies and network theory to explain how ideas and behaviours spread like viruses. Such books highlight how much we can understand about human behaviour by observing the laws and concepts that govern the physical universe.

Newton's concept of momentum, in particular, provides a deceptively simple and constructive way to view group dynamics on a large scale. For in Newtonian terms, it could be argued that today we are dealing with increasingly weightier issues (mass) and a world that is moving at much greater speed (velocity), than at previous stages in history, which generates more momentum. We know, for instance, that just a minor increase in Earth's average temperature would displace millions of people, and a rapidly mutating lethal flu virus would spread through our interconnected transport system and cause mass devastation. And recently we saw how a slump in one part of the US housing market (i.e. the subprime market) eventually threatened the foundations of the global financial system. We have a lot of 'mass' to deal with.

Simultaneously, the 'velocity' factor has increased exponentially. The global integration of communications, technology, business, communities and economies has accelerated the speed at which events unfold. An action in one part of the global network resonates almost immediately throughout the entire network. Each part of the system is so interconnected and interdependent that actions are amplified by mutual reinforcement. For example, the world's major banks are now six times more interconnected than they were two decades ago. This creates a multiplier effect, which means that even relatively small actions can have large and unintended consequences. This applies not just to banks but to all large interconnected systems. Consider for a moment how the tiniest software flaw can disrupt an electricity grid. Or how, as mentioned earlier, a natural event such as the eruption by the Eyjafjallajökull volcano in Iceland in 2010 reverberated through the world's transport system and had a domino effect on many economies. Everything affects everything else.

This phenomenon is further magnified and accelerated by all-pervasive and instantaneous media that make the world more transparent and reactive to events. We expect to know more, and we expect to know it now. When an issue arises that attracts the attention of this integrated media network, it can quickly escalate into a major event and take on a life of its own, fuelled by its own momentum. Ominously, this self-generating media machine works most efficiently when it harmonises at a particular 'spin-rate', or storyline, which becomes the galvanising focal point. So when alternate or contradictory facts arise which challenge the original storyline, they tend to be ignored or re-interpreted to fit the narrative structure. This phenomenon helps explains why, for example, it took the mainstream media in the United States a number of years to seriously challenge the precepts used to justify the Second Iraq War and why it took the British media so long to repudiate the false claim that the MMR triple vaccine causes autism in children. To draw a parallel with physics again, when a moving body only experiences positive feedback, it eventually spins out of control. It needs negative feedback to stay in equilibrium, just as the media must be able to absorb contradictory information to remain balanced.

The combination of global integration, media convergence, increased velocity and the weightiness of the issues we face has created a momentum-driven society. If Sir Isaac Newton were alive today he might say there is a lot of *quantitas motus* about. Momentum is no longer simply part of the equation; it has evolved to become the driver of the equation.

This new dynamic has a profound effect on the way organisations such as corporations and governments operate. It encourages people in power to do things because they believe they have momentum on their side. As in the UBS story, the pros and cons of their decisions become less relevant than the momentum factor. Once the momentum gains traction, it is difficult to change course, no matter how perilous that course turns out to be. This does not mean that individuals should be absolved for making bad judgements or that their actions are simply a product of social physics but, rather, that errant behaviour is likely to manifest in a momentum-driven environment. Unfortunately, such environments are becoming increasingly common today, for reasons we shall now explore.

Chapter 2

The Equilibrium Delusion

While working at UBS in London, I would often walk to the office by using the Millennium Footbridge, a skeletal steel structure that spans the River Thames from the Tate Modern art gallery to St Paul's Cathedral. When the weather is good – always a consideration in London – the bridge provides a wonderfully scenic view up and down the bustling river. What's truly interesting about this bridge, though, is that, despite being relatively new, it already has a substantial history.

When it was declared open on 10 June 2000 by Queen Elizabeth II, the Millennium Bridge, with its bold, futuristic lines, seemed to symbolise the innovative spirit that had enabled London to become a leading global financial centre. The bridge was designed by renowned architect Sir Norman Foster and the sculptor Anthony Caro, together with the engineering firm Ove Arup. The bridge opening attracted so much public attention that when the ribbon was cut, thousands of people began to walk across it.

Then things became wobbly. The bridge began to sway from side to side in such a violent manner that it was abruptly closed. Initially it was assumed that too many people had crossed at the same time, overloading the bridge. So it was reopened a few days later, when traffic was lighter, but the same thing happened again. Suspicion fell on other possible causes, such as the foundations or the wind factor, but these were soon ruled out.

It eventually became clear to the engineers at Ove Arup that the wobbly effect was caused by something that had been totally unaccounted for. This is the way that people tend to lock in step with each other, so that even a minor lateral movement in the bridge can become exaggerated. The more the bridge sways, the more people adapt their footsteps to the sideways movement by synchronising their steps – greatly magnifying the effect. This self-reinforcing process, which the engineers described as 'synchronous lateral excitation', upset the dynamic equilibrium of the bridge. It was rectified by the installation of ninety-one shock absorbers, and the bridge reopened almost two years later, in February 2002.

In retrospect, the experience of the Millennium Bridge, which has come to be known as 'the wobbly bridge', provided a symbolic prophecy of things to come. It demonstrated what happens when people move en masse and synchronise their actions to such an extent that they magnify inherent flaws in the system – which then develops its own self-perpetuating dynamic. I am talking here, of course, about the conditions that precipitated the global financial crisis.

The wobbly-bridge episode also demonstrated that when things go out of kilter, we cannot assume that they will automatically return to a state of balance or equilibrium.

But dispelling this assumption is easier said than done. This is because much of our understanding of the way the natural world works is based on the idea that everything tends towards a state of equilibrium or balance. From our earliest school years we are taught that everything around us exists in a state of balance with everything else and that any upheavals will soon settle down. So if we shake up a bottle of water and dirt, for instance, the dirt particles will eventually sink to the bottom and the system will rebalance itself. So conditioned are we to see this tendency towards equilibrium as the normal state of the universe that we automatically assume it applies to social and economic behaviour.

We transpose our knowledge of the 'physical' world, with all its clockwork sureties, onto the 'human' world.

Modern economic thinking, for example, is based largely on the concept of equilibrium, known technically as 'general equilibrium theory'. That is, no matter how erratically the markets behave, it is expected that they will eventually rebalance themselves, without external inference from governments. They are self-equilibrating. Hence, when the powerful chairman of the US Federal Reserve Bank, Alan Greenspan, famously warned of 'irrational exuberance' in the markets, it was assumed that it would eventually settle down.[1]

However, as was so vividly demonstrated by the recent global financial meltdown, this assumption of equilibrium may be a delusion – at least in a behavioural sense. The renowned investor George Soros observed: 'The idea that financial markets are self-correcting and tend toward equilibrium remains the prevailing paradigm on which the various synthetic [financial] instruments . . . are based. I contend that the prevailing paradigm is false and urgently needs to be replaced . . . The contention that markets tend toward equilibrium does not correspond to reality.'[2]

If market 'equilibrium' is, in fact, a chimaera, this could help explain the puzzling research findings of Dimson, Marsh and Staunton of the London Business School, that momentum plays a bigger role in market behaviour than it ought to. Because if the power of equilibrium is less than we assume – or even a delusion – then it is unlikely to slow down the momentum. It cannot put the brakes on to rebalance the system. However, this still doesn't explain why in certain circumstances momentum does not just slow down but actually seems to speed up, as we saw in the lead-up to the global financial crisis.

In our quest for answers to this conundrum, let's turn briefly to the somewhat spooky world of astrophysics.

In 1998, two groups of experimenters discovered that the universe is expanding at an accelerating rate. This discovery shocked the scientific community because it had been assumed that the forces of gravity, being attractive, would pull the galaxies closer together and slow down the expansion created by the Big Bang billions of years ago. But stars and galaxies are flying apart at an ever-increasing rate. Alan Guth, a leading cosmologist at MIT, said the discovery 'was not expected theoretically, at least not by most of us, and is very hard to understand in the context of the theories that we have been using all these years'.[3] Other cosmologists expressed outright shock at the findings. Brian Schmidt, of the Mount Stromlo and Siding Spring Observatory in Australia, leader of the High-Z Supernova Search Team that reported the results, said, 'My own reaction is somewhere between amazement and horror. Amazement, because I just did not expect this result, and horror in knowing that [it] will likely be disbelieved by a majority of astronomers, who, like myself, are extremely sceptical of the unexpected.'[4]

It turns out that we know far less about the laws that govern the universe than we realised. There appear to be forces capable of resisting the force of gravity and speeding things up, especially over large-scale, intergalactic distances. Professor Ray Norris, an astrophysicist at the Commonwealth Scientific and Industrial Research Organisation (CSIRO) in Australia, told me, 'This phenomenon is weird. Really weird. We suspect there may be a type of "dark energy" involved but we have no idea what it is.'[5] And when quantum physics is applied to help us understand the phenomenon, it gives nonsensical answers. Whatever the anti-gravity mechanism is, said Adam Riess, of the University of California at Berkeley, 'We're seeing the universe take off.'[6]

It would, of course, be drawing a long (and rather nonsensical) bow to suggest that such a mysterious energy may play a role in accelerating the velocity and, therefore, the momentum in our society. Yet we cannot discount the possibility that momentum, like other forces in the universe, may be influenced by scale and complexity. That is, if a small system develops too much momentum, it will tend to automatically slow down. But if the system is sufficiently large and complex, such as the global financial system, then perhaps it doesn't automatically slow down and return to a state of equilibrium. Perhaps if it reaches a critical mass, the internal momentum can keep feeding on itself until the system spins out of control before eventually collapsing. Indeed, our world may be inherently more wobbly than we think.

This misplaced faith in equilibrium has consequences that extend way beyond the financial markets. It influences how we respond to other global challenges such as climate change, technological development, religious extremism and geopolitical conflict. For it encourages us to believe that, given time, everything will naturally return to a state of normality. So if we just adopt a 'hands-off' approach, things will settle themselves. The trouble is that if a large, complex system achieves a certain level of momentum, this may not be the case. Quite the reverse, in fact. Consider the vexing issue of climate change. Scientists are constantly having to revise their estimates of how quickly the changes are occurring and the severity of those changes. They continually underestimate the cascading effect, whereby small incremental changes lead to other larger changes, which in turn become cumulative and self-perpetuating. This is not just a matter of scientific conservatism but the result of a deeply conditioned belief by scientists that Nature will somehow keep things in a state of equilibrium and therefore slow the pace of change.

Indeed, it is illuminating to note the extent to which the concept of equilibrium permeates every branch of science, particularly biology, physics and chemistry. This influence is reflected in a vast lexicon of equilibrium-esque terminology, which includes 'thermodynamic equilibrium', 'quasistatic equilibrium', 'Doonan equilibrium', 'diffusion equilibrium', 'radiative equilibrium', 'hydrostatic equilibrium', 'punctuated equilibrium', 'equilibrioception', 'Nash equilibrium' and 'Schlenk equilibrium', to name but a few. These applications of the equilibrium concept are usually based on sound scientific principles.

More recently, however, the concept of equilibrium has begun to influence other disciplines, such as psychology, sociology, politics and finance, where it tends to be applied rather loosely and often carelessly. Psychologists, for example, will sometimes refer to a patient's 'emotional equilibrium', which is a state that is not only difficult to define but almost impossible to measure in a meaningful way. In the field of sociology, a community is said to be in 'social equilibrium' when there is a dynamic working balance among its interdependent parts. But how you would go about defining such a 'dynamic working balance' is anyone's guess.

Like many specialist terms that enter common parlance, people interpret equilibrium in a way that suits them. And in these unsettling times it is reassuring to believe there is a force that automatically restores everything to a state of balance, no matter how badly things are messed up. We just have to utter the magic word 'equilibrium' and all will be OK.

This blind faith in equilibrium is so entrenched in our collective psyche that it is reflected in the way we use our language. Consider, for example, how we usually say 'return to' equilibrium, rather than 'achieve or reach' a state of equilibrium, the implication being that equilibrium is the natural default position and, therefore, does not require any effort on our part. The terminology of equilibrium is also used to obscure or rationalise unpalatable actions. How often do we hear that a new drilling platform will not 'upset the natural equilibrium of the local ecosystem', or that 'as soon as this war in the Middle East is over we will return to a peaceful equilibrium'; or: 'Don't worry, after just one more stimulus package the financial system will return to its natural state of equilibrium. We can always trust in the efficient market to restore balance.'

The distinguished mathematical biologist Lord Robert May, zoology professor at Oxford University and former president of Britain's Royal Society, says, 'The more I hear about financial economics, the more I am struck by its similarity to ecology in the 1960s.'[7] The way economists talk about 'efficient' or 'perfect' markets reminds him of ecologists talking about 'the balance of nature' forty years ago – a time when it was assumed that nature would always be able to take care of itself.

More broadly, this almost childlike faith in equilibrium also distorts social values. Consider, for example, the fundamental issue of how wealth is earned and distributed. Many people, especially economists and government finance ministers, like to believe that, over time, our 'efficient' free-market economy will automatically balance things out – and reduce any great disparities of wealth. The idea behind this is that the forces of competition will foster a level and equitable playing field and make it difficult for anyone to dominate the market or accumulate too much wealth. However, this is not borne out by the facts. Over the past three decades in the United States, wealth has continued to be transferred to those at the apex of the economic pyramid. Two-thirds of all the income gains from the years 2002 to 2007 went to the top 1 per cent of Americans, and the so-called trickle-down effect from the richest to the poorest has been almost negligible in real terms.[8] The United States isn't the only country where the rich keep getting richer, a similar trend has occurred in most other developed countries.

In the corporate sector, in particular, the salaries of top-tier executives has continued to skyrocket, even when their companies failed spectacularly. Indeed, executive salaries, particularly for CEOs, seem to obey some kind of law of disequilibrium rather than equilibrium. Market forces push them towards the extremes rather than the middle. Figures compiled by Lucien Bebchuck of Harvard Law School and Yaniv Grinstein of Cornell's School of Management show that the average CEO's compensation package has risen from 24 times the pay of the average worker in 1965 to 275 times that in 2007.[9] To cite a few examples from the banking industry: in 2006, Richard S Fuld, Jr, CEO of the now defunct Lehman Brothers, was paid $40 million; Lloyd Blankfein of Goldman Sachs was paid $54.72 million; Stanley O'Neal, CEO of Merrill Lynch, was paid $48 million; John Mack, CEO of Morgan Stanley, was paid $41.41 million; James E. Cayne, CEO of Bear Stearns, was paid $33.85 million; and Charles Prince, CEO of Citigroup, was paid $25.98 million (these figures include bonuses, options and stock).[10] Put another way, this handful of men were paid almost a quarter of a billion dollars for a year's work. By the time Lehman Brothers and Bear Stearns collapsed in 2008, the top five executives in both companies had collectively taken home $2.4 billion in salary, bonuses and stock since 2000 – nearly a quarter of a billion dollars each.

Bebchuck and Grinstein's report says that the pay of the top five executives in publicly traded firms now amounts to 10 per cent of those companies' earnings, up from 5 per cent a decade earlier. The researchers found that 80 per cent of this increase was unexplained and not attributed to increases in corporate productivity.[11] It's also interesting to note that the highest salary increases occurred in those industries most susceptible to momentum, or Big Mo, such as banking, entertainment, the media, sports and technology. Yet the productivity of many senior executives, particularly those in the banking industry, is questionable. The business writer David Bolchover, in his book *Pay Check: Are Top Earners Really Worth It?*, suggests that the surge in CEO pay bears almost no relation to their 'talent' or 'performance'. For the most part, they just happened to be in the right place at the right time. 'Whether [the CEO] had talent or not was irrelevant,' he says; 'the company would probably have performed the same under a different leader.' It's like paying a ship captain a massive bonus for riding an incoming tide while bragging about his ability to get the craft moving forward. But when the tide goes out, they take no responsibility.

A study conducted by the New Economics Foundation in late 2009 calculated that UK bankers had destroyed £7 of value for every £1 they earned and were a drain on the country. By contrast, the foundation said, hospital cleaners created £10 of value for every £1 they were paid.[12] Yet, for the most part, these disparities are rarely challenged because of the deep-seated belief that everything will 'balance' out in the long run, in the same way that most of us probably assumed the global financial crisis would correct itself.

The equilibrium concept has emerged as one of main 'lenses' through which we view our world, as reflected in the ubiquitous use of this term in the mass media and everyday language. As such, it exerts a pervasive influence on the way we interpret and respond to important issues. It underpins our collective understanding of the way things work. Yet equilibrium is less a reality than something we yearn for. It is a fervent hope that everything will be OK in the long run if we just stop meddling and don't interfere with the 'natural order' of things. By promising salvation, however, our faith in equilibrium blinds us to the true state of our world and, in particular, to the nature of large-scale momentum and its tendency to spiral out of control.

Every so often, some influential individuals do rebel against the equilibrium concept, but their voices are few and far between. Nearly forty years ago the great financial analyst Benjamin Graham wryly described the self-balancing efficient-market hypothesis as a theory that 'could have great practical importance if it coincided with reality'.[13] And for many years, from the early 1960s to his death in 1996, the economist Hyman Minsky warned that the free-market system was inherently unstable, not self-balancing, and prone to huge blow-ups.[14] At the time, his warnings fell on deaf ears. More recently, George Soros and a handful of market commentators have echoed these concerns.

Beyond the financial markets, however, there have been other more broadly based criticisms of the equilibrium concept, mostly from academics and philosophers. One of the most notable of these is Jean Baudrillard, the French cultural theorist and philosopher, who observed, 'The world is not dialectical – it is sworn to extremes, not to equilibrium, sworn to radical antagonism, not to reconciliation or synthesis . . .'[15] In other words, the natural state of the world tends towards imbalance, not equilibrium. People's reluctance to engage with such an uncomfortable reality has been articulated with considerable poignancy by the Nobel Prize-winning novelist Albert Camus: 'In our wildest aberrations we dream of an equilibrium we have left behind and which we naively expect to find at the end of our errors. Childish presumption which justifies the fact that child-nations, inheriting our follies, are now directing our history.'[16]

Let's now consider some of these follies, and where they are leading us.

CHAPTER 3

Non-Friction

If we believe that equilibrium will automatically restore balance to a system, then we are less likely to place controls on that system. We expect the system to correct itself, so we adopt a hands-off approach. In fact, we might go even further by removing any points of friction in the system to ensure it operates as 'efficiently' as possible. Those of us who live in 'developed nations' like efficiency because, since the advent of the Industrial Age, we have been conditioned to believe it is invariably a good thing, as it enables us to operate with more speed and productivity.

In our relentless drive towards a more 'efficient' world we have eliminated many of the impediments, or 'points of friction', that previously slowed things down. Nowhere has this trend been more apparent than in the global financial system, where 'efficiency' has become synonymous with 'deregulation', as successive governments have systematically removed barriers to the free flow of capital between markets. Alan Greenspan, former chairman of the US Federal Reserve Bank, once decried the foolishness of those who called for more regulation: 'Why do we wish to inhibit the pollinating bees of Wall Street?' he asked rhetorically in his book *The Age of Turbulence*.[1] The mantra became: 'What's good for Wall Street is good for Main Street.'

The first big wave of deregulation in the United States – the most globally influential market – took place in the 1980s under Ronald Reagan, when savings and loans (S&L) institutions (similar to building societies) were allowed to offer a wider range of products with less regulatory oversight. This encouraged many of them to engage in high-risk lending activities, which eventually resulted in the collapse of nearly eight hundred S&L companies. Cleaning up that mess cost taxpayers around $300 billion in today's terms. But this did not deter the free-market ideologues like economist Milton Friedman, who, at the time, was the best-known evangelist for a form of capitalism known as 'laissez-faire' – a French phrase meaning 'leave alone'. He also had Reagan's ear and was a member of the President's Economic Policy Advisory Board. Martin Anderson wrote in *Revolution* that 'Reagan's eyes sparkled with delight every time he engaged in a dialogue with him [Friedman]'.[2] Central to Friedman's view, and Reagan's, was that a free market was an indispensable means towards the achievement of political freedom, and that therefore, laissez-faire capitalism was as much a moral issue as an economic imperative.

Friedman (as well as Greenspan) was an ideological descendant of Adam Smith, the eighteenth-century Scottish economist and philosopher whose opus *The Wealth of Nations* promoted the idea that free markets are not only efficient, but also self-correcting – and that therefore there was little need for market regulation. The 'invisible hand' of the market, as Smith called it, would take care of everything.[3] The ideas espoused in Smith's book, which incidentally was published in 1776, the same year as the American Declaration of Independence, continue to resonate to this day and underpin the general equilibrium theory. Two centuries later, Milton Friedman carried Smith's ideological torch forward in his book *Free to Choose*, which was launched in 1980 and translated into seventeen languages, including samizdat editions in Poland and the Soviet Union. Friedman's views converged with those of many other influential economists at this time – especially with individuals associated with what became known as the 'Chicago School' of economics, which promulgated the efficient markets theory and the need for more deregulation. The Chicago School also championed the idea that, in terms of economics, people would always behave rationally and act like a kind of new species which they dubbed *Homo economicus* – the utility-maximising autonomous individual. Human nature, with all its capricious whims and flaws, was amputated from economic theory.

The ideological transformation was now complete. Whereas once economists and intellectuals like Milton Friedman, Friedrich Hayek, Sir Keith Joseph and Arthur Laffer were regarded as far-right cranks, now they were seen as part of the establishment. You could say they had a lot of Big Mo on their side.

So much so that, on 12 November 1999, the free-market ideologues succeeded in their quest to repeal the Glass–Steagall Act, which was created in 1932 by the US Congress to ensure, among other things, a separation between the risk-taking investment banks and the more conservative commercial banks. This legislation had been introduced for the same reason as ships are compartmentalised, so that if there is a leak in one section, the leak doesn't spread and sink the whole ship. The legislation had acted as a considerable brake on the global financial system for over sixty years and prevented the high-rolling activities of the investment banks from influencing the traditional commercial banks: in effect, stopping them from turning into casinos. Now it was gone – all in the name of efficiency.

It had cost the banks over $300 million in lobbying fees over a period of twenty years to remove Glass–Steagall – fees which enabled many Washington lobbyists to put their kids through college – but the banks' persistence finally paid off. The new law, known as the Financial Services Modernisation Act, would allow banks and investment banks to merge and create giant financial supermarkets. The deregulators were so proud of their achievements that in 2003 the top US banking regulators staged a photo-opportunity in which they used a chainsaw and garden shears to cut up stacks of paper representing regulations.

But there was more cutting to be done. The investment banks were unhappy that they were required to maintain large reserves to cushion them against potential losses on their investments, which prevented them from taking on too much debt. So, on a bright spring afternoon on 28 April 2004, five members of the Securities and Exchange Commission (SEC), the key US regulator, met in a basement hearing room to consider the bankers' plea. Fifty-five minutes later, with the stroke of a pen, the members agreed to relax the rules, thus unshackling billions of dollars which the bankers could now use to make even bigger bets. One of those petitioning firms was Goldman Sachs, headed by Henry M Paulson, Jr, who would become treasury secretary two years later.[4]

Meanwhile, across the Atlantic, the crusaders for deregulation were also in full swing. Continuing the free-market traditions of Margaret Thatcher decades earlier, Britain's chancellor (treasurer) Gordon Brown did his best to remove restrictions from the financial markets. In 2004 he told an audience of bankers: 'In budget after budget I want us to do even more to encourage the risk-takers,'[5] and later admitted that he had resisted pressure to impose a British version of the Sarbanes–Oxley legislation, which was introduced in the United States to ensure greater corporate transparency and accountability in the wake of two massive financial debacles, Enron and WorldCom.[6]

At the global level, new banking rules were also introduced called the Basel II Guidelines, which stressed the need for capital *efficiency* and had the perverse effect of imposing the greatest capital restrictions on the smaller banks – which posed the least risk to the system – while the large, highly interconnected super-banks were given more freedom. These guidelines also relied heavily on the banks' internal models to monitor risk – in effect, to police themselves. Andrew Haldane, executive director, financial stability, at the Bank of England, quipped that the new Basel rules 'vaccinated the naturally immune at the expense of the contagious; the celibate were inoculated, the promiscuous intoxicated'.[7] All over the world – in both developed and emerging markets in Europe, Asia and America – the push was on to free up the financial global system as much as possible. It wasn't only banks, however, that were being freed up. Many other types of financial institutions were allowed to offer more banking-style products and services with little regulatory oversight, thus spawning what would become known as the 'shadow banking system'.

The cumulative impact of all this deregulation has created a hands-off (laissez-faire) environment in which money flows freely and instantaneously between markets in staggeringly large volumes, facilitated by modern technologies that emphasise speed and efficiency over stability. For instance, whereas once a big cross-border equities transaction would involve a painstaking amount of paperwork and cross-checking, and sometimes regulatory approval, now it happens at the click of a few buttons. This lack of 'friction' (or 'negative feedback') in the financial system enables market activity to rapidly develop a powerful momentum (or Big Mo) which can easily become destabilising. Science and history show that a dynamic system needs negative feedback to stay balanced. Conversely, when momentum turns negative, the lack of friction accelerates the downward trend because there are few impediments to slow down the collapse. In other words, the lack of friction in the system accelerates both the upward cycle (boom) and the downward cycle (bust).

What makes the financial system so acutely vulnerable to this boom–bust phenomenon is that, unlike other industries, it doesn't have to build new assembly lines, rent space or hire new people in order to expand its business. Finance is an 'intangible' business, so banks can write new contracts instantaneously, without limits, greatly multiplying the scale and speed of business flows: no new bricks and mortar required.

Any problems that arise within this frictionless financial system also spread more quickly around the world because the global financial system has become a lot more tightly linked. Consequently, big economies now experience the kind of contagion, or domino effect, previously associated with emerging economies. This is why, for instance, the collapse of the US subprime market was able to reverberate so quickly around the world.

This global boom–bust contagion is further compounded by the fact that central banks apply a rather schizophrenic approach to managing their economies. In his book *The Origin of Financial Crises: Central Banks, Credit Bubbles and the Efficient Market Fallacy* author George Cooper says that central banks tend to follow one economic theory during an expansion and another during a contraction. When things are bubbling along, central banks are

> Friedmanites who leave the market to do its thing. But when they get a whiff of a downturn, they turn Keynesian, and rush to stimulate the economy with rate cuts . . . As a rule, we favour capitalism in an expansion and socialism in a contraction . . . Had Isaac Newton subjected himself to the same standards, he would have given us three laws of gravity: one telling us how an apple behaves when thrown up into the air; another quite different law telling us how it then falls back to earth; and a third law telling us the apple never moves at all.[8]

Newton would have also observed that such inconsistency is a recipe for generating more momentum because by adopting a hands-off attitude during boom times, it accelerates the velocity of the system, which in turn magnifies the scale of the problem when the economy turns downward – at which point, governments often overreact by pumping too much money back into the system, thus laying the foundation for the next boom.

This is exactly what happened in the credit markets in the first few years of this century. After the bursting of the dot.com bubble in 2000 and the 9/11 attacks, the US government was keen to keep money flowing, so they took their foot off the regulatory brakes by drastically reducing interest rates. Alan Greenspan, as chairman of the Federal Reserve, slashed interest rates from 6.5 per cent to 1 per cent in the space of just two years, which made money incredibly cheap to borrow.[9] Much of this cheap money went into the booming real-estate market, particularly the low (that is, subprime) end of the US mortgage market, which catered to low-income people with shaky credit ratings and little prospect of repaying the money. A typical example was a Mexican strawberry picker in Bakersfield, California, with an income of $14,000 and no spoken English who was loaned every penny he needed to buy a house for $720,000. Loans were often made to people known in banking circles as 'ninjas', that is, people with 'no income, no job or assets'.[10]

These alarmingly lax lending criteria ensured America's debt-fuelled housing frenzy soon reached fever pitch. The volume of US subprime-related mortgages rose from $120 billion in 2001 to over $600 billion in 2006. This credit was then repackaged into complex derivatives, such as collateralised debt obligations (CDOs) and credit default swaps (CDSs), which were sold all around the world and dragged the European banks into the high-stakes game. This process is called 'securitisation' and has been described by economist Paul Krugman as follows: 'Loans no longer stayed with the lender. Instead, they were sold on to others, who sliced, diced and puréed individual debts to synthesize new assets. Subprime mortgages, credit card debts, car loans – all went into the financial system's juicer. Out the other end, suppos-edly, came sweet-tasting AAA-rated investments. And financial wizards were lavishly rewarded for overseeing the process.'[11]

Private-equity firms and hedge funds took advantage of these new types of credit and the historically low interest rates to borrow vast sums of money to buy out companies. Now that they no longer had to rely on the banks for credit, it was boom time for borrowers. Consequently, by 2008 the total US credit market debt had grown to $51 trillion, which is 3.5 times the gross domestic product of the United States. To put that into perspective, in 1929, on the edge of the Great Depression, total US debt was just 1.8 times gross domestic product.[12]

The flow of money through the system was further acceler-ated by the behaviour of the ratings agencies, such as Moody's, Standard & Poor's and Fitch. These agencies determine the quality of companies' investment offerings so that people can make informed choices about whether to invest in them. Positive ratings speed things up by encouraging people to invest; negative ratings slow things down by prompting investors to be more cautious. Unfortunately, the ratings agencies have a strong incentive to deliver positive ratings on the products they review because they are paid by the companies selling the investment, not the buyers, and charge up to $500,000 for a rating. So when, for example, a bank submitted a complex product which was designed to spread and lower risk, but which actually contained toxic, or unviable, levels of debt, the ratings agencies helped the banks to disguise the problem by awarding the product an AA or AAA rating. Of the AAA-rated subprime-mortgage-backed securities, issued in 2006, 93 per cent had been downgraded to junk status by 2010.

But it wasn't just the blatant conflict of interest that distorted the agencies' judgements; it was also the calculation models they used. When Steve Eisman, a New York-based hedge fund manager, called Standard & Poor's and asked what would happen to default rates if real estate prices fell, the man at S&P couldn't say – its model for home prices had no ability to accept a negative number. 'They were just assuming home prices would keep going up,' Eisman said.[13] The credit boom was a bonanza for the ratings agencies, and Moody's in particular, which saw its earnings grow by 900 per cent and its stock price increase sixfold.[14]

By acting as lubricants for the financial system, rather than as friction points, the ratings agencies accelerated the velocity at which money flowed through the system. But there was also another factor that was speeding things up. This was the emergence of complex new financial models.

When beautiful models turn bad

Up until a few decades ago, bankers had to laboriously and meticulously analyse their figures before completing a transaction, whereas today they rely on computer-simulated models to conduct business at lightning speed and in staggeringly large volumes. These models are designed by people known as 'quants' who operate in an arcane world of numbers and statistics. They are usually brilliant PhD-wielding graduates drawn from top universities like MIT in Boston, USA, and Cambridge University in the UK, who can apply their quantitative magic to simulate practically any scenario in the 'real world'. But whereas once they spent their time deciphering string theory in the hope of winning a Nobel Prize, now they look for ways to make money in an industry where multimillion-dollar bonuses are not uncommon. They have struck a Faustian bargain with Wall Street and the City of London.

Computer-simulated models can also be very seductive. Just like their human counterparts, they can be elegantly sophisticated and convey a sense of reassuring confidence. They employ artificial intelligence and concepts like 'stochastic volatility' and 'the superstatistics of labour productivity' to penetrate the mysteries of market behaviour. For bankers, the most seductive type of model is the 'risk management' model, which promises to minimise the amount of financial risk in an investment or loan and therefore protect a portfolio. They also help bankers to sleep at night. Consequently, over the past decade, banks have invested many millions of dollars in the development and acquisition of these models.

Most bankers did not understand how or why these models worked. It simply became an article of faith that they did. After all, they were paying a lot of money to the brilliant quants on their payrolls to make sure they did. During the boom times the models certainly seemed to be doing their job and were applied to all manner of newfangled financial products like credit default swaps and complex derivatives arrangements. They enabled traders and investment bankers to conduct business in quasi-scientific language and take huge risks that neither they nor their customers understood. In the lending markets, the only way the lenders could keep up with all the complicated business being done was to move away from using human judgement and rely increasingly on automated underwriting systems and computerised credit-scoring models. The models had become the new 'emperors' of the financial system.

That is, until the global credit crisis revealed they weren't wearing any clothes. It turned out that many of the risk-management models didn't work, and worse than that, they actually increased risk. They enabled bankers to be wrong with infinite precision. This is because most risk-management models focus on managing the small day-to-day fluctuations in risk and don't account for the rare event of a significantly big risk happening. They are based largely on the work of the mathematician Carl Friedrick Gauss (1777–1855), who observed that the probability of events follows a bell curve, with few big surprises. Gaussian models provide an illusion of greater safety, much like a boat that makes for smooth sailing in choppy waters but is dangerously unstable in stormy weather. The boat's ability to insulate you from small choppy water lulls you into a false confidence and so you ignore the tsunami looming on the horizon.

This 'insulating' effect of models can foster a sense of false optimism. A paper by four Federal Reserve economists, 'Making Sense of the Subprime Crisis', explored why so many Wall Street analysts and economists failed to foresee the surge in subprime foreclosures in 2007 and 2008.[15] It concluded that the analysts had stubbornly clung to their models, which suggested that because housing prices had continued to climb for decades, they would continue to do so, and therefore the possibility of collapse was very low.

To be fair, predicting the price of any asset, such as a house, can be a difficult thing. This is because the price reflects not only the owner's beliefs about what the asset will be worth, but also many other people's beliefs too. It's these hierarchies of beliefs and behavioural factors – all intangible – that are so hard to model.

The Nobel Prize-winning economist Edmund Phelps says that risk-management models were never well founded. 'There was a mystique to the idea that market participants knew the price to put on this or that risk. But it is impossible to imagine that such a complex system could be understood in such detail and with such amazing correctness . . . The requirements for information [have] gone beyond our abilities to gather it.'[16]

One of the biggest victims of a 'beautiful model turned bad' was my former employer, UBS bank. Its risk department used the same VaR (value at risk) formulae and Gaussian copula techniques that many other banks adopted, and calculated that the bank would never lose more than 2 per cent on its exposure to derivatives. This encouraged the bank to splurge on a particular type of derivative known as super-senior CDO notes, which carried a triple-A rating and were presumed safe. The bank's ex-chairman, Peter Kurer, recalled, 'Frankly, most of us had not even heard the word "super-senior" until the summer of 2007', by which time the bank had increased its exposure to these markets from almost zero a few years earlier to over $50 billion.[17] Few people within the bank were concerned about this mounting exposure because the risk models suggested the exposure would be capped to just 2 per cent, and even this small amount was further protected by a mono-line insurance policy – making the entire portfolio appear risk-free. But of course, the risk models used turned out to be hopelessly inadequate for dealing with a complete market meltdown. By late 2007 it became clear that UBS, once a paragon of prudently conservative financial management, was now sitting on the biggest single pile of toxic debt of any of the world's major banks.

When an organisation falls under the hypnotic trance of a model, it can be difficult for the users of the model to snap out of it. Ron den Braber was a statistical expert working in the CDO department of Royal Bank of Scotland (RBS) during the 1990s. He was concerned that the bank's models were significantly underestimating the risks of super-senior CDO investments and voiced his concerns. 'I started saying things gently,' he recalls. 'In banks you don't use the word "error", but what I was trying to say was important. The problem is that in banks you have this kind of mentality, this group-think, and people just keep going with what they know, and they don't want to listen to bad news.' It wasn't long before den Braber was asked to leave the bank.[18]

A decade earlier, Emanuel Derman, a physicist-turned-financier who played a central role in the development of models for derivatives, warned his employer Goldman Sachs of the limitations of derivatives models – he compared their relationship to reality to that between a child's toy car and an actual automobile. More recently, Derman, who is now a professor at Columbia University and the author of *My Life as a Quant: Reflections on Physics and Finance*, wrote, 'It's difficult or well-nigh impossible to systematically predict what's going to happen. You may think you know you're in a bubble, but you still can't tell whether things are going up or down the next day.'[19] He also cheekily co-authored a financial modeller's version of the Hippocratic oath, which pledges, among other things, 'I will remember that I didn't make the world, and it doesn't satisfy my equations.'

Bright people like Emanuel Derman who challenge the status quo, however, are usually the exception. For it doesn't matter how sophisticated or intelligent a person (or organisation) is, they can be just as vulnerable to the influence of destructive models as a less intelligent person, and in some cases more so. This is because from a psychological perspective, intelligent people are often more comfortable dealing with synthetic simulations of reality which may be intellectually sound but not practical in the real world. Albert Einstein once described this tendency in a letter to Sigmund Freud, on 30 July 1932, 'Experience proves that it is rather the so-called "intelligentsia" that is most apt to yield to these disastrous collective suggestions, since the intellectual has no direct contact with life in the raw but encounters it in its easiest, synthetic form – upon the printed page.'[20] Think for a moment of all those brilliant bankers and analysts who bet the lot on the basis of some beautiful but deeply flawed models.

Apart from disguising the real risks in the financial system, the other major effect of the models has been to further accelerate the level of momentum in the system by simplifying and speeding up complex decision-making processes – by removing the 'human' element. For instance, as discussed in chapter 1, analysts estimate that up to 60 per cent of trading in equity markets is now driven by mathematical algorithms used in computer programs. These allow trading to take place automatically in response to the latest market data and news, deciding when and how much to trade. And it all happens instantaneously, in less than the blink of an eye. Some 'high-frequency' traders trade more than a billion shares a day, and they are very short-term bets – a typical stock being held for just eleven seconds.

In a deregulated, frictionless environment, such model-driven programs have enabled money to flow freely between every sector of the global economy at dizzying speeds, on a scale never seen before. No one seemed to mind how fast the money flowed because it was seen as evidence of 'efficiency' and therefore was a sign of progress.

But was it really?

Let's look at this from the perspective of the natural world. The ecosystem tells us that there are often serious consequences when a system 'speeds up' beyond its natural capacity. Consider, for example, how water moves across a landscape. Professor David W Orr, the Paul Sears distinguished professor of environmental studies and politics at Oberlin College and a James Marsh professor at the University of Vermont, points out that if water moves too quickly it does not recharge underground aquifers. The results are floods in wet weather and droughts in summer. Similarly, Orr says,

> Money moving too quickly through an economy does not recharge the local wellsprings of prosperity, whatever else it does for the global economy. The result is an economy polarised between those few who do well in a high-velocity economy and those left behind . . . There is an appropriate velocity for water set by geology, soils, vegetation, and ecological relationships in a given landscape. There is an

appropriate velocity for money that corresponds to long-term needs of whole communities rooted in particular places and the necessity of preserving ecological capital.[21]

Orr believes that, having exceeded the speed limits, our society is vulnerable to ongoing ecological degradation and economic arrangements that are unjust and unsustainable. His analogy is not just theoretical. It is now widely recognised that the real cause of the Asian financial crisis in 1997 was too much money flowing too quickly in and out of these developing countries, which resulted in economic devastation to the region. Even the International Monetary fund, which has for long preached the virtues of free capital flows, has recently come to recognise the inherent dangers of too much money moving too swiftly through the system. In February 2010, the fund's deputy director of research, Jonathan D Ostry – along with five other authors – wrote that in the aftermath of the global financial crisis, officials were 'reconsidering the view that unfettered capital flows are a fundamentally benign phenomenon... Concerns that foreign investors may be subject to herd behavior, and suffer from excessive optimism, have grown stronger; and even when flows are fundamentally sound, it is recognized that they may contribute to collateral damage, including bubbles and asset booms and busts.'[22]

There are clearly natural speed limits to how fast money should flow through the system. Yet, for the most part, our society is not even aware of these speed limits, let alone their consequences, because we have become so deeply conditioned to believe that speed and efficiency are always a good thing – and that, in any case, the magical forces of 'equilibrium' will curb any excesses.

CHAPTER 4

Gorillas on Speed

So far we have looked at the factors that have increased the 'velocity' in our world, using the financial system as an example. But what about the other half of the equation? Newton's law is made up of mass times velocity. As we shall see, the mass (or scale) we are dealing with has grown exponentially in recent years. Let's start with some numbers.

A quadrillion is a number that is normally only used by astronomers when calculating, say, the number of stars in a galaxy, or by people in universities with lots of chalk on their coats. It is 1,000,000,000,000,000 or one thousand trillion – a mind-bogglingly large number. Over the past few years, however, an entirely new category of people has begun using such numbers and tossing them around with an unsettling familiarity. These people couldn't be more different from astronomers and academics. They are invariably chalk-free, slickly attired and extremely well paid. They are the derivatives traders.

Derivatives are the 'black holes' of the financial world. They are vast in number, virtually incomprehensible and tend to suck everyone into them. They have been described frequently as financial 'weapons of mass destruction' and many analysts blame them for the recent global financial crisis. Over the past twenty years, more money has poured into derivatives than into all other investment vehicles combined. According to the Bank of International Settlements, by 2009 the total amount of derivatives outstanding was $680 trillion, which is well over half a quadrillion.[1] By comparison, the entire economic output of the world (GDP) is about $50 trillion. Given their importance to the world economy and their pivotal role in the momentum-generating process, let's delve into derivatives in some detail.

A step removed from reality

Derivatives are financial products that 'derive' their value from things like stocks, bonds, currencies, commodities or interest rates. They don't have an intrinsic value of their own but offer investors a way to buy or sell something at an agreed price at a later date. The defining feature of derivatives is that they are one step (or many steps) removed from the real, tangible asset on which their value is based. For example, a home-insurance policy is a form of derivative. This concept can be difficult for a non-financial person to grasp. Perhaps the simplest explanation has been provided by Linda Davies in her book *Into the Fire*, in which she says that the job of a derivatives trader is like that of 'a bookie once removed, taking bets on people making bets'.[2] These bets include financial products like 'options', 'futures' and 'swaps'.

Investors are keen on derivatives because, unlike the stock or bond, a legal contract for a derivative is a form of promise, and can therefore be more flexible and generate high profits. The downside of this contractual flexibility is that derivatives come with complex arrangements which hinder transparency, making it difficult to grasp the true nature of the deal. For example, an investor would in theory need to read as many as 1.125 billion pages to understand the components in the type of derivatives-based security known as a collateralised debt obligation squared, or CDO^2, which could contain portions of nearly a hundred million mortgages.[3] It is also easier to borrow money to purchase a derivative, whereas, under US law – which governs a large proportion of the global market – a purchaser can borrow only up to a certain percentage of the stock's value. So you can make bigger bets on derivatives without putting up so much collateral, or sometimes none at all. Indeed, some derivatives traders sit on astronomically large levels of credit risk.

To calculate the value of derivatives, many financial institutions employ mathematicians and physicists to develop sophisticated financial models. In 1997, the Royal Swedish Academy of Sciences awarded the Nobel Prize in Economics to Professor Robert C Merton of Harvard University and Professor Myron S Scholes of Stanford University to honour the method they jointly developed to calculate the value of options derivatives. One year later, however, a derivatives-based hedge fund in which Merton and Scholes were principal shareholders, Long Term Capital Management (LTCM), had to be rescued at a cost of $3.5 billion when the Federal Reserve Bank decided that its collapse would pose a serious threat to the stability of the American markets.[4] Merton and Scholes had thought that their model for 'dynamic hedging' was next to foolproof.

It defies belief that a hedge fund that trades in financial instruments designed to reduce risk, and includes two Nobel Prize-winners in Economics among its shareholders, can make such huge losses and shake the foundations of the financial system.

Yet LTCM isn't the only contemporary example of a derivatives-heavy institution to generate negative momentum in the global marketplace. Almost ten years later, in 2007, one of Wall Street's most blue-blooded firms, Bear Stearns, was brought down by complex derivatives trading in hedge funds – making it the first major victim of the financial crisis. Shortly thereafter, Goldman Sachs also revealed it had lost billions through hedge-fund derivates trades. However, a fundamental difference between the original LTCM collapse and the more recent Bear Stearns and Goldman Sachs losses is that hedge-fund investing is no longer the preserve of the rich: nowadays about 25 per cent of hedge-fund money comes from large pension funds seeking to maximise their returns. So any derivatives-based collapse is now felt by average workers and not just the well-off.

Warren Buffet, the CEO of Berkshire Hathaway and known as the 'sage of Omaha', is one of the world's most successful investors. He has, for many years, warned about the risks of derivatives trading. In his now-famous 2002 chairman's letter to his shareholders, he described derivatives as time bombs and wrote, 'The range of derivatives contracts is limited only by the imagination of man, or sometimes, so it seems, madmen.' The derivatives businesses, he continued, are 'like Hell, easy to enter and almost impossible to exit'.[5]

According to Buffet, at the heart of the devilment of derivatives is the fact that the actual money transaction will take place at some future date, and the price will depend on many variables. But, in the meantime, even before the contract is settled, the companies involved can record profits or losses based on their derivatives deals 'without so much as a penny changing hands . . . and these reported earnings are often wildly overstated . . . The inaccuracy may not be exposed for many years.' Compounding the problem, he argues, is that the valuation of the derivatives may be greatly exaggerated by, say, a trader eyeing a multimillion-dollar bonus or a CEO who wants to report impressive 'earnings' (or both). It is only much later, after the bonuses are paid, that shareholders discover that the reported earnings were a sham.

In closing his letter to shareholders, Buffet warned about the derivatives business expanding unchecked: 'The derivatives genie is now well out of the bottle, and these instruments will almost certainly multiply in variety and number until some event makes their toxicity clear . . . Central banks and governments have so far found no effective way to control, or even monitor, the risk posed by these contracts.'[6]

Charlie Munger, Buffet's long-time business partner, said during the annual general meeting, 'There is an electronic herd of people around the world managing an amazing amount of money, who make decisions based on minute-by-minute stimuli.'[7] It is not just the herd mentality and the nature of derivatives that are of concern, however, it is the type of institutions that increasingly drive the derivatives markets. These are the giant hedge funds and private-equity groups.

Hedging their bets

The author Tom Wolfe described the hedge-fund managers as the 'new masters of the universe',[8] and for good reasons. They operate in a shadowy, largely unregulated world and hold unparalleled influence over the financial markets, accounting for more than one-third of all stock trades and controlling over $2 trillion worth of assets. Hedge funds operate by pooling massive amounts of capital, gathered mainly from super-wealthy individuals or large institutions, which is invested in sophisticated financial instruments, particularly derivatives. They are managed by the world's smartest and most highly paid traders – who are willing to take sizeable risky bets on any kind of market and borrow enormous amounts of money to magnify their investing impact. In Newtonian terms, the hedge funds wield a lot of 'mass' and generate a lot of momentum.

Most of the US hedge funds are based in Greenwich, Connecticut, or 'Hedgistan', as it is often called. As the benefactors of the deregulation movement, they are not controlled by any federal agency in the United States, are not required to reveal much about either their investment philosophy or trading activities and pay relatively low taxes. Not surprisingly, the chairman of the US Securities Exchange Commission, Christopher Cox, was moved to say that hedge funds operated in a 'gap' in the SEC authority.[9] Hedge funds are also difficult to understand. Newly appointed Federal Reserve chairman Ben Bernanke required a face-to-face refresher course from fund managers in August 2007 to get to grips with how they operated.[10]

Despite their 'dark arts' aura, hedge funds have been enormously profitable and remained so even during and after the financial crisis of 2008–9, with a number of top hedge-fund management companies earning over $1 billion per annum. To make the 2009 list of the twenty-five highest-paid hedge-fund managers published by *AR: Absolute Return+Alpha* magazine, an individual had to make $350 million – up from $75 million a year earlier. In total, the top twenty-five earned a collective $25.3 billion, beating the previous 2007 record high by a wide margin. Topping the list was David Tepper, an ex-Goldman Sachs executive, whose fund enabled him to earn $4 billion. That's more than $1.9 million an hour, or $32,000 per minute. The runner-up was George Soros, a perennial name on the rich list of money-makers, who earned $3.3 billion.[11]

Hedge funds also wield considerable geopolitical power, as the global economist David Hale explained to me: 'The Asian financial crisis of 1997 was actually caused by a hedge-fund attack on the system of pegged currencies operating there,' which, as described earlier, greatly accelerated the flow of money through the system. Hale says that hedge funds are even more powerful today.[12] Their influence now extends to every sector of the global economy and they are often at the epicentre of market events.

So here we have a tiny group of people managing trillions of dollars, through financial instruments that are little understood, making ever bigger bets and motivated by dizzyingly high bonuses, with minimal regulatory oversight and low taxes, in an industry that helps to underpin the economic welfare of the planet. If ever there was a sure-fire recipe for Big Mo, this would be it.

Private equity

Apart from hedge funds, another whopping big gorilla on speed is the private-equity firm. Unlike hedge funds, which make much of their money through investments, private equity firms focus on company takeovers – buying, selling and restructuring companies to extract maximum profits for their partners and clients. Private-equity activity now accounts for about one-third of all takeover deals, whereas a few decades ago it accounted for a tiny percentage of such deals. Private-equity firms now target even the largest publicly owned multinationals, a scenario that would have been unthinkable in previous eras. No prey is too big for this voracious new gorilla. The first mega-sized deal occurred in 1989, when the huge food and tobacco conglomerate RJR Nabisco was taken over by the private equity group KKR in a $31.1 billion leveraged buyout deal. So acrimonious and notorious was this deal that it was chronicled in the book (and later a made-for-TV movie of the same name) *Barbarians at the Gate: The Fall of RJR Nabisco*. By 2007, a record $686 billion of private equity was invested globally, up over a third on the previous year and more than twice the total invested in 2005.

Private-equity firms, like hedge funds, have been permitted to operate in a world far away from the prying eyes of the media and the regulatory authorities that scrutinise public companies. Like their hedge-fund counterparts, the partners in private-equity firms make extraordinary amounts of money and pay relatively little tax. US hedge-fund employees, for example, pay only 15 per cent tax on the income they generate through capital gains, and in Britain the tax system enables multimillionaire venture capitalists to effectively pay less tax than a cleaner.[13] The historian Niall Ferguson quipped in London, on 2 July 2007, while attending a London Business School event, 'Why are we here attending conferences when we should be setting up private equity firms?'[14]

Another observer of the private-equity scene, Roger Cohen, writing in the *International Herald Tribune*, said the 'tax authorities in the United States and Britain resemble dinosaurs pursuing space ships. They have lost touch with the super-rich, as has most of humanity.'[15]

Sovereign wealth funds

The other big gorilla to emerge in recent years is the 'sovereign wealth fund' (SWF). These are huge funds that have been accumulated by foreign governments, particularly those which have built up large reserves through their oil revenues or exports, such as China, Russia and Middle Eastern countries. Like hedge funds and private-equity companies, the SWFs operate with little transparency, and there is minimal international regulatory framework governing the activities of SWFs. The US Treasury estimates that the total investments in SWFs could be up to $2.5 trillion, which is more than all the world's hedge funds combined. According to Morgan Stanley, this figure will increase to $12 trillion by 2015, which is equal to the gross domestic product of the United States.

Up until recently SWFs have attracted scant public attention because they invested mainly in currencies or government bonds and acted primarily as passive investors, willing to sit on the sidelines and receive their commercial return on investment. That has changed since the SWFs have begun to significantly expand their portfolios. In 2007 the Chinese government bought a $3 billion stake in Blackstone, a US private-equity company that, through the various businesses it controls, is one of America's largest employers. This was followed by major Chinese investments in resource companies in Australia, Asia and Africa. In March 2008 Dubai International Capital bought 3 per cent of the European defence company EADS, which makes the Eurofighter.[16] Then came the global financial crisis, which enabled big SWFs to invest in troubled Western banks and businesses, often at bargain prices.

The recent purchases by SWFs not only signalled a tectonic shift in the balance of world capital markets, they also raise an important geopolitical question: will governments continue to use their SWFs purely as financial investment tools, or will they be used as an implement of political muscle? That is: will these giant gorillas remain politically agnostic? Lawrence Summers, the Harvard economist and now President Obama's top economic adviser, suspects not. He wrote in a July 2007 *Financial Times* opinion piece, 'It's far from obvious that [the search for profit] will be the only motivation of governments as shareholders.' He said that the concerns raised over SWFs are 'profound and [go] to the nature of global capitalism.'[17]

Whether these SWFs remain politically agnostic or not, one thing is certain: their power and influence will continue to grow.

The cumulative impact of these 'gorillas on speed' – the giant hedge funds, private-equity companies, derivatives traders and sovereign wealth funds – has been to create a lot more financial 'mass'. This mass is able to operate with much greater 'velocity' in the frictionless, deregulated environment of the modern financial system, which in turn can generate a lot of momentum. It is an environment where Big Mo meets Big Money.

However, as we shall see in the following chapter, it would be a mistake to confuse size with strength.

CHAPTER 5

The Paradox of the Strong

Earlier we looked at the possibility that momentum may be sensitive to issues of scale and complexity. That is, once a system becomes sufficiently large and complicated, its internal momentum may continue to accelerate rather than slow down. This has disturbing implications because it means our society will have to rethink many assumptions that underpin its approach to designing organisations. For example, it is generally assumed that bigger, more integrated organisations are better, because they can produce economies of scale and efficiency that lead to greater productivity (and profit). We tend to think of our big organisations as being the rock-solid pillars of society and the economy. The trouble is that momentum feeds on internal integration and efficiency to become self-perpetuating, and in a very large organisation this effect can be magnified to such an extent that it disrupts the organisation's state of equilibrium.

The great paradox is, therefore, that a 'strong' organisation can be more vulnerable to momentum than a weak one. It is similar to the way some types of virus thrive in organisms that are particularly healthy – the virus can take advantage of the internal robustness. The deadly 1918 flu pandemic, for example, was most lethal for the young and healthy because it triggered their efficient immune systems to massively overreact.[1]

Consider for a moment which organisations were most affected by the global financial crisis. It wasn't the medium-sized regional banks and building societies whose computer networks and systems hadn't been updated for years. It was the global behemoths of the banking and financial world, like Citibank, Bear Stearns, Lehman Brothers, Merrill Lynch, Fannie Mae and Freddie Mac, Royal Bank of Scotland and UBS – organisations whose annual turnovers exceeded the gross domestic products of some medium-sized countries. It used to be said, until quite recently, that such mighty banks were simply 'too big to fail', yet it was these banks that experienced the greatest declines relative to their size.

It was the same for other industries too. The General Electric Corporation, one of the twelve original companies in the Dow Jones industrial average in 1896, saw its share price plummet to one-tenth of its peak value. The once impregnable General Motors Company filed for bankruptcy. The size and strength of these companies did not protect them. Quite the opposite, in fact.

Very big companies are not simply more vulnerable to destructive momentum, they are also more likely to spread it because they are more interconnected to the rest of the system. To borrow again from the flu analogy, they are 'super-spreaders'. When the giant American insurance group AIG suffered a liquidity crisis in 2008, it threatened the entire US financial system because AIG was so deeply intertwined with numerous banks and other companies. The US government had to effectively bail it out by providing financial support of over $180 billion. The once seemingly impregnable AIG was on its knees and dragging everyone else down with it.

This paradox of the strong extends beyond corporations to the wider economy. A disturbing analysis published in the *IMF World Economic Outlook* in October 2008, which looked at 113 episodes of financial stress in 17 countries, argues that the economic impact of financial shocks may be bigger in countries with more sophisticated financial markets, such as those applying the Anglo-Saxon model, with its emphasis on deregulation and efficiency.[2] Also, those countries which rapidly modernised and reformed their economies to be state-of-the-art financial centres, such as Iceland (the Nordic tiger), Estonia (the Economic miracle) and Ireland (the Celtic tiger), fell hardest and fastest when the global financial crisis hit.

So what's going on here? Why would the strongest, fittest and best governed economies be the most vulnerable?

One possibility is that such economies generate more momentum because, like big companies, they are more efficient and integrated – and therefore more prone to the momentum effect. They also tend to be more deregulated, so there is less 'friction' to slow them down. But there is another factor that makes sophisticated economies particularly vulnerable to the momentum effect. This has to do with 'network behaviour'.

Network behaviour

Economies (and corporations) are really large networks of inter-connected parts or 'nodes'. People who study networks, such as Albert-Laszlo Barabasi (a physicist at Notre Dame University and the author of Linked: The New Science of Networks) and Steven Strogatz (a Cornell mathematician), tell us that as a network grows, there is a natural tendency for some nodes to become better connected than others.[3] We see this pattern in our social lives, where some people are better connected and more plugged in to what's happening. In a really large network, such as the economy, these highly connected nodes evolve into 'hubs'. For example, the global financial network is now dominated by a few very large hubs, which are the global banks. By contrast, fifty years ago there were no global banking hubs, just thousands of regional and local banks that were only loosely connected. A similar evolution has occurred in many other industries, and for good reasons. Concentrated networks are easier to control than dispersed ones. They are also cheaper to run because they channel resources more efficiently.

However, when a hub breaks down, the whole system can be

affected. It's easy to observe this phenomenon in the airline industry when, say, a major hub like Chicago Airport is closed for a day because of snow. This causes ripple effects throughout the US network and even overseas, not just for passengers but for freight and mail deliveries.

Similarly, during the global banking crisis, a few highly interconnected superbanks (i.e. hubs) felt the full force of the liquidity shock and their internal systems responded by generating so much negative momentum that it threatened to bring down the entire financial system (i.e. their efficient 'immune systems' overreacted). This is precisely what happened when the giant American investment bank Lehman Brothers failed, which, unlike AIG, was not bailed out by the government. Lehman Brothers was such a critical hub of the network that many analysts believe that its collapse was the trigger point for the global financial meltdown. The BBC's financial editor, Robert Peston, said that Lehman's collapse 'caused a massive panic and suddenly funds were being withdrawn from any bank anywhere in the world that was perceived as remotely vulnerable. That was the moment people thought, "Crikey, we're on the verge of a depression."'[4]

It was also the moment the world realised that some banks had indeed become 'too big to fail', because if they did, they could bring down the entire system. Simon Johnson, professor of entrepreneurship at MIT's Sloan School of Management and the former chief economist at the International Monetary Fund, says, 'When large companies can 1) shape their regulatory environment, 2) take advantage of lax regulation to take on more risk than they can manage, and 3) put the downside losses onto the taxpayer, we should be very afraid. This exact problem has repeatedly slapped us in the face over the past 12 months with almost every development in the financial sector, and it remains inherent in every "too big to fail" bank.'[5]

The last time there was such deep concern about 'bigness' in the United States was a century ago, following the emergence of a handful of giant industrial trusts that came to dominate American business. This led to 'antitrust' legislation which limited the size and scope of big companies for the next half-century. These rules, however, were watered down during the 1990s under strong pressure from the deregulation movement and their pursuit of a 'frictionless' environment (as discussed earlier). By the turn of the twenty-first century it was fashionable to be big again.

But as the banks became bigger, the financial system grew more concentrated, and therefore more vulnerable to the momentum effect.

Interestingly, this concentration-related vulnerability appears to be mirrored in the workings of the human brain, which is actually a highly complex network comprising a hundred billion nerve cells, called neurons, each interconnected to thousands of other neurons. In March 2008, two researchers from the University of California's Department of Anatomy and Neurobiology, Robert Morgan and Ivan Soltesz, discovered that when a small number of neurons in the hippocampus become highly connected, they develop into neural 'hubs', which begin to circulate and amplify signals (i.e. boost momentum) to such a degree that they overwhelm the brain's networks, leading to epileptic seizures. This transforms a healthy brain into an epileptic one, which is more prone to fits. In effect, the hubs become the conduits for seizures in the network. 'The structure of the epileptic brain differs substantially from that of a healthy one, and our discovery of this hub network offers insight into how epilepsy may develop,' Morgan explained.[6]

The parallels between the epileptic brain and the modern global financial system are disturbing and suggest that the emergence of a few highly connected and powerful banking hubs has made the system more prone to periodic fits and seizures. They create the conditions for a financial version of a 'grand mal' seizure – a Big Mo seizure.

More broadly, the dangers of concentrated networks extend beyond the financial system into the wider community. These dangers are vividly demonstrated in the UK, where, in recent decades, local and regional power has been centralised in London and managed by bureaucratic super-hubs that govern practically every aspect of British life. So once-great regional centres and towns find themselves stripped of their local autonomy and are at the mercy of bureaucratic decisions made many kilometres away. According to the British writer Phillip Blond, who grew up in working-class Liverpool, centralisation is having a devastating impact on local communities and creating a 'broken' society. 'I lived in the city [Liverpool] when it was being eviscerated. It was a beautiful city, one of the few in Britain to have a genuinely indigenous culture. And that whole way of life was destroyed.'[7] In a much-discussed essay in *Prospect* magazine in February 2009, Blond wrote, 'Look at the society we have become: We are a bi-polar nation, a bureaucratic, centralised state that presides dysfunctionally over an increasingly fragmented, disempowered and isolated citizenry.'[8]

This centralisation has been accelerated by the free-market economic revolution that enables giant supermarkets like Tesco to squeeze out local stores and small banks to be gobbled up and absorbed within the global financial monoculture. Perversely, the more social problems this centralisation creates – such as alienation, poverty and rising crime – the more centralised measures are put in place to combat them. These measures include security cameras (Britain now has over four million) and an endless array of government targets and quotas which provide the illusion that something is being done, whereas in reality, these measures disguise and exacerbate the underlying problems, like the bankers' models discussed earlier; they make the system more vulnerable to upheavals.

Across the English Channel, meanwhile, the European countries have been grappling with the consequences of centralising their currencies into a single unit, the euro. Everything was going well until April 2010 when Greece teetered on bankruptcy and threatened to bring down all the other European nations with it. Unlike in the pre-euro days, the Greeks could not make their economy more competitive by reducing the value of their currency (the old drachma) which would have had the effect of making

Greek wages cheaper against, say, the Germans. This flexible option was no longer available to them. They were stuck. The other European countries were forced to bail them out at a cost of billions of euros, with no guarantee that such a scenario might not occur again with another European country. Such is the price of centralisation and concentration.

Brittleness

Apart from being more vulnerable than they appear to be, the other disturbing aspect of concentrated networks is that they provide less warning when something is about to go seriously wrong. Everything can be humming along smoothly, when suddenly it all goes 'kaput' because a major hub of the network has collapsed. This helps to explain why the financial markets were so confident right up until the eve of the crash. Even the International Monetary Fund remained bullish in its outlook up until the last minute, predicting that prospects for 2007 and 2008 had actually improved and that world economic growth would be 3.9 per cent in 2009 – a far cry from what was about to happen.

The reason why concentrated networks provide so little warning of a collapse is that there are fewer connection points to progressively relay and absorb the impact of a shock. In other words, there is no 'crumple zone' of the sort that is incorporated into the design of a modern car to reduce the dangers of a crash. The impact happens instantaneously, without warning. Engineers refer to this behaviour as 'brittleness'. They use the term when describing a material that may appear to be strong and hard but which snaps when the stresses become too great. In some industries this issue of 'brittleness' can have life-or-death consequences. Modern aircraft, for example, are increasingly built using a high proportion of composite plastic materials, such as carbon-fibre-reinforced epoxy, instead of traditional aluminium. These new state-of-the-art composites are lighter, stronger, and enable a higher cabin air pressure, which makes for a more comfortable flight. But they are also more brittle, so when they do break down they tend to collapse catastrophically and suddenly (at 30,000 feet!). On the other hand, good old-fashioned aluminium creaks and groans and warns of its demise. You can see visible signs of wear in aluminium, whereas it is difficult to detect stress in a composite material, even using X-rays and ultrasound. A composite can appear perfectly fine right up until the second it explodes into a million splintered fibres. Also, composites don't always behave the way that computer simulation models predict they should, which makes it difficult for engineers to understand how a composite aircraft will respond to the stresses of actual flight. Challenges such as these caused significant delays to the development of Boeing's new 787 Dreamliner and Airbus's A380 super jumbo, both of which are built with a high proportion of composites. This is not to suggest these planes are unsafe, but rather that the 'unknowability' factor has increased.[9]

Indeed, the topic of composite plastics exemplifies a conundrum of recent technological progress. That is, by insulating consumers from discomfort (turbulence), these new technologies create the illusion of more stability. Consequently, we can barely feel the vibration and momentum building up in the system until it is too late, at which point we may be faced with a sudden catastrophic shock to the system. The technology blinds us to what is actually happening and lulls us into a false sense of security. To illustrate how dangerous this phenomenon can be, let's look at another aeronautical example.

On 21 October 2009, a Northwest Airlines plane, Flight 188, carrying 144 passengers en route from San Diego to Minneapolis, overshot its destination airport by 240 kilometres because its pilots had become so immersed in their computer screens that they became oblivious to their location. For retired Pan Am 707 captain, Arnold Reiner, this incident came as no surprise and he commented that this behaviour is symptomatic of a wider systemic problem afflicting the aviation industry. He wrote in the *New York Times* on 17 December 2009 that decades of technological enhancements and automation have made flying undeniably much safer but have also fostered a subtle disconnect between pilots and the planes they fly. The automated systems on a modern plane can leave pilots so detached from flying that they become almost like passengers on their own flights, which is what happened on Northwest flight 188. Reiner said, 'The pilots were so deeply preoccupied with their computer screens that their situational awareness went out the window and even radio calls were tuned out. The plane was on its own, and this crew was along for the ride just like the folks in the back.'[10]

But what really got the crew into trouble, Reiner said, was 'thousands of hours in highly reliable, automated planes that over time made them ever more confident and blunted their need to be involved in the tasks of flying'. In contrast, when he had co-piloted planes in the late sixties, he explained, few cockpit controls and systems were fully automated. 'Most required periodic attention and resetting to operate properly . . . These disciplines required extreme accuracy and skill. And with all the numbers and variables of this demanding work, errors were expected and occurred . . . In short, *even when things were going smoothly during level cruise flight, cockpit crews had to be more actively involved to get where they were going.*' (Italics added.)[11] By the 1980s, aircraft had become so automated and computerised that most of the manual work for pilots had been eliminated. Reiner recalls that when he qualified to be a captain of the new, highly automated 'fly-by-wire' Airbus A310, pilots would joke that to pass the FAA simulator check ride, they needed to type fifty words a minute. 'I had evolved from the hands-on flier of my earlier years to a systems manager, controlling the plane with a flight management keyboard.'[12]

The problems with automation also extend to the automobile industry, where 'drive-by-wire' systems have been recently implicated in a string of accidents. In early 2010, Toyota, the largest car company in the world, recalled a number of best-selling models in the United States because some of the cars suddenly accelerated for no apparent reason, resulting in fatal crashes. Suspicion soon fell on the complex electronic accelerator mechanism which replaced the old mechanical version. Antony Anderson, a Britain-based electrical engineering consultant who investigates electrical failures and has testified in sudden-acceleration lawsuits, had this to say: 'With the electronic throttle, the driver is not really in control of the engine. You are telling the computer, will you please move the throttle to a certain level, and the computer decides if it will obey you.'[13] Sometimes, it appears, the computer decides not to. Cars have become scary again.

These examples illustrate how, once again, new technologies intended to ensure a smoother and safer ride can expose us to catastrophic outcomes. Perhaps nowhere has this paradox been more evident than in the banking industry, where, like a faulty car throttle, computer-driven models helped to accelerate the entire industry over a cliff in 2008–9. More recently, as discussed in Chapter 1, such programs were blamed for the largest single drop in Dow Jones' history when, on 6 May 2010, it suddenly fell almost 1,000 points – wiping nearly $1 trillion off equity values. It eventually bounced back a few hours later but the sheer scale and speed of the drop disturbed and mystified regulators and the financial industry. The system was not supposed to work this way. There were supposed to be safeguards to prevent this sort of thing. The fact that almost a trillion dollars in value could evaporate almost instaneously, without anyone knowing why, raised serious questions about the nature and robustness of the financial system that we have created.

In response to the Dow's mysterious fall, or 'flash crash', as it has come to be known, two US senators, Ted Kaufman, D-Del., and Mark Warner, D-Va., called for the Securities and Exchange Commission and the Commodity Futures Trading Commission to conduct a through study of high-frequency trading and other tools that move markets in milliseconds. 'We saw a living, breathing, real-time example today of the potential catastrophe that takes place if we don't have an ability to make sure we adequately use this technology,'[14] Warner said. 'Right now, there is no way to know what is happening in this marketplace,' Kaufman added.

These new technologies enable trading to occur on such a massive scale, so quickly that they generate a powerful momentum capable of feeding a dangerous and self-reinforcing volatility. Indeed, some computer-trading programs are deliberately designed to kick-start momentum in the market by, for example, initiating a series of rapid-fire buy or sell orders that are then cancelled. The techniques used to achieve this 'momentum ignition' range from legitimate trading to illegal scams, such as false rumours. Worse still, it is almost impossible to detect a problem until after it has made an impact. Bernard Donefer, a finance professor at Baruch College, New York, and author of the study 'Algos Gone Wild', fears that the 'speed of these high-frequency algorithm-based trading programs, and their capacity to impact so many markets simultaneously, could turn even a minor coding error into a spiralling disaster.'[15]

Which brings us to the issue of systemic risk.

CHAPTER 6

Systemic Risk

So far in this book, among other things, we have looked at the factors that have increased the velocity and scale of the global financial system, which in turn generates powerful momentum. This momentum, or Big Mo, is now such a significant force that it has become one of the key drivers of the global economy. Yet, remarkably, we can barely detect its presence.

This is because momentum affects the entire system simultaneously; it operates at what is called the 'systemic' level. And despite all the technical and analytical know-how of the finance industry, we are largely in the Dark Ages when it comes to understanding or detecting systemic risks. In fact, the main reason that the global financial crisis caught everyone by surprise is that there is no way of analysing the economy in a holistic way. There are numerous economic indicators but no integrated, big-picture view that would highlight a pervasive risk threatening the whole system simultaneously.

And we are not likely to see such a big-picture view any time soon. A 2006 report co-sponsored by the Federal Reserve Bank of New York and the US National Academy of Sciences concluded that even defining systemic risk was beyond the scope of any existing economic theory.[1]

This inability to define or measure systemic risk explains why such a dangerous level of momentum was allowed to build up in the global financial system without it being detected. But why is it so difficult?

Firstly, there are a great many variables in a large, complex system, and each new input creates an exponential number of possible outcomes. Complexity is obviously a key factor.

The other main reason is that it is only relatively recently that economists (and scientists) have woken up to the extreme dangers of systemic risks. It was assumed that the big threats to, say, the global financial system, would be external – such as the impact of a war, serious earthquake, terrorism or a pandemic. It was not anticipated that the biggest threat of all would emerge *from within the system itself*. And even if it did, it wasn't expected to have a major impact and so was accorded a low priority.

In any case, as discussed in chapter 2, it was assumed – misguidedly – that large systems would usually return to a state of equilibrium, thus averting any such problems. The global financial crisis changed all that, because economists realised that this was not the usual bubble gone bust: it was a complete systemic breakdown that would not be corrected by the power of 'equilibrium'. It was a wake-up call to look at the bigger picture.

In fact, not all economists were so behind the curve. One enterprising economist did attempt to create a model capable of looking at the entire economy in a big-picture way. But we have to go back in time sixty years to find it.

Back to the future

In November 1949, a chain-smoking ex-POW and former crocodile-hunting New Zealander named Bill Phillips ushered a group of students into a seminar room at the prestigious London School of Economics. There they were confronted by a mass of interconnected transparent pipes, tanks, sluices and valves in a glass-fronted box, which was connected to a cannibalised pump from an old Lancaster bomber. Phillips pulled a lever here and there, and the contraption gurgled to life as water sloshed around the system, while some of the students struggled to contain their mirth. But this machine was no joke. For Phillips had created the world's first dynamic model of an economy which showed how all the different parts worked together in real time. As he pulled each lever, coloured water rose and fell, representing the flow of money from the treasury to tanks representing health and education. Other flows represented the growth and decline in savings or tax revenue in the UK economy, and the interactions between them. Different economic parameters, such as investment and tax rates, could be manipulated by setting the valves which controlled the flow of water about the machine. So users could experiment with different settings to see the effect on the model. The contraption was crude. It was rudimentary. But it worked. It did what no amount of elegant diagrams and flow charts had ever done before: depict a 'live' model of a large economy at work.[2]

The machine soon attracted worldwide interest, and fourteen more machines were constructed and sold to institutions like Oxford, Cambridge and Harvard universities, Roosevelt College (Chicago, USA), the Ford Motor Company and the Central Bank of Guatemala. It became known as the 'moniac', an acronym for Monetary National Income Analogue Computer. Today only two of the machines survive, one of which is exhibited in the Reserve Bank of New Zealand.

The significance of Phillips's machine, however, is not is its novelty or improvised engineering. It is in what it stands for, which is a radical departure from the way academics and scientists have tried to solve complex, interconnected problems.

For the past few centuries, the tendency of science has been to break down (i.e. reduce) everything into its smallest component parts in order to understand a complex problem or system. This is known as 'reductionism'. For example, if someone is sick the doctor will often request a blood test which provides a micro-analysis of the patient's cells. Similarly, economists will tend to focus on specific aspects of the markets, such as interest or bond rates, and try to extrapolate from this information a broader view of what's going on. The intention is to use such 'micro-information' to build the bigger picture. Unfortunately, this reductionist process often becomes an end in itself, and no meaningful attempt is made to pull the pieces together in a holistic way. It becomes easier for, say, a doctor to talk about the specific readings of the blood test than to launch into a speculative and holistic analysis of what could really be making the patient sick. It is safer to stick to the specifics, where the margin of error is less, and an expert is less likely to be wrong or, in litigious societies, to be sued for malpractice (a real concern with doctors). Such concerns drive much of science and economics towards reductionism rather than its opposite, expansionism. It is so much easier to focus on the specifics than on the bigger picture.

The trouble is that the only way to understand a complex, interconnected system is to take an expansive view which shows how the dynamic feedbacks work. This is exactly what Bill Phillips's gurgling collection of pipes and pumps did. But even though Phillips applied the principles of flowing water to demonstrate how the economy worked, he was the antithesis of someone who allows himself to be carried along with the current. He was not afraid to challenge the system, as borne out by his remarkable life story.

Alban William Housego (Bill) Phillips was born on a New Zealand dairy farm in 1914. Shortly after leaving school he moved to Australia and then left for China in 1937, where he narrowly escaped ahead of the Japanese invasion of that year by boarding the Trans-Siberian Railway to Britain. He studied electrical engineering for a couple of years in London and joined the Royal Air Force at the outbreak of World War II. He was posted to Singapore, which soon fell to Japanese forces, but Phillips managed to escape to Java on a troopship. Along with thousands of other Allied servicemen he was soon captured by the Japanese and became a POW – but no ordinary one. No sooner had Phillips settled into the camp than he risked his life by constructing a makeshift radio from bits and pieces he had 'borrowed' from the camp commander's office and which he hid in a clog (Java was originally under Dutch rule). He also created a simple immersion element that surreptitiously drew power from the camp's lighting and was able to make hot cups of tea for hundreds of fellow prisoners.

For his heroic wartime efforts Phillips was awarded an MBE and a New Zealand Forces scholarship, which enabled him to attend the London School of Economics in 1946, where he studied sociology and then economics and, of course, was able to build his revolutionary moniac machine. He also went on to develop a coherent way of understanding the relationship between inflation and unemployment through a graph which came to be known as the Phillips curve. By any measure, Bill Phillips was an extraordinary and highly original person. He also had a unique insight into the ways that systems worked – whether it was the POW camp system or the economic system – which enabled him to make constructive sense of the bigger picture. He was no more constrained by orthodox thinking than he was by the barbed wire of his POW camp's perimeter. He was an 'out of the box' thinker long before the term was coined. In 1966 Phillips moved back to Australia and taught for some years at the Australian National University, before eventually retiring to New Zealand, where he passed away in March 1975.

It is a shame there are not more people like Bill Phillips around today. For his approach to holistic, dynamic modelling was way ahead of its time, and we could certainly do with a twenty-first-century version of his machine to help us understand how our global financial system operates. In the absence of such a holistic model, our financial system remains acutely vulnerable to systemic forces that we cannot easily detect – and in particular, momentum, or Big Mo.

But it is not just the economy that is increasingly threatened by systemic risks. The more interconnected and interdependent our world becomes, the more aspects of our lives are impacted by such risks. Let's explore a couple of other examples.

Cyber risks

The Internet is certainly one of the great technological triumphs of our age. It was originally designed in the 1960s to provide the US Defense Department with a way to communicate in the event of a nuclear holocaust. So it had to be robust. Since then it has evolved into the digital backbone of our world and underpins much of our technological and communications infrastructure. It is hard to imagine life without it.

Given that it is a man-made system, designed and built from the ground up, it would be logical to assume that plenty of people have a good idea of what it looks like in terms of its structure. But nobody does. The fact is that the Internet has grown so rapidly, and organically, that it has evolved pretty much spontaneously. Apart from some protocols about communication links and domain names, the Internet is largely unregulated and uncontrolled.

Recently researchers at Bar Ilan University in Israel set out to create the first comprehensive 'map' of the Internet. They discovered that it consists of a dense core of about eighty critical nodes (connection points) surrounded by a middle layer of approximately fifteen thousand peer-connected and self-sufficient nodes, and a further outer layer of five thousand sparsely connected, isolated nodes.[3] What is disturbing about this structure is just how concentrated the Internet is, especially given the trillions of transactions and the volume of data that daily pass through the connection points. And as we learned in chapter 4, 'concentrated networks' are not a good thing. Meanwhile, the amount of traffic flowing through this concentrated network is increasing exponentially. In 2008, for example, a single video site named YouTube, owned by Google, consumed as much bandwidth as the entire Internet did in 2000, and the growth of multimedia downloads and sharing is putting a huge burden on the system, not just in terms of the bandwidth required, but also in terms of the energy needed to power the system and the effort involved in keeping such a complex network running smoothly.

Nevertheless, the Internet will continue to grow and accelerate because, according to 'Metcalf's Law' (a sacred creed of computer scientists), a network's 'value' increases in proportion to the square of the number of people or devices in it. So the more people connected to the network, and the more data flowing through it, the more useful it is.

It's safe to say that the Internet is generating a lot of Big Mo.

But as with the global financial system, people assume that the Internet will evolve and be able to cope with this dramatic increase in velocity and scale. And of course, there are always those handy forces of 'equilibrium' to ensure a balance between internet capacity and usage.

Although the Internet has proved to be remarkably resilient until now, and continually confounds predictions of its impending collapse, it remains to be seen for how long this will be the case. It is not just an issue of technical robustness and network concentration, but one of growing dependence. Many businesses today almost come to a stop when their email service breaks down, which it frequently does. For example, during 2009 Google's Gmail service (which is one of the more reliable on offer) suffered two serious collapses, causing mass disruption among millions of users – and sending entire regions into a virtual communications blackout.

This dependency will further increase given the trend for businesses to move their key software applications to external online servers, which can only be accessed through the Internet. This development is referred to as 'cloud computing' because it is as if the software exists in a cloud. The trouble with this new approach, however, is that when the Internet goes down for whatever reason, businesses don't just lose access to their email, their entire computer systems become redundant. In today's highly interconnected world, this can have a knock-on effect that, in turn, can generate a powerful negative momentum. Yet the systemic threat posed by cloud computing is not generally recognised because, as previously explained, we tend not to take a big-picture view of the entire system. Cloud computing is being viewed in the same way as people looked at the subprime element in the US housing markets, as something that can be quarantined.

As the world's computer networks become more connected and concentrated, they become more susceptible not only to accidental failure but also to deliberate attack by cyber terrorists or foreign powers intent on sabotage. Most of our critical infrastructure, including energy supply, air-traffic control, transport grids, water supplies and communications, is controlled by interconnected computer networks. During 2008, infrastructure networks were subject to over fifty thousand incidents of malicious cyber activity in the United States alone. To protect against such threats, national intelligence authorities are seeking to reduce the number of government Internet access points so they can better monitor and control them. Although this might sound like a good idea in principle, it may have the opposite effect to what is intended, because making a network more concentrated also makes it more vulnerable. Wesley Clark, the ex-supreme commander of NATO and Peter Levin, a cyber security expert, articulated this challenge in an article in *Foreign Affairs*. 'The problem is that bundling the channels in order to better inspect them limits the range of possible responses to future crises and therefore increases the likelihood of a catastrophic breakdown. Such "stiff" systems are not resilient because they are not diverse.' Clark and Levin believe that rather than concentrate the US electronic infrastructure, it should be diversified. 'In the virtual world, just as in a natural habitat, a diversity of species offers the best chance for an ecosystem's survival in the event of an outside invasion.'[4]

Speaking of the natural habitat, let's look at another example where systemic risk poses a grave and imminent threat. This is the issue of climate change, where once again humanity is flying blind in terms of its capacity to detect and understand the risks involved. For, as with the models used to monitor the economy, the focus tends to be on just a few key indicators, such as the rate at which the polar ice caps are melting or average temperatures. Given an extremely cold winter or a hot summer, it's easy to conclude that the Earth is cooling or warming. But these indicators can be as misleading as interest rates were in the lead-up to the global financial crisis and are liable to distort the true picture. The reality is that, despite some unseasonably cold weather in the northern hemisphere during the past few years – according to figures from NASA's Goddard Institute for Space Studies, which monitors temperature fluctuations at thousands of sites round the world – the decade beginning January 2000 was the warmest decade since modern records began in 1880, and 2009 was the second warmest year recorded.[5]

Current models don't take into account the numerous ways climactic forces interact with each other to generate a powerful cumulative effect, or momentum. It is this cumulative effect that worries climate scientists like James Hansen of the Goddard Space Institute. He says that recent data have led him to conclude that most estimates of sea-level rises triggered by rising atmospheric temperatures are too low and too conservative. Whereas the Intergovernmental Panel on Climate Change predicts a rise of between twenty and sixty centimetres by the end of the century,[6] according to Hansen, the situation is moving much faster. He claims feedbacks in the climate system are already accelerating ice melt and are threatening to lead to the collapse of ice sheets, which will cause sea-level rises to be far greater and cause devastating flooding of many of the world's major cities and low-lying areas in Holland, Bangladesh and other nations.

Meanwhile, the increased amounts of greenhouse gases in the atmosphere are causing the oceans to become more acid with a lower pH value. This, in turn, will lead to food shortages because organisms in water live within a narrow band of pH levels and face extinction if the pH level is too high or too low. The knock-on effects of these changes will have a devastating impact on vast regions of the Earth, and destabilise our food and water supplies, as numerous environmental forces feed on themselves to accelerate change. When this momentum effect becomes self-perpetuating, the system is likely to spin out of control, just as it did with the global financial crisis. Unlike the financial world, however, nature doesn't do bail-outs.

It is difficult to grasp the cumulative nature of these changes because we citizens of the early twenty-first century have no Bill Phillips-style machine to help us see how all the factors interact with each other. We are not capable of seeing the system in its entirety, nor are we conditioned to even try. We prefer to focus on the specifics. The trouble is that, increasingly, the major threats to our world are occurring at the systemic level. They attack the whole system simultaneously. This is exactly what momentum does; it feeds on the system itself to become self-perpetuating, and it is very difficult to detect.

Shortly after it became apparent just how destructive was the BP oil spill in the Gulf of Mexico in 2010, David Brooks wrote in the *New York Times*, 'Over the past decades, we've come to depend on an ever-expanding array of intricate hi-tech systems. These hardware and software systems are the guts of financial markets, energy exploration, space exploration, air travel, defense programs and modern production plants. These systems, which allow us to live as well as we do, are too complex for any single person to understand. Yet every day, individuals are asked to monitor the health of these networks, weigh the risks of a system failure and take appropriate measures to reduce those risks. If there is one thing we've learned, it is that humans are not great at measuring and responding to risk when placed in situations too complicated to understand . . . People have trouble imagining how small failings can combine to lead to catastrophic disasters.'[7]

Let's now turn our attention to a very different kind of 'systemic threat'. This is the system that provides us with information, news and entertainment: the modern media. As we shall see, the media play a pivotal role in the creation of a momentum-driven society.

CHAPTER 7

Perpetual Prime Time

Over the past few decades, the news media have undergone a profound transformation. This has much to do with the way news is presented. Whereas once the media provided us with relatively unvarnished reports of current events with little hype, now they increasingly tend to operate as magnifiers and sensationalisers of news stories. This trend is particularly prevalent on television, where news stories are often 'talked up' out of all proportion to their intrinsic newsworthiness and then repeated relentlessly through the twenty-four-hour news cycle. News has become infotainment. Let's look at how we arrived at this point, and consider the consequences.

During much of the twentieth century in countries such as the United States, Britain, Canada, France, Australia and other developed nations the news business was dominated by people who had an affection and respect for the news. They were often journalists who had risen through the ranks to become executives or were members of illustrious media families such as the Grahams, Chandlers, Sulzbergers and Luces. When television became a major force in the 1950s and 1960s, it was the professional news teams that became the 'stars' of the television networks – people like Walter Cronkite in the United States. Such was the aura of credibility and authority of such figures that they cast a positive halo over their entire network, and were deemed as being integral to its success. Then things changed.

During the 1980s and 1990s there was a fundamental shift in the way that companies, including media organisations, perceived their role in society. As more people started buying shares in public companies with the aim of maximising their returns, those companies increasingly saw themselves as being in the business of creating 'shareholder value', that is, enriching their shareholders to the exclusion of all other measures. Traditional perspectives, such as a company's usefulness to society, public service, employee satisfaction and environmental record, all became subordinate to the share price. The mantra of shareholder value, or SV, was popularised by books such as Alfred Rappaport's *Creating Shareholder Value*, and soon dominated all aspects of business management and philosophy.[1]

The newsrooms of the big media organisations were among the first casualties of this shift towards shareholder value and profitability. Whereas previously they were allowed some leeway because of their special role in society, now they were transformed into dedicated 'profit centres' like any other part of the media business. They came under pressure to reduce costs, which resulted in fewer journalists, fewer foreign bureaus, reduced travel budgets and, ultimately, a reduced capacity to dig deep on important stories over sustained periods of time. Simultaneously, they took steps to boost their audiences by simplifying complex news stories, highlighting the emotional and sensational aspects of a story and employing newsreaders for their telegenic qualities rather than their journalistic credentials. They became masters of the autocue. As Dan Rather, former CBS anchor, observed, television news has been 'dumbed down and tarted up'.[2] Meanwhile, the culture of the advertising and entertainment industries, with their emphasis on attention-getting and instantaneous reactions, permeated the television newsrooms. So news is now delivered in staccato bursts of headlines – stripped of contextual meaning.

Conditioned to succumb

The cumulative effect of these changes in the media is to create a perceptual environment in which the world around us seems to be moving faster. Events appear to happen more frequently and evolve more rapidly. They also seem to be more important and consequential, as if every news story is a big story. This makes us feel we should know about them, and so we 'plug into' this fast-moving machine to get our daily 'fix' of the news, which for many people can be quite addictive. We become conditioned to see the world as a series of rapidly escalating events that generate a powerful, self-perpetuating momentum. Voyeuristically and vicariously, we ride the wave of these events, as they ebb and flow.

Gradually, over time, this conditioning can affect the way that we, as news consumers, experience our own 'real' lives. We become more accustomed to a momentum-driven world in which it seems normal to be swept along, to observe rather than participate or challenge. This is particularly so for the really big issues of our time, which develop enormous momentum. As individuals, we are less inclined to resist such powerful momentum – to form our own views – and may even see such resistance as futile. It is so much easier to surrender to the flow.

This conditioning may not just be a matter of how people perceive the world. Recent studies of the human brain using functional magnetic resonance imaging (fMRI) technology indicate that the persistent use of communications technology activates reward pathways that have been linked to addiction. The brain appears to rewire its neural pathways through a process called 'neuroplasticity'.[3] In other words, there may be a biological basis to some people's apparent addiction to the fast-moving news cycle. This is also reflected in the amount of television being consumed, which averages now around four hours a day in developed countries (and over five hours in the United States) and accounts for the major share of people's leisure time.[4]

Apart from seeming to speed up the news, media momentum

also causes news stories to take on a life of their own and become 'stuck in the groove'. This is because when a newsworthy event happens, the media develop a storyline around it, which is then magnified and reinforced by the globally integrated nature of the media. Eventually this storyline develops its own powerful momentum, so that even when facts arise that contradict it, they are resisted or ignored and ultimately overwhelmed by the media juggernaut, which is already moving in a certain direction. This is why so many news stories, particularly big ones, seem to have a predetermined air about them. Rarely are we surprised by a sudden turn of events.

One of the most destructive stories promulgated by the media in recent times was the idea that debt didn't matter because people could get richer through rising house prices. The economist Paul Krugman wrote in the *New York Times* on 16 February 2009,

> Until very recently Americans believed they were getting richer, because they received statements saying that their houses and stock portfolios were appreciating in value faster than their debts were increasing. And if the belief of many Americans that they could count on capital gains forever sounds naïve, it's worth remembering just how many influential voices – notably in right-leaning publications like the *Wall Street Journal*, *Forbes* and *National Review* – promoted that belief, and ridiculed those who worried about low savings and high levels of debt.[5]

Once a storyline becomes established in the public mind, even if it is false, it becomes difficult to dislodge. Long after it became clear just how serious the global financial crisis was, people were still rushing in to buy homes they couldn't afford and ramping up their credit-card debts. It was as if they didn't want to hear the bad news.

This is one of the great paradoxes of the modern media: they actually condition people to be less able to absorb real news.

It's like someone who is always babbling at you and hyping everything up: when he actually has something consequential to say, you don't hear it. As the social commentator and columnist Frank Rich observed:

> One of the most persistent cultural tics of the early 21st century is Americans' reluctance to absorb, let alone prepare for, bad news. We are plugged into more information sources than anyone could have imagined even 15 years ago. The cruel ambush of 9/11 supposedly 'changed everything', slapping us back to reality. Yet we are constantly shocked, shocked by the foreseeable.[6]

Rich lists numerous examples of major stories that didn't sink into the public consciousness until long after the evidence was made public. '[The use of] steroids, torture, lies from the White House, civil war in Iraq, even recession: [those are] just a partial glossary of the bad-news vocabulary that some of the country, sometimes in tandem with a passive news media, resisted for months on end before bowing to the obvious or the inevitable.'[7]

This resistance to reality is consistent with the behaviour of people who have become swept up in a fast-flowing current and who block out the sound of the waterfall up ahead. They would prefer to insulate themselves from the world outside by listening to the same song being played over again on their iPod – with the familiar lyrics that never change.

The juggernaut aspect of the media is often used to good effect by politicians and their Machiavellian handlers. They know that if they can create enough momentum for their cause, keep feeding it, and stay 'on message', it will soon become a self-perpetuating force that is difficult for their opponents to stop. Any contradictory factual evidence that emerges to challenge their campaign, or the credibility of their candidate, can be swamped by the sheer impetus of the media juggernaut. A similar tactic is used by the advertising industry, which strips down the proposition (story) into a slogan (sound bite) and repeats it over and over again until it sticks in the consumer's mind. This, in a nutshell, is the basis for modern political campaigning. As former President George W Bush explained to a public forum in 2005, 'See, in my line of work you got to keep repeating things over and over again for the truth to sink in, to kind of catapult the propaganda.'[8] In other words, to give the storyline some Big Mo.

Reinforcing these practices, increasingly, the only way established news networks can gain regular access to the halls of power is by 'behaving'. If journalists step out of line by being too confrontational in their questioning, they often find themselves excluded from press conferences, or their phone calls aren't returned. Conversely, if they behave, in the United States they may eventually find themselves drinking Kool-Aid on Air Force One, or in Britain being feted by the Downing Street PR maestros. Over time, journalists learn to be more compliant and complicit in the way information is disseminated by their government. They go along with the information flow. It is telling that many of the most consequential stories are now produced by freelance journalists working outside the big networks, such as Michael Hastings, whose article about the Afghanistan War in *Rolling Stone* in June 2010 forced President Obama to fire General Stanley McChrystal for making insubordinate comments. Hastings could do this because he was an 'outsider' and wasn't afraid to 'burn bridges' with people he may need to access in the future.

Another tactic that politicians and newsrooms have borrowed from the advertising industry is the use of fear as a persuasion tool. Advertisers have long used fear to promote products: fear of ageing and not looking good sells cosmetics; then there's fear of disease; fear of germs, and so on. In recent years, newsrooms have become adept at hyping the fear level out of all proportion to the actual threat. Consider, for example, the issue of terrorism. Notwithstanding the wars in Iraq and Afghanistan, and intermittent terrorist attacks, research suggests the world overall is experiencing the lowest levels of global violence since the 1950s. Steven Pinker, Johnston family professor in the Department of

Psychology at Harvard University, speculates that, according to the evidence, we are living 'in the most peaceful time of our species' existence'.[9] *Newsweek*'s international editor, Fareed Zakaria, writes in his book *The Post-American World* that

> part of the problem is that as violence has been ebbing, information has been exploding. The last 20 years have produced an information revolution that brings news and most crucially, images from around the world all the time. The immediacy of the images and the intensity of the 24-hour news cycle combine to produce constant hype. Every weather disturbance is the 'storm of the decade'. Every bomb that explodes is breaking news. Because the information is so new, we – reporters, writers, readers, viewers – are all just now trying to put everything in context.[10]

Then there is the age-old issue of censorship. Although media proprietors today rarely intervene directly in editorial policy, this does not mean censorship does not occur. It just happens more subtly. For the pressure on journalists emanates from the 'corporate culture' of the organisation for which they work, which encourages a kind of self-censorship. In a very strong culture, journalists instinctively know what the boundaries are. A survey conducted in 2006 by Roy Morgan Research in Australia, where media ownership is highly concentrated, revealed that half the journalists surveyed claimed they were unable to be critical of the media organisation they worked for, and a third said they felt obliged to take into account the political views of their proprietors when writing stories.[11] Philip Adams, an iconoclastic and influential writer, suggested that his regular column in the predominantly right-wing *Australian* newspaper, owned by News Limited, was window dressing to 'demonstrate pluralism'. But he is reported as saying there were topics that might offend management, on which even he would tread carefully.[12]

The combination of corporatisation, sensationalised news stories and declining journalistic standards has not gone unnoticed by the public. A poll conducted by the Washington-based Pew (public opinion poll) Research Center suggests that more than half of Americans believe that US news organisations are politically biased, inaccurate and don't care about the people they report on.[13] This represents a significant fall in the public's opinion about the news media since 1985, when a similar survey was conducted. Meanwhile, media diversity is in decline everywhere, particularly with regard to news coverage. Although there are now over sixteen hundred network and cable channels in the United States (up from just a handful twenty-five years ago), most of these amplify news feeds from a small number of major media companies.[14] Thousands of local, independent newspapers have closed down across the country, further reducing the diversity of viewpoints. The number of television channels in Britain has increased from 11 in 1990 to 530 today, but the number of newsrooms has actually decreased. In a case of 'more is less', most major media companies in the Western world have simultaneously reduced their independent news-gathering resources while expanding their distribution networks.

Alternative news sources

The precipitous decline in news quality has been a catalyst for the growth in alternative news and current affairs formats, such as documentary-style films, which provide deeper analysis and a broader context about topical issues. The most high-profile of the new breed of documentary film-makers is Michael Moore, whose films include *Bowling for Columbine*, an anti-gun manifesto; *Fahrenheit 9/11*, a scathing portrait of President George W Bush; and *Sicko*, an exposé of the US health-care system. Former vice president Al Gore used the documentary format to powerful effect to draw attention to climate change with his Academy Award-winning film *An Inconvenient Truth*.

Documentaries have the capacity to challenge strongly entrenched beliefs and the established momentum-driven storylines of the mainstream news. Errol Morris, whom the *Guardian* newspaper named as one of the top ten documentary film-makers in the world, is best known for his film *Thin Blue Line*, which helped exonerate an innocent man accused of murdering a policeman in 1976. 'The police were convinced they knew who the killer was,' Morris explained. 'They had a narrative about what had happened, and they had a deeply invested interest in believing that narrative. People fall into patterns of belief. It's not that they consciously choose to believe one thing or another. Often people do this because it's simpler to or it answers some social need. It doesn't have to be true. And once you choose to believe something or end up believing it, you surrender that belief reluctantly – if at all.'[15]

Notwithstanding the growing influence of documentary films, their weakness is that they are usually 'one-shot wonders' (albeit well-aimed ones) and can't tap into the continuity and repetition factor of the mainstream media. Without this constant reinforcement their impact can fade quite rapidly.

Another popular type of alternative news source is, paradoxically, 'fake news' programmes, which parody the mainstream format and provide satirical perspectives on the big issues of the day. Such programmes were pioneered on television in the early 1960s by Britain's *That Was The Week That Was* and have evolved into a potent media format that is now emulated around the world by shows such as Italy's *RockPolitik*, Pakistan's irreverent *Pillow Talk*, Japan's groundbreaking *Hikari Ota*, and *The Stephen Colbert Show* and *The Daily Show* in the United States. These programmes are all huge ratings successes and are highly influential. For example, despite *The Daily Show* being a 'fake news' show, 35 per cent of young Americans aged fifteen to forty now use it as their main source of news.

This begs the question: how is it possible in these serious times of global financial crises, wars and environmental upheavals that comedy news shows can challenge the established 'straight' news outlets? Perhaps, by performing the role that court jesters did during the Tudor era, they are able to speak truth to power without getting their heads cut off, while the other media act more like imperial court functionaries and cheerleaders. Consider this exchange – televised on 14 March 2009 – between *The Daily Show* host, Jon Stewart, and Jim Cramer, the manic host of CNBC's *Mad Money* show, who was renowned for his exuberantly bullish statements about the markets right up until the crash. The segment began with the usual irreverent banter but the mood abruptly soured.

'Listen, you knew what the banks were doing,' a visibly angry Stewart said, referring to the banks' profligate behaviour, 'and yet you were touting it for months and months. The entire network was, and so now to pretend that this was some sort of crazy, once-in-a-lifetime tsunami that nobody could have seen coming is disingenuous at best and criminal at worst.'[16] Stewart went on to accuse Cramer of turning finance reporting into a 'game', and said that CNBC, as the leading financial news network, had shirked its journalistic duty by believing corporate lies, rather than being an investigative 'powerful tool of illumination'.[17]

The interview crystallised the public mood of the time, and was broadcast around the world and through YouTube, the world's leading purveyor of online video. It was even acknowledged by the Obama administration. Stewart had articulated the anger and bewilderment of millions of people who wanted to know how the so-called financial masters of the universe could possibly have got away with their destructive behaviour for so long without being challenged. And, in particular, why had the media conformed so blatantly to the will of the financial institutions, instead of asking the hard questions? This unwillingness to ask such questions is, of course, symptomatic of the momentum effect.

Hub Brown, chair of communications at Syracuse University's SI Newhouse School of Public Communications, explains, '*The Daily Show* seems to understand the [truth] better than the networks do. I think it's valuable because when the emperor has no clothes, we get to say the emperor has no clothes.'[18]

In his 2004 paper '"The Daily Show" and the Reinvention of

Political Journalism', Geoffrey Baym, associate professor of media studies at the University of North Carolina, Greensboro, said, '"The Daily Show" can be better understood not as "fake news" but as an alternative journalism, one that uses satire to interrogate power, parody to deconstruct contemporary news, and dialogues to enact a model of deliberative democracy.' Baym believes that in an age in which few power-holders are willing to speak clearly and honestly, '"The Daily Show" . . . uses humor as the license to confront political dissembling and misinformation, and to demand a measure of accountability.'[19]

Despite their growing popularity, however, alternative news sources like *The Daily Show* are no antidote to the malaise that afflicts the modern news media. Rachel Smolkin, writing in *American Journalism Review*, said:

> Perhaps the hardest lesson to take away from 'The Daily Show' is the most important one. How can journalists in today's polarized political climate pierce the truth, Edward R. Murrow style, without being ideological or appearing ideological? . . . The mainstream media cannot and never will be 'The Daily Show'. The major news of our time is grimly serious, and only real news organizations will provide the time, commitment and professionalism necessary to ferret out stories such as [the] *Washington Post*'s exposé of neglected veterans at Walter Reed or the *New York Times*' disclosures of secret, warrantless wiretapping by the federal government. But in the midst of a transition, our industry is flailing. Our credibility suffers mightily.[20]

Everything old is new again – online

But what about the Internet? Doesn't the Internet transform the whole media equation by providing an open forum for more independent viewpoints to be expressed? Doesn't it challenge the momentum of the mass-media juggernaut by encouraging us to look at things differently, to question the status quo and step out of the flow?

Yes and no. The Internet certainly provides access to information on an unprecedented scale, and search engines like Google make it easy to rapidly sift through millions of web pages to find what one is looking for. But the Internet, by its very nature, is highly fragmented. It is a cacophony of different voices all struggling to be heard – a kaleidoscopic conglomeration of data, words, images, sounds. The Internet is really a 'splinternet'.

Unlike the mainstream media, the Internet cannot create and perpetuate a contextual framework for assimilating information. It cannot pull together all the pieces of data like a major media organisation does. Whereas the mainstream media converge information around a storyline, the Internet diverges information outwards into ever-increasing circles. Its impact is viral and incremental. For example, when, in November 2009, the *National Enquirer* magazine first broke the story about golfer Tiger Woods's affairs, the Internet swirled with rumours, and anyone following the story on the net could easily have become confused about what had really happened. There were so many contradictory bits and pieces of information floating around. It wasn't until the mainstream television news began to pull all the pieces together and went prime-time with it that the whole sorry tale came into full view. It also made the story more credible, especially for disbelieving die-hard Tiger fans. Similarly, when the online whistleblower site Wikileaks released 92,000 classified military documents about NATO's war in Afghanistan in August 2010, it did so through old-fashioned national newspapers: the *New York Times*, the *Guardian*, and the German weekly *Der Spiegel*. These publications propelled the leaked information into the media stratosphere and conferred on it a legitimacy and importance that it would not otherwise have had if it had been released directly into cyberspace. The Internet can certainly 'light a fire' by introducing new information, in a blog for instance, but it cannot guide and manage that fire in the way that mainstream media do. For an idea to hit the big time, it will need to be simplified and amplified by television. The Internet cannot compete with mass-market television for defining the essence of a story and driving this story home to millions of households simultaneously.

One of the more disappointing, and counter-intuitive, aspects of the Internet is that it is not the free and open marketplace of ideas that we would like to believe. Many of the world's most popular Internet news sites are owned by the major news organisations such as CNN, the *New York Times*, News Limited and the BBC, which, unsurprisingly, leverage the editorial from their own television and newspaper outlets. During the first quarter of 2009, websites owned by newspaper groups in the United States attracted over seventy million unique visitors on average, which according to Nielson Online Research was a record number that represented a significant percentage increase over the same period the previous year. Of the twenty-five most visited news websites, twenty-two were owned by the hundred richest media companies in 2008.[21] In effect, we are seeing the emergence of an online oligarchy dominated by the old guard. Some media companies have invested huge resources in their online sites, which provide lucrative revenue because advertisers are able to more accurately track the audiences and their response rates to online advertising. People gravitate to the big established online news sites because they are distrustful of a medium that, as Jon Stewart points out, 'combines the credibility of anonymous hearsay with the excitement of typing'.[22]

Skimming not diving

Apart from boosting momentum by creating a perceptual environment in which everything seems to be speeding up, the modern media are affecting us in another important way. They are changing the way we think.

At the dawn of the Internet Age in the mid-1990s, many pundits predicted that the Internet would empower billions of people to become smarter, or at least better informed, simply by making so much information easily accessible. Indeed, by 2009, the average American consumed three times as much information per day as they did in 1980. They spent an average of 11.8 hours a day sucking up, in aggregate over the year, 3.6 zettabytes of data and 10,845 trillion words.[23]

But information is not knowledge. People don't automatically become smarter by being immersed in a sea of data any more than security guards in an art gallery become art experts through a process of osmosis. Information must be chewed over, tested and digested before it can become knowledge. Indeed, too much information can be a bad thing. This is because the only way that most of us can cope with vast oceans of data is to skim the surface and glean the fragments of information that seem most relevant. Many of us are able to scan vast amounts of information by jumping from hyper-link to hyper-link with astonishing dexterity.

Although it may appear that skimming is simply the Internet version of 'speed reading', this would be to underestimate its influence on the way we process information. Nicholas Carr, writing in the *Atlantic* magazine, says:

> What the Net seems to be doing is chipping away my capacity for concentration and contemplation. My mind now expects to take in information the way the Net distributes it: in a swiftly moving stream of particles. Once I was a scuba diver in the sea of words. Now I zip along the surface like a guy on a jet ski. I'm not the only one. When I mention my troubles with reading to friends and acquaintances – literary types, most of them – many say they're having similar experiences. The more they use the Web, the more they have to fight to stay focused on long pieces of writing. Some of the bloggers I follow have also begun mentioning the phenomenon.[24]

Carr highlights one of the paradoxes of the modern media – and particularly the Internet – which is that, despite offering so much depth of information, they encourage our thinking to be more shallow. Another writer, Scott Karp, who regularly comments on online media in his blog, says he has stopped reading books altogether. 'I was a lit major in college, and used to be [a] voracious book reader . . . What happened? What if I do all my reading on the web not so much because the way I read has changed, i.e. I'm just seeking convenience, but because the way I THINK has changed?'[25]

Reading, unlike speaking, is not an instinctive skill for human beings that is coded in our genes. It has to be learned and practised. Over time, the way we read – and process information and ideas – conditions the way we think, which in turn rewires our brain through the process of neuroplasticity. For centuries, reading has been a means not just to acquire and broaden knowledge but also to reflect on the human condition and the world we live in, through works of literature and philosophy. Deep reading is indistinguishable from deep thinking.

Nowadays, however, technology is conditioning us to read in the 'shallows' and never dwell on one subject for too long. The playwright Richard Foreman believes this process is transforming us into 'pancake people'[26] – spread wide and thin as we connect with the vast network of information accessed by the mere touch of a button. Even the businesses that run the Internet don't like us staying on one site too long, or surfing at too leisurely a pace. This is because they derive their advertising revenue from the number of sites visited, and the faster we move from one site to another, the better.

People don't just move between Internet sites, they also skip from medium to medium – selecting from emails, phone calls, blogs, Facebook, text messages, Twitter, television and radio. Our evolution into media omnivores is also affecting the way we think. A recent study led by Clifford Nass of Stanford University in California investigated whether cognitive abilities might be affected by the range of media people regularly use. The results of the study were surprising, and suggest that heavy 'multi-taskers' – that is, people who often switch between many tasks – are actually slower at identifying changes to content than 'light' multi-taskers. The heavy multi-taskers also had more trouble filtering out irrelevant information, greater difficulty in concentrating on particular activities and, perhaps most surprisingly, more difficulty in moving between tasks in an effective way. Up until now it was generally assumed that heavy multi-taskers would be more adept at responding quickly and accurately to content changes, but the reverse seems to be the case. The researchers concluded that 'human cognition is ill-suited both for attending to multiple input streams and for simultaneously performing multiple tasks'.[27] It seems that our brains literally suffer information overload when so many media are competing for our attention.

The entire multimedia system is a momentum-generating machine, designed to accelerate the 'mass' of information and the 'speed' at which it flows. Multi-tasking and skimming make us more vulnerable to this machine because they keep us floating on the surface – where, as with a river, the water flows faster and we are more likely to be swept along like a leaf. By contrast, individuals who dwell more deeply on information are more able to resist the current.

There are certain professions that breed multi-taskers and 'super-skimmers': people whose job it is to scan and process information at lightning speed. Financial traders are such people. They are immersed in a sea of BlackBerrys and Bloomberg screens gushing out torrents of financial data, which they rapidly sift through in order to optimise their trades. It is not a job for the slow or dimwitted. Traders are usually acutely bright young men. Yet they were among the first to be drowned by the tsunami of the global financial crisis. Why? Because they couldn't detect the tectonic shifts occurring on the ocean floor that would generate the destructive wave. They were skimmers trying to cope with too much information.

In the 1960s an interesting experiment was conducted that demonstrated the folly of having too much information. Two groups of people were shown a fuzzy but indistinct outline of a fire hydrant. The resolution was gradually increased for one group, through a series of ten steps. For the other group, however, the resolution was increased over just five steps. Then the process was stopped at a point where each group was looking at an identical picture and the subjects were asked what they could see. It turned out that the members of the group that saw fewer intermediate steps recognised the picture earlier than the group presented with more steps. The extra information encouraged the latter group to speculate more about what the image was, clouding their judgement. The first group saw the fire hydrant more directly for what it was, unhindered by too many layers of information.[28]

The Internet too has a multilayer structure – so many layers, in fact, that you can easily get lost. Paul Kedrosky, a senior fellow at the Kauffman Foundation, commented that the Internet was supposed to be 'the great democratizer of information. It was supposed to empower individual investors, make murky financial markets more transparent, and create a new generation of citizen investors . . . It was supposed to shrink the world and turn it into a village, where everything happened in the public square and corruption and greed would have no place to hide. As the 1990s mantra went, "information wants to be free".'[29]

However, this new 'freedom of information', created a giant jigsaw puzzle comprising a zillion pieces of information that were constantly and frenetically changing. All the relevant information was there, but there was no way to look at it in a way that made sense. The sheer abundance of financial information available online created a smog of data. Even the most sophisticated financial analyst found it difficult to grasp the whole picture and comprehend the scale of the emerging problem. This was compounded by the illusion that any misconception, mistake or blunder could be rectified by accessing more information online. Simultaneously, the Internet also greatly accelerated people's ability to make transactions, thus generating more momentum in the markets, which in turn fuelled the global financial bubble that led to the crash.

'We are in the first financial crisis of the internet age,' said

Kedrosky, 'a crisis caused in large part by the tightly coupled technologies that now undergird the financial system and our society as a whole.'[30]

The Internet doesn't just encourage thinking to become shallower, it also encourages it to be narrower. This is because, unlike traditional media such as a newspaper or a television show, we consumers can choose to see only the information we want to see. So when we go online, we act as our own editor and gatekeeper for the news and tend to screen out opposing viewpoints. In fact, we often look for information and perspectives that confirm our existing mindsets and prejudices. We live in information cocoons. Nicholas Negroponte of MIT calls this self-censored media product 'The Daily Me', and is convinced it represents another step towards a world in which people increasingly isolate themselves in a bubble of self-sustaining beliefs and immerse themselves in like-minded communities.[31] Although we may think we like the idea of a debating chamber, in reality we prefer an echo chamber.

In one classic US study, Republicans and Democrats were offered various research reports from a neutral source. Both groups were most eager to receive coherent arguments that corroborated their pre-existing mindsets. Bill Bishop, the author of *The Big Sort: Why the Clustering of Like-minded America is Tearing us Apart*, says that as the United States grows more politically segregated, 'the benefit that ought to come with having a variety of opinions is lost to the righteousness that is the special entitlement of homogeneous groups'.[32] A twelve-nation study found that Americans, particularly highly educated ones, are the least likely to discuss politics with people of different views.[33]

This political polarisation is compounded by the ideologues who have stepped into the vacuum created by the demise of journalists – who have been laid off in huge numbers – and whose commentary is really a search for political ammunition. I am referring to the bloggers who preach only to the choir and inflame the partisan debate by selectively using, or exaggerating, information that supports their own view. They are the storm troopers of the post-journalistic world.

People's tendency to confirm their existing beliefs encourages them to form like-minded communities on the web, such as social-networking sites and virtual worlds. Communities such as Facebook, MySpace, SecondLife and the Twitterscape help connect millions of people in online environments that are conducive to building relationships. They also offer the potential for new types of democratic processes such as direct voting online, and the scope for alternative views to be put forward. The downside to web communities is that they can cause people to become more cut off from the rest of society. In their paper 'Electronic Communities: Global Village or Cyber Balkans', professors Marshall Van Alstyne and Erik Brynjolfsson wrote that 'individuals empowered to screen out material that does not conform to their existing preferences may form virtual cliques, insulate themselves from opposing points of view, and reinforce their biases . . . This voluntary Balkanisation and the loss of shared experiences and values may be harmful to the structure of democratic societies.'[34] They warned that we should have no illusions that the Internet will create a greater sense of community.

The danger is that when people suppress or are oblivious to information that contradicts their existing mindset, they are far more likely to believe they are heading in the right direction and ignore warning signs.

Momentum is the message

Given the fragmented and tribal nature of the Internet and its tendency to create information overload, people will continue to rely on mainstream news to pull all the pieces together into a narrative that makes sense of the world. Meanwhile, the nature of mainstream news will continue to evolve in its current direction, which means a greater level of corporatisation, more simplified and sensationalised news, momentum-driven storylines, fewer objective viewpoints and fewer dedicated news resources. This will make it more difficult for courageous journalists to ask the hard questions. Even publicly funded media organisations, like Britain's BBC or the ABC in Australia, find themselves increasingly having to justify their existence in commercial terms – and therefore are under pressure to emulate some of the mass-market compromises of the privately funded networks. The cumulative effect of these trends will be to continue to foster the ongoing development of a momentum-driven society – a society in which it is becoming increasingly difficult for individuals and organisations to avoid being swept up in waves of momentum that propel them along in a particular direction, even when that direction is no longer valid.

Nearly fifty years ago the Canadian English professor and philosopher Marshall McLuhan proclaimed: 'The medium is the message' – meaning that the medium is not just a passive provider of information but also shapes the thinking process.[35] Today, it may be more accurate to say that momentum drives the message.

Part 2

Behavioural
Momentum

CHAPTER 8

The Coherent Domain

In this book we have now explored a range of factors that have conspired to produce a momentum-driven world, such as the advent of new technologies, deregulation, network behaviour and globalisation. We have looked at some false assumptions that have enabled momentum to escalate, such as the erroneous belief that equilibrium will always restore balance, the over-reliance on models that accelerate decision-making while disguising the real risks, and the outdated mantras of 'bigger is better' and 'efficiency is king'. We have seen how the modern media exacerbate these problems by creating a perceptual environment in which events appear to be moving faster and every story is treated as important breaking news. This environment fosters thinking that is shallow and narrow, and individuals – overloaded with information – are less able to think for themselves or resist the flow. The cumulative impact of these forces has been to accelerate both the speed at which events unfold and the scale of their impact. In a Newtonian sense, this generates more momentum in our world.

Thanks to Newton's laws, readers of *The Big Mo* should have a good idea of the 'physics' that is creating this momentum-driven environment. What is less clear, though, is how momentum operates at the psychological level to influence human behaviour.

This is where things become more subtle. For, as described earlier, momentum seems to pull us into a directional flow which influences our behaviour. It tends to creep up on us and envelop us in such a stealthy way that we are barely aware of its effect. Our thoughts begin to align themselves in the direction of the momentum. One thought leads to another, each one reinforcing the next, producing an internal cascading effect. We begin to self-justify our direction and suppress information that challenges it. By this stage we are deeply immersed in the flow. Eventually, our self-justifications may become entrenched in our psyches as belief systems, which manifest in behaviours that further reinforce our beliefs.

This cognitive process has always been integral to our human behaviour. What is different today, however, in this more hectic, media-driven world, is that we have less and less time to challenge our innermost thoughts, and so we react more unconsciously and automatically to the stimuli around us. This makes us more vulnerable to the tides of momentum that now drive our world. Dr Jon Kabat-Zinn of the University of Massachusetts Medical School explains:

> We are often being pushed through our lives by the pace of the world [momentum], without the luxury of stopping and taking our bearings, of knowing who is doing the doing. Our actions are all too frequently driven by thoughts and impulses that run through the mind like a coursing river, if not a waterfall. We get caught up in the torrent and it winds up submerging our lives as it carries us to places we may not wish to go and may not even realize we are headed for.[1]

Sometimes, when we are caught in such a torrent, there is a feeling that we are being propelled forward by unseen forces. It's as if everything around us has fallen into alignment, urging us forward in a particular direction. The German writer Goethe described a similar phenomenon in his oft-quoted observation on commitment. He wrote, 'The moment one definitely commits oneself, then Providence moves too. All sorts of things occur to help one that would never otherwise have occurred. A whole stream of events issues from the decision, raising in one's favour all manner of unforeseen incidents and meetings and material assistance, which no man could have dreamed would have come his way.'[2]

Sports psychologists have a particular interest in momentum because of its influence on performance. *The Oxford Dictionary of Sports Science and Medicine* defines psychological momentum as 'the positive or negative change in cognition, affect, physiology, and behaviour caused by an event or series of events that affects either the perceptions of the competitors or, perhaps, the quality of performance and the outcome of the competition'.[3] Positive momentum is associated with periods of competition, such as a winning streak, in which everything seems to 'go right' for the competitors. In contrast, negative momentum is associated with losing streaks.

While sports psychologists are willing to define behavioural momentum, they readily admit they are at a loss to explain how it operates, or how to go about measuring it.

Over the years, there have been attempts to quantify the nature and impact of behavioural momentum, with varying degrees of success. In 1982, a research team led by John Nevin, professor emeritus of psychology at the University of New Hampshire, together with Charlotte Mandell and Jean Atak, wrote a paper called 'The Analysis of Behavioral Momentum', in which they explored why certain behaviours can become persistent over time.[4] The team drew heavily on Newtonian physics to explain the nature of behavioural momentum, which is perhaps not surprising given that the team leader, Professor Nevin, also had a BE in mechanical engineering from Yale University. In effect, the researchers said that people's tendency to continue to behave in a certain way, and resist change, is dependent on the type of reinforcement they receive. This resistance to change is characterised as behavioural momentum. The team even developed a method for calculating the impact of behavioural momentum, based on the Newtonian formula: $\Delta V = f/m$, in which ΔV is the change in velocity or, in behavioural terms, response rate; velocity (V) refers to the response rate; mass (m) refers to the response strength, and force (f) refers to the change in the contingencies for the behaviour (i.e. environment change). This equation is analogous to Newton's second law of motion, which states that the change in velocity of a moving object when an outside force is applied is directly related to that force and inversely related to the object's mass.

The pioneering work of Nevin, Mandell and Atak has been highly influential in the development of social and health-care policies, such as drug rehabilitation programmes, where behavioural persistence (momentum) and relapse are critical issues. By providing a powerful and workable framework for addressing these issues, they also introduced the concept of behavioural momentum into mainstream psychology for the first time.

However, subsequent research has revealed some inconsistencies and limitations in the model originally developed by Nevin's team.[5] Although these inconsistencies do not undermine the value of the work, they highlighted the limitations of using a Newtonian model to comprehend the infinitely complex nature of human behaviour.

To overcome such limitations, some researchers into human behaviour have recently turned their attention to the realm of quantum physics, and in particular to 'field' theory. According to this perspective, the world is not simply a 'machine', as Sir Isaac Newton and René Descartes characterised it, but rather it can be seen as a complex web of interconnected packets of energy, operating at various frequencies and manifesting in myriad different ways. In certain circumstances, subatomic particles begin to cooperate through common electromagnetic fields and resonate in phase with each other. They move away from randomness and disarray towards order and alignment to create a perceived sense of order, which physicists refer to as negentropy. They enter into what is known as a coherent domain.

A similar tendency has been observed in people in group environments. Experiments have shown that in certain situations the brain of each member of the group becomes less highly tuned to their own separate information and more receptive to that of other group members. In effect, they pick up someone else's information from the 'field' as if it were their own. Perhaps this is what members of a winning sports team experience when they 'enter the zone'.[6]

The idea that we are susceptible to such unseen forces, or coherent domains, may rankle the more rational among us. But the underlying premise is sound, because we, as humans, exist within a sea of quantum energy, and at our most elemental level we are not a chemical reaction but rather an energetic charge. As such, we are likely to be susceptible to the energetic forces or 'fields' around us. It is not uncommon, for example, for people to feel there is an overpowering mood or energy present in certain group environments. I, for one, have experienced this many times in corporate life – you can feel it the moment you enter the room. It is almost palpable.

Unlike more orthodox psychological models, field theory may help explain why momentum can exert such a powerful influence over human behaviour and group dynamics. It suggests that at the quantum level the momentum effect may actually be a type of coherent domain which aligns a range of disparate forces together to drive people in a certain direction. So we are not dealing with a simple Newtonian equation of mass times velocity equals momentum. We are dealing with a complex range of quantum forces that combine to produce a cumulative effect that influences our psychology and behaviour.

Field theory would also explain the immersive quality of momentum and the stealthy and subtle way it influences human behaviour. A field, or coherent domain, tends to permeate a situation and influence it through a process of osmosis that is barely detectable. It becomes the water that people swim in, the context in which they operate. It helps to explain why even highly intelligent, powerful or even cynical people often don't realise they are being swept up in a momentum trap until it is too late. Their objective cognitive processes become sublimated within the momentum 'field' and realigned, much like iron filings on a magnet.

It's possible that we are more susceptible to changes in our environmental field than we may realise. This is because, according to recent psychological research, our characters are much less 'situationally stable' than previously thought. That is, we don't really have a single character that expresses itself consistently in all situations, but rather we have a multiplicity of tendencies which are activated in different environments. For example, a person can be scrupulously honest at work, but may constantly shade the truth in his personal life. A woman may demonstrate great courage when serving as a police officer, but may be cowardly in her personal relationship. Different environments, or fields, bring out different character traits, which in turn become further reinforced by those environments.

Paul Bloom, professor of psychology at Yale University, says that individuals are a community of competing selves. These different selves 'are continually popping in and out of existence. They have different desires, and they fight for control – bargaining with, deceiving, and plotting against one another.'[7] So although we may tell ourselves that our behaviour fits into a consistent, coherent story, we are really driven by a variety of unconscious tendencies that get aroused by different environments. This view is supported by research conducted by Richard Thaler, professor of behavioural science and economics at the University of Chicago, and Cass Sunstein, professor of jurisprudence at the University of Chicago Law School, which suggests that individuals comprise different personalities. Specifically, they propose that we have within us a far-sighted-planner personality (a Dr Spock type) and a myopic 'doer' personality who is more like Homer Simpson. 'The Planner is trying to promote your long-term welfare but must cope with the feelings, mischief, and strong will of the Doer, who is exposed to the temptations that come with arousal.' When people are in a 'hot state' (i.e. aroused), their decision-making will be different from when they are in a 'cold state' and are thinking more rationally, with more consideration for the long-term consequences of their actions. Our inner Dr Spock is often in conflict with our inner Homer Simpson, and one will inevitably lose.[8]

The idea that we have multiple selves is not new. Plato alluded to it 2,500 years ago, and the eighteenth-century Scottish philosopher David Hume wrote, 'I cannot compare the soul more properly to anything than to a republic or commonwealth, in which the several members are united by the reciprocal ties of government and subordination.'[9] Celebrated late nineteenth-century poet Walt Whitman famously observed, 'I am large, I contain multitudes.'[10]

More recently, these subjective observations have been supported by brain-imaging studies which suggest that a person's multiple selves activate the brain in different ways, pointing to a possible physiological basis for the concept.[11]

More broadly, this model of behaviour also appears to operate at the collective level. We know, for example, that at certain times in human history the environment changes in such a way that some behavioural traits are more likely to manifest than others and to have a greater impact on the world. Times of plague or war, for example, tend to bring out different dominant behaviours in society from times of prosperity and peace, as do periods of great technical innovation or creativity.

So what kind of dormant behavioural traits are likely to be aroused by today's momentum-driven environment? Obviously, it would be helpful to be responsive to changes in such a fast-flowing environment – so responsiveness is a trait that may be activated. It may also help to be more efficient and focused to deal with the increased complexity and speed. Other traits likely to be activated, however, may not be so benign. In my experience in the financial world, a momentum-driven environment can encourage people to behave opportunistically and selfishly, with scant regard for the longer-term consequences of their actions. It can incite some people to become greedy or ruthless or to gamble recklessly, fearful of missing out on a fast-moving opportunity. It can also foster a superficial perspective because, as discussed earlier, this is the only viable way to deal with overwhelming amounts of fast-flowing information: to skim the surface and not dig deeper.

For most people, however, the most prevalent behavioural trait to be aroused by a momentum-driven environment is a generalised submissiveness in which they are perfectly willing to surrender to the flow. This is not for lack of objectivity or courage but simply because it is easier to submit than resist what appears to be inevitable.

But people don't just surrender to momentum because it is the path of least resistance. They also defer to it because the flow itself is perceived as a kind of guiding authority, whose legitimacy is based on the fact that everyone else is moving in the same direction, and in the absence of clear signposts the crowd *must* be right. The stronger the momentum, the more authority it exerts over people. This explains why people who are caught up in a powerful momentum flow are sometimes willing to compromise their values; they believe they have authority on their side.

It is disturbing what people are capable of doing for the sake of authority. In one of the most famous, and oft-cited psychological experiments of the 1960s, the Yale University psychologist Stanley Milgram showed that people would be willing to administer painful electric shocks to a stranger if they were told to do so by a scientist (i.e. authority figure). In summing up his experiment, Milgram said, 'Ordinary people, simply doing their jobs, and without any particular hostility on their part, can become agents in a terrible destructive process. Moreover, even when the destructive effects of their work become patently clear, and they are asked to carry out actions incompatible with fundamental standards of morality, relatively few people have the resources needed to resist authority.'[12]

One of the least understood implications of the Milgram

experiment, even today, is that 'authority' doesn't have to be in the form of a scientist in a white coat; it can also take a more generalised form, such as an ideological cause or a powerful dynamic like momentum. In fact, the dynamic forms of authority tend to be more destructive because they can permeate the collective consciousness and become self-perpetuating. They affect the environment, or coherent domain, in which people operate, which can sometimes bring out the worst in them.

To help understand how an environment can activate destructive behavioural tendencies, let's return again to the example of UBS, where a subtle change in the bank's field, or coherent domain, led to devastating consequences – not just for the bank, but for the entire Swiss financial industry.

Farmers and hunters

During my time working at UBS, my colleagues and I used to divide the bank into two distinct camps: farmers and hunters. The farmers represented the bank's wealth management business, which helped clients to grow their assets over time – hence the agricultural label. Their work was relatively slow, painstakingly detailed, and required a lot of patience. It was necessary to build trust with a client over time, sometimes over generations when dealing with a family. There were no real short cuts in this type of business.

The Swiss were very good at it because they were natural farmers, having learned over the centuries how to optimise and protect the resources of their tiny Alpine country. They were also natural diplomats, having had to operate between the great powers of Europe, which were often at war. In such an environment, the Swiss learned the value of discretion. These qualities permeated the cultural DNA of the UBS wealth-management business and helped it become so successful that by 2008 it was the largest private bank in the world, managing nearly $3 trillion on behalf of investors, including nearly one-third of the world's billionaires. It was also a relatively predictable and stable business. In terms of field theory, you might say the business tended towards a state of negentropy.

The hunters represented the investment-banking business of UBS, which was a relatively new area for the bank to be involved in. It focused on the world of high finance, corporate buyouts and complex equity deals or, as they say, the 'big end of town'. The behavioural qualities of an investment banker, particularly the high-octane Wall Street variety, are the antithesis of the conservative, nurturing Swiss wealth manager (farmer). Investment bankers are constantly on the hunt for new deals – the bigger and riskier, the better. More risk means higher returns, and higher returns mean staggeringly large performance bonuses. Investment bankers operate in a world of Big Mo, where things move quickly on a massive scale. It is not an environment for the faint-hearted. In terms of quantum physics, you might describe this world as embodying chaos theory.

To give you an idea of the surreal environment in which some investment bankers worked during the heady days before the financial crash, consider this recollection by an ex-UBS investment banker named Philipp Meyer:[13]

I'd been working for the bank for about five weeks when I woke up on the balcony of a ski resort in the Swiss Alps. It was midnight and I was drunk. One of my fellow management trainees was urinating onto the skylight of the lobby below us; another was hurling wine glasses into the courtyard. Behind us, someone had stolen the hotel's shoe-polishing machine and carried it into the room; there were a line of drunken bankers waiting to use it. Half of them were dripping wet, having gone swimming in all their clothes and been too drunk to remember to take them off. It took several more weeks of this before the bank considered us properly trained.

UBS apparently thought pretty highly of me, because despite my lack of a financial background, they put me onto the derivatives trading desk. This was a coveted spot

– the derivatives traders were viewed as the elite – the baddest of the bad-asses . . . By the time I arrived on Wall Street in 1999, the link between derivatives and the real world had broken down. Instead of being used to reduce risk, 95 per cent of their use was speculation – a polite term for gambling . . .

I put on 45 pounds [20 kilos] in my first year at the bank, and, as you might guess, it was not from eating McDonalds . . . My standard strategy was to order half a dozen appetisers, plus a steak and lobster, plus a few desserts and as much wine as I could drink, as long it was under a few hundred dollars a bottle . . . Being a junior employee, I couldn't really order bottles that cost more than a few hundred dollars, but the senior guys could get nicer stuff – Opus One, Chateau Latour. As long as we were out with a client, the bank paid. I remember being stunned the first time I saw a dinner bill for ten grand. But that was just the beginning . . . I never saw anyone literally set fire to money, but I did drink most of a bottle of 1983 Margaux [$2,000].

The mornings after, with our thousand-dollar hangovers, my colleagues in corporate finance would set up deals and make a few hundred factory workers redundant. I helped build derivatives that funnelled income to offshore holding companies so rich people and big corporations didn't have to pay taxes. We had lawyers on retainer in the Cayman Islands and Jersey – a quick phone call and it was all set, no more taxes.

For a long time, and for obvious reasons, the worlds of the farmer and hunter were kept quite separate at UBS, and there was little overlap between their respective businesses. Their corporate cultures did not contaminate one another. Then in 2004 UBS did something that was considered to be quite revolutionary at the time. It integrated all its various businesses into a 'one bank' strategy, in order to streamline its operations and 'unlock synergies' within the business. No global megabank had achieved this before. Although most megabanks operated under single brands, their businesses remained separate in all but name. Now UBS was taking integration to a whole new level. The new 'one bank' strategy was launched with much fanfare and an expensive advertising and PR campaign, which was well received by the media and shareholders. After all, it made intuitive sense to bring everything together. As the Swiss like to say, 'There is strength in unity.'

Unfortunately for UBS, however, there is also the paradox of the strong, as discussed in chapter 5. Large, highly integrated organisations tend to generate a powerful internal momentum which becomes self-perpetuating. The momentum feeds on internal efficiency and scale, which can be magnified to such an extent that it pushes the organisation beyond a state of equilibrium.

The 'one bank' strategy unleashed a powerful new dynamic within UBS. But it wasn't the only factor at play. For some time there had been insistent rumblings among the ranks of the wealth-management business that they were effectively bankrolling the huge corporate bets and lavish lifestyles of the investment bankers. This inequality eventually prompted UBS to introduce a new performance-based remuneration system in the wealth-management business that enabled the farmers to earn big money for the first time, provided they achieved ambitious new targets. This new fairness, however, came at a price. The combination of aggressive business targets and generous performance incentives fostered a powerful internal momentum that encouraged some people within the wealth-management business to do whatever it took to achieve their targets, even if it meant cutting corners and being less prudent with the affairs of their clients. Their 'bad selves' were activated, as the Yale psychology professor Paul Bloom might say. The Big Mo dynamics of the investment-banking world began to permeate the wealth-management business at UBS. In doing so, it fundamentally altered the coherent domain in which the farmers had operated. This would have far-reaching consequences.

In 2008 it emerged that a group of UBS private bankers had helped some of their wealthy US clients avoid paying tax to the Internal Revenue Service (IRS). Bradley Birkenfield, a former UBS private banker based in Geneva, revealed to a US Senate inquiry how he squeezed diamonds into tubes of toothpaste to help his clients transfer assets without detection by the IRS. Others used counter-surveillance techniques, such as encrypted computers and code names, to enable US clients to hide their assets in Switzerland. Such clients may have been seeking a safe haven for their posterity fund, which was the hypothetical amount they needed to salt away to preserve their lifestyle if things ever turned sour. It would enable them, for instance, to continue paying their grandchildren's private-school fees or the gardener at their Lake Como villa. Sometimes this amount of money is referred to as 'the nut'. 'Every Master of the Universe knows the number,' wrote Tom Wolfe in *The Bonfire of the Vanities*.[14]

One wealthy client in search of a safe sanctuary for his money told how he was given a secret tour of the UBS headquarters in Geneva, where he was taken five storeys below ground to a bomb-proof vault protected by facial recognition and thumbprint software. He had entered the inner sanctum of a mysterious, self-protective world.

Bradley Birkenfield knew this world well. The son of a successful neurosurgeon in Boston, he moved to Switzerland in his late twenties, where his smooth, well-spoken manner helped him to thrive in the rarefied club of Swiss banks, enabling him to own a BMW and a chalet in Zermatt. He also knew he had to be careful. A September 2006 UBS document warned its bankers to always maintain a 'clear desk policy' in hotel rooms; use secure infrastructure (travel notebook, PDA); be aware that cellphones were prone to eavesdropping; cross borders without client-related documents. Swiss bankers were operating like spies.[15]

When I moved from New York to Zurich in 2002, one of the first things I noticed was that the windows on every house on my cobblestoned street were heavily shuttered – as they were throughout the city, even for large office blocks. At first I assumed this was to keep out heavy snowfalls and bad weather, but after a while I came to believe the shutters served a secondary purpose: they kept prying eyes out. The more I came to know the Swiss through working and socialising with them, the more aware I became of their innate respect for privacy. It was so different from living in midtown New York, where people wanted to know my business from the outset and were all too happy to regale me with their life story, often in excruciating detail. By contrast, the Swiss were more reserved and cool, sometimes glacially so. It took quite some time before my neighbours thawed sufficiently to welcome me into their confidence, and began to address me as Mark rather than Herr Roeder. The upside of this love of protocol and privacy is that Switzerland is a remarkably safe place to live. I would have no hesitation in leaving the flat without locking it, or leaning my unchained bike against the railing outside – behaviour that would be unthinkable in New York or London. More broadly, at the risk of stereotyping, I have come to believe that the Swiss are one of the great humanitarian societies on Earth – in the sense that they really do care about the plight of others less fortunate. It is no accident that Switzerland is the headquarters for an inordinate proportion of the world's altruistic enterprises, including the International Committee of the Red Cross, Doctors Without Borders (Médecins Sans Frontières) and the United Nations High Commission for Human Rights, to name just a few.

Ironically, it is this humanitarian tradition that provides the backdrop for the banking-secrecy laws that have earned the Swiss so much enmity in recent years.

In the early 1930s, Swiss politicians became concerned about some ominous developments in neighbouring countries. The Nazis in Germany had just introduced a law that made it a death-penalty crime for its citizens to hold assets outside the country, and there was a huge scandal in socialist France over Swiss bank accounts held by prominent citizens, including the wealthy Peugeot brothers and Françoise Coty of the perfume family. The

Swiss looked out across their Alpine borders and saw an increasingly chaotic world of rising fascism, communism, despots, bank collapses and militarism. They decided to lock the vault. The Swiss parliament introduced the Swiss Banking Act of 1934, which made it a criminal offence to pass on client information to an external party. It also paved the way for the introduction of numbered bank accounts, where the name of the bank client is replaced by a number or a code word and the client's name does not appear in documents, such as bank-account statements. The identity of the client was restricted to a select number of bank employees. These stringent banking laws did not merely protect client confidentiality; they also earned Switzerland a reputation as a tax haven, which attracted wealthy clients from around the globe. The rest of the world tended to turn a blind eye to such activities up until the events of 9/11 in 2001, when it became clear that terrorist organisations could hide their funds in secret bank accounts. This prompted a push for greater transparency, which was subsequently further accelerated by the global financial crisis, when governments which were pumping billions into failing banks realised they could not afford to lose tax revenue to secret offshore accounts.

Against this background, the proactive tax-evasive actions of the UBS executives went too far. They triggered an aggressive investigation by the US Department of Justice that cast an unwelcome spotlight on Swiss bank secrecy – or bank privacy, as the Swiss prefer to call it. It was the last thing UBS needed. Having already lost billions, and with its reputation in tatters, it was now responsible for prompting an attack on Switzerland's special status as a tax haven, which underpinned the Swiss banking industry. 'This is a very dangerous situation because the banking sector has been critical to Switzerland's wellbeing,' said Charles Wyplosz, director of the International Centre for Money and Banking Studies in Geneva.[16] At about $2 trillion during the 2007–8 financial crisis, the balance sheet of UBS was four times as large as Switzerland's gross domestic product. A downturn in the Swiss banking industry had consequences for the rest of the country's economy.

The much-publicised investigation into UBS encouraged the G20 group of leading industrial countries, in April 2009, to place Switzerland on a 'grey list' of countries to keep a close eye on for tax-evasion activities, and undermined the Alpine nation's status as a global financial centre. Eventually, after protracted negotiations, UBS and the Swiss government reached a settlement with the US Department of Justice in August 2009, and the Swiss banking system emerged from one of the darkest periods in its history, albeit with its reputation for providing privacy considerably diminished. Switzerland had been forced to agree to new laws ensuring that clients could no longer hide taxable assets in their banks.

So what caused the normally cautious UBS private bankers to overstep the mark? Some commentators have blamed their errant behaviour on the opacity of tax-haven laws, which are notoriously grey. More broadly, others have blamed financial regulators for creating a 'loose money' environment in the first place. Luis E Rinaldini, a former partner at the investment bank Lazard Frères, disagrees. 'Bankers are paid to be cautious when there's loose money around. If you had a bus driver who went 100 miles an hour [on an icy road], you'd think he was crazy. But if his boss said, "It's our policy to drive faster as the road gets icier," you wouldn't be surprised if the boss ended up in jail.'[17]

In any case, these loose-money factors had been present, to varying degrees, for decades before the UBS bankers went haywire. It is also not sufficient to pin the blame on the bank's ambitious performance targets, because other banks had introduced similar programmes without the devastating consequences. What really changed was the environmental field in which the UBS bankers found themselves operating. UBS had succumbed to a powerful momentum dynamic that permeated and resonated throughout every aspect of the organisation. This activated dormant opportunistic behaviours in some bankers who had previously been constrained in the old conservative environment.

The same Big Mo dynamic that propelled the bank headfirst into the toxic subprime markets drove its private bankers to make reckless decisions about their clients' US tax affairs. And the bank clung to this precarious path long after it became evident how dangerous it was. In fact, one of the defining symptoms of being caught in a momentum trap is a compulsion to keep going in the same direction no matter what, right till the very end.

In his final appearance as chairman of UBS – at the bank's emotionally charged annual shareholders' meeting in April 2008 – Marcel Ospel closed his presentation by saying, 'It was a bad storm. It whipped our sails, but it didn't throw us off course.'[18]

CHAPTER 9

The Rise of the Momentum Surfer

Why should the lord of the country
flit about like a fool?
If you let yourself be blown to and fro,
you lose touch with your root.
If you let restlessness move you,
you lose touch with who you are.

Lao-Tzu, Tao-te-Ching

What sort of person thrives in this increasingly momentum-driven world? What behavioural species, in a Darwinian sense, most successfully adapts to this new environment and rises to the top?

It seems logical that such a person would be particularly sensitive to the presence of momentum and may feel a natural affinity with it. They can tap into the 'coherent domains' and 'energy fields' described in chapter 8, and their finely tuned antennae can sense infinitesimal variations in the amplitude and direction of these fields – not consciously, of course, but intuitively. They see how momentum ebbs and flows and evolves with the situation. They also have an appreciation of its power and influence. They may have witnessed this power first-hand in their own life, and seen its capacity to effect change and make things happen. They appreciate its ability to catapult individuals or organisations to success in a relatively short time. And so they see momentum in a purely positive light. Most importantly, they know how to ride these unseen waves of momentum that propel our world. They enjoy the feeling of being lifted up and swept forward by this surging force. It doesn't really matter which direction the wave is heading, as long as it is big enough and powerful enough for them to ride it. Such a person is a momentum surfer.

Everyone goes with the flow sometimes; how can anyone avoid it? And sometimes it makes sense to do so. But momentum surfers are in a different league. They represent the apotheosis of a momentum-driven society. Such people live for the rush of going with the flow. The momentum dynamic is central to the way they operate in life. It is what drives them at the visceral level, and in some cases may even come to define them. Momentum surfers tend to be rather energetic and dynamic personalities, as they resonate with the energy that feeds them. They can also be charismatic and convey a sense of inner certainty, which gives the impression to those around them that they know where they are going. It is little wonder that a very adept momentum surfer can rise to a leadership position. This is where the problems start.

When a momentum surfer takes charge, or is put in a position of authority, their instinctive tendency is to discern where the momentum is already heading and then to magnify and accelerate it. This is fine for an organisation that is on an upward trend and already heading in the right direction, but it can be disastrous for an organisation that has already peaked, or is near the top of its game, and is seeking new direction. It is even worse for an organisation that is on the downward slope and is looking for leadership to pull it out of a spiral. In these situations, a momentum surfer will almost inevitably transform the wave into a destructive tsunami by accelerating the company in the perilous direction in which it is already heading. They are not capable of challenging the existing strategy, although they are often adept at dressing it up to appear different. This behavioural weakness is not always apparent, though, because many momentum-driven CEOs have an uncanny knack for switching companies just before things go belly-up and finding another wave to ride. It is only much later that the damage caused by their tenure is revealed.

A major problem with the momentum style of leadership is that leaders of this kind tend to surround themselves with teams who think and act like them; they can't tolerate roadblocks and only work well with people willing to wave the traffic full speed ahead, cheering all the while. Momentum surfers tend to interpret dissenting views as applying the brakes, because friction is the enemy of momentum. Surfers see their job as aligning everyone in the same direction and pressing the accelerator. Hence, momentum-style leaders often find themselves surrounded by acquiescent supporters who don't seriously question the given direction. Rather, they reinforce and amplify it through their words and actions and play an integral part in the momentum-building process. The author Joseph Heller described this scenario all too well in his wicked 1979 political novel *Good as Gold*, in which a presidential aide named Ralph tells a job applicant: 'This President doesn't want yes-men. What we want are independent men of integrity who will agree with all our decisions after we make them.'[1]

In the pre-global financial crisis days at UBS, there was one individual who exerted an inordinate influence over all those around him. This was the bank's legendary chairman, Marcel Ospel, the most powerful businessman in Switzerland at the time. The influential business magazine *Euroweek* in 2002 painted a picture of Ospel as a leader who filled positions at UBS with his friends and admirers, reporting that dissension was not allowed: 'When you pass the great man, you no longer say, "*Guten Morgen*, Herr Ospel," but, "Hail, Caesar!".'[2]

Ospel, the son of a baker-turned-engineer, started work at Swiss Bank Corporation (SBC) in 1977 after graduating from Basel's School of Economics and Business Administration. Before leaving SBC, the bank's general manager wrote in his evaluation of Ospel, 'Very ambitious, thinks materialistically, could make mistakes because of big ambition. Therefore needs control.'[3] Ospel later returned to SBC, quickly rose through the ranks to a senior position and eventually engineered the successful merger between the SBC and the Union Bank of Switzerland that resulted in UBS. Ospel was appointed CEO of the new organisation, and eventually became its executive chairman. His declared ambition was to make UBS the number one investment bank in the world. Over the next few years, under his leadership UBS quickly acquired various companies, employed some high-octane executives from Wall Street (guys with 'street cred') and built new premises, including a huge trading floor in Stamford, Connecticut. UBS soon emerged as a global financial powerhouse that managed nearly $3 trillion dollars of clients' money. In 2006 *Forbes* magazine ranked it as the tenth-largest company in the world.[4] The stakes were now very high and the momentum was extremely powerful.

UBS had nowhere to go but onwards and upwards. The shareholders demanded it, and Ospel and his team were determined not to let them down. They would do whatever it took to propel the bank forward, even if it meant moving aggressively into potentially high-risk markets. Momentum had become the name of the game. UBS had transformed into a Big Mo bank and, at some point along the way, it seems that Ospel and his team succumbed to the power of the flow and were eager to ride the wave – no matter where it took them.

But this is precisely where perhaps the most dangerous aspect of momentum-based leadership kicks in. Leaders who are momentum surfers usually develop a critical blind spot, because they are so focused on the 'motion' of the game; they often lose sight of the game strategy. They think opportunistically rather than strategically, always on the lookout for the next move, the next play. They want to keep the game moving forward at any cost, so obstacles are downplayed or ignored. Maintaining momentum is paramount. In a corporate environment this problem is exacerbated by the fact that senior executives are generously rewarded through share options, whose rising value is dependent on the company 'moving forward'. In this kind of environment it is difficult to get an executive to understand something is wrong, when their salary depends on it being right.

This behaviour was aptly illustrated by the financial journalist Camilla Cavendish, who wrote in *The Times* on 30 August 2007 before the financial crisis reached its peak, 'I have been talking to bankers who already knew that things had got out of hand. But as one said to me yesterday: "When something is bleedin' obvious for a while, and still no one does anything about it, you just go with the flow." They knew it couldn't last – but nor could they bear to leave the party.'[5] Charles (Chuck) Prince, the ex-chairman and CEO of Citigroup, expressed a similar view when he told the *Financial Times* on 15 November 2007, 'As long as the music is playing, you've got to get up and dance. We're still dancing.'[6] Shortly thereafter, Citigroup announced huge write-downs and Mr Prince left the group.

The momentum-driven leader, or momentum surfer, is a funda-mentally different breed of executive from the model prescribed by the renowned management philosopher Peter Drucker, which has dominated management education for the past fifty years. According to Drucker, the ideal executive is strongly driven by a set of values and ethics. Such a leader constantly asks, 'What is the best thing to do here? How do we respond to this in the right way and make a difference? What are the implications?'[7]

A momentum-driven leader asks, 'How do we keep moving forward? How do we get people on board? How can we take advantage of this situation?' Such a leader is not necessarily a 'bad' or malevolent person, or motivated purely by greed or a lust for power (although some certainly are). They are more likely to be 'values-agnostic', in that either they are oblivious to ethical standards or they see them as something to pay lip service to. In other words, they may say all the right things, but they are rarely motivated by values.

These differing perspectives have far-reaching consequences for our society, because increasingly, the highest echelons of business and government tend to be occupied by leaders with a momentum-driven outlook rather than a values-driven one. The renowned social anthropologist Dr Janine Wedel, who has written extensively on this subject, describes such people as 'flexians' – people who are willing to bend every which way in order to get what they want. One high-powered member of a think-tank explained his modus operandi to her, 'I tend to operate in a just in time mode, sort of like Toyota, because I realize that busy, important people tend not to plan ahead much. They tend to pivot this way and that in a high-flex mode given constantly changing priorities.' Wedel's research suggests that in today's corporate and public environment, flexibility is everything; employees are expected to constantly reinvent themselves, take job insecurity as a given and go where the wind takes them.[8] This trend is being exacerbated by a new wave of management literature that extols the virtues of flexible momentum-based strategies without warning of their inherent dangers.

Perhaps more troubling, though, is that when a momentum surfer in a leadership position does fail, they rarely pay a price for it, especially if they work for a large corporation. There is a tendency to blame the wave not the surfer. Yet the surfers are happy to take credit when things are going well. It is remarkable that in the aftermath of the global financial crisis no one has been brought to account for it – not individually or collectively – it is as if it just sort of happened. Nassim Nicholas Taleb, author of *The Black Swan*, told the 2009 World Economic Forum in Davos, Switzerland, that the biggest problem of the financial crisis 'was that nobody was willing to pay the price for failure'.[9] He was referring to the fact that the executives responsible for overseeing the global financial carnage would, effectively, get off without any punishment and would often walk away with millions of dollars in severance pay. Indeed, at the height of the global financial crisis in January 2009, while the global financial system teetered on the brink, the New York State comptroller reported that employees in New York financial companies would collect an estimated $18.4 billion in bonuses for the year, almost as much as when the economy was booming a few years earlier. This figure jumped to a massive $55 billion a year later, when the banks began to bounce back – largely funded by government bail-out money. On *The Daily Show*, Jon Stewart rolled a clip of Merrill Lynch's former CEO, John A Thain, defending bonuses as a way to 'keep your best people'. Then Stewart quipped, 'You don't have the best people! You lost $27 billion!'[10]

Sometimes, however, the price of failure is measured not just in treasure but in blood. When a country goes to war, the cost in human casualties and suffering can be immeasurable. An ill-fated or misjudged war is not only physically destructive, but it can also inflict lasting damage on a nation's collective psyche and undermine its standing in the world for generations to come. Some wars are unavoidable, and others are wars of choice. It is incumbent upon a nation's leader to know the difference. However, when events are moving swiftly and unpredictably, a leader can become swept up in the escalating crisis and feel compelled to act – to show leadership and resolve. This temptation can be particularly strong for a personality with a momentum-driven outlook. Such people don't like to wait and analyse the situation. Their instinctive tendency is to jump into the game and rally the troops.

This brings us to the Second Iraq War. Although it may appear that, after so much exhaustive analysis on this subject in recent years, we have a good fix on why it happened the way it did, this is far from the case. We have about the same level of understanding of the war, and particularly the dynamics that drove it, as we have of the recent global financial crisis – that is to say, relatively little.

So let's look at the war again, but this time through the prism of what we have come to learn about momentum and Big Mo.

The cheerleader

George Walker Bush knew about momentum from an early age. His father, George Bush senior, saw momentum – or Big Mo, as he called it – as essential to political success. After he won the Iowa caucuses in 1980 in his quest for the Republican nomination, and was facing further contests, Bush Senior said, 'Now they will be after me, howling and yowling at my heels. What we will have is momentum. We will look forward to Big Mo being on our side, as they say in athletics.'[11] Eventually the Big Mo favoured Ronald Reagan, but the lesson was not lost on young George. Politics is a momentum game.

Momentum is, of course, the essential element of the cheerleading process. An effective cheerleader reads the ebb and flow of the game, knows instinctively when things are not going well, when they are going right and, most importantly, when there is an opportunity to turn the tide – to seize the momentum and turn the game around. A cheerleading team can sometimes make the difference between success and failure.

George W Bush was head cheerleader – a male role then – for the football team during his senior year at the prestigious Phillips Academy in Andover, Massachusetts, and he was good at it. His natural enthusiasm, gregarious personality and competitive nature, tempered with a self-deprecating sense of humour, made him a natural booster of team spirit. The dean of students, G Grenville Benedict, said that the young Bush had raised Andover's school spirit to the highest level in over thirty years.[12]

Bush's qualities as a cheerleader would serve him well in his political career and, along with his family connections, helped propel him into the fast lane. As governor of Texas his ability to galvanise people, particularly his supporter base, helped to push his agenda forward. Bush then turned his attention to the greatest prize of all, the presidency. It was the year 1999. The timing seemed right. America was in a triumphalist mood following the collapse of the Soviet Union, years of rising prosperity and a renewed sense of American ascendancy. Bush's sunny nature and inner certainty resonated with the buoyant mood of the time. Once again, he drew on his innate cheerleading skills and rapidly generated a sense of momentum that propelled his campaign all the way to the finish line.

But just as the presidency appeared to be within his grasp, a controversy over the voting procedures in Florida caused a recount, and eventually the final verdict had to be decided by the US Supreme Court. It could be argued that even at this critical juncture, when the election result hung on a knife edge, momentum once again played a pivotal role. The Bush campaign had built up such a groundswell of support, and he radiated such confidence, that a result against Bush would have seemed to defy natural gravity. There was an air of inevitability about his ascension. And so Bush won the presidency. Such is the power of Big Mo.

The greatest test was yet to come. The tragedy of 9/11 catapulted Bush into dangerous and uncharted territory, as it would have any president. His initial and instinctual response was to personify the public's outrage, proclaim rightful retribution and reach out for support both domestically and internationally. He did this brilliantly. His standing atop the burning rubble of the Twin Towers, loudspeaker in hand and surrounded by firefighters, was exactly what was needed. At this moment, perhaps more than at any time in its history, America needed a cheerleader-in-chief, and they had one.

A few months later, the Bush administration and its allies achieved a rapid and decisive victory over the Taliban in Afghanistan, who had supported and provided sanctuary for the 9/11 perpetrators. Bush was seen as the leader for his time – decisive, focused, committed and unrelenting – and he had much of the world in support. Most significantly, he had momentum on his side. The question for Bush and his advisers now became what to do with all this positive-approval momentum? How best to apply this once-in-a-century opportunity?

There were basically two options: 'stay focused' or 'think big'. Staying focused meant single-mindedly pursuing the mastermind of 9/11, Osama Bin Laden, and his cohorts in Afghanistan and the border areas of Pakistan, and putting enough resources there to ensure Bin Laden could never strike again.

Thinking big, however, meant looking beyond the immediate problem of Bin Laden and addressing the wider threat that he represented – that is, a global, Islamic-inspired jihadist movement against the West that had been steadily growing in potency for a number of decades, albeit largely below the radar.

The trouble with the 'stay focused' option was that although it was the most surgically precise response – and, with the benefit of hindsight, might have been more effective in terms of neutralising the threat and sending a message to other would-be perpetrators – it did not match the proportionality of response demanded by an outraged American public. It also failed another key test: it would not enable the Bush team to capitalise on the enormous positive momentum they had at their disposal following the 9/11 attacks. This was an extremely rare opportunity to seize the initiative and do something really big and transformative.

But what, exactly? How and where could the Bush administration apply the power of this momentum? Some influential people within the administration already knew the answer. They had been working on such a transformative game plan since 1997. It was known as the 'Project for the New American Century' (PNAC) and had been drafted by a neoconservative think-tank that included people such as William Kristol, Robert Kagan and Paul Wolfowitz. The stated goal of the project was 'to promote American global leadership', as articulated in a ninety-page report in September 2000 called 'Rebuilding America's Defenses: Strategies, Forces, and Resources for a New Century'.[13]

The controversial report proposed:

> America should seek to preserve and extend its position of global leadership by maintaining the pre-eminence of US military forces ... The American peace has proven itself peaceful, stable and durable. It has provided the geopolitical framework for widespread economic growth and the spread of American principles of liberty and democracy. Yet no moment in international politics can be frozen in time; even a global Pax Americana will not preserve itself.

The report went on to list the specific ways that American military dominance could be maintained – through modernisation and exploiting the revolution in military affairs – and suggested: 'The history of the [twentieth] century should have taught us that it is important to shape circumstances before crises emerge, and to meet threats before they become dire.' In short, it was a manifesto for a pre-emptive approach to US military intervention.

From its inception, the PNAC specifically pushed for the invasion of Iraq, as evidenced in the PNAC's letter to President Bill Clinton on 16 January 1998, which urged him to embrace a plan for 'the removal of Saddam Hussein's regime from power'.[14] The letter said Saddam posed a threat to the United States, its Middle East allies and oil resources if he succeeded in maintaining what they asserted was a stockpile of weapons of mass destruction. In effect, the PNAC had developed a far-reaching and comprehensive game plan for the way forward.

Bush was susceptible to such a game plan. It was bold, audacious and grand. If successfully implemented, it would simultaneously address the 9/11 outrage, prevent Saddam from developing weapons if he had not already done so, remove an ongoing threat to Middle East oil supplies, and help cement America's pre-eminent position in the world. On a personal level, it would enable him to eclipse the achievements of his father and possibly assure himself a place as one of America's greatest presidents. This was a game plan big enough to capitalise on the vast amount of Big Mo available to his administration.

Donald Rumsfeld, Bush's secretary of defense, pushed aggressively for the plan from the outset. Richard Clarke, chief counter-terrorism adviser to the White House, recalls,

> That night, on 9/11, Rumsfeld came over to join the others, and the president finally got back, and we had a meeting. And Rumsfeld said, You know, we've got to do Iraq, and everyone looked at him – at least I looked at him and [Secretary of State Colin] Powell looked at him – like, What the hell are you talking about? And he said – I'll never forget this – There just aren't enough targets in Afghanistan. We need to bomb something else to prove that we're, you

know, big and strong and not going to be pushed around by these kinds of attacks. I made the point . . . and I think Powell acknowledged it, that Iraq had nothing to do with 9/11. That didn't seem to faze Rumsfeld in the least.[15]

Bush was not fazed either and did not appear to be much interested in questioning or challenging the game plan itself. His job was to boost the war effort and build the momentum. He was the cheerleader-in-chief. Bob Woodward, the famed *Washington Post* journalist who decades earlier broke the Watergate scandal with Carl Bernstein and brought down the Nixon presidency, recounts in his book *State of Denial* that by October 2003, just six months after the commencement of the war, 'there was little or no evidence that he [Bush] engaged in much substantive policy debate at this point in the war cabinet meetings. His role was to express confidence and enthusiasm.'[16]

What is remarkable about the Second Iraq War is the extent to which momentum was a driving force from the outset. In many of the earliest discussions about the war by senior US policy officials, the momentum factor drove the decision-making process, influenced or accelerated it. Woodward described a scene leading up to the resignation of Andy Card as White House chief of staff. 'Like so many of Bush's decisions, such as the decision to invade Iraq, there was a momentum, the big and the little incremental steps that suddenly converged.'[17]

Bush now found himself in a fast-moving, high-stakes game with everything to play for. He was in his element, and it showed. Richard Haass, the director of policy planning at the State Department under President Bush, recounts an hour-long conversation he had with Bush and Colin Powell on Air Force One in April 2003 while flying back from the Northern Ireland summit.

What struck me more than anything was how comfortable Bush was with his decision to attack Iraq. Here we were, three weeks into the war, and he appeared totally at peace with what he had decided and how it was unfolding. It was real confidence, not bluster. But I was struck too, by how unconcerned the president seemed to be with all the complications that I and others had predicted would come his and our way. He had a penchant for the big and dramatic and was not about to allow the doubts of others or the details to sidetrack him. How did George W Bush reach this point? I will go to my grave not fully understanding why. There was no meeting or set of meetings at which the pros and cons (of going to war) were debated and a formal decision taken. No, this decision happened. It was *cumulative* [italics added].[18]

Haass later told an interviewer: 'It was a decision that *happened* more than it was *made*. And increasingly, the conversation simply assumed it.'[19]

This cumulative quality is, of course, symptomatic of the way Big Mo operates. It creates a sense that events just sort of happen, rather than being consciously directed or pushed – much like a wave that gradually builds on itself and becomes ever more powerful.

The tsunami

In many ways, George W Bush was the consummate momentum surfer. From his earliest days as a football cheerleader he demonstrated an instinctive ability to read the flow of the game, to ride the surge of momentum and boost it. When he saw the game plan for the Iraq War, he immediately sensed an opportunity to harness the powerful momentum generated by the outrage of the 9/11 attacks. He rode this huge wave of momentum with all the skill of a big-wave surfer, and for a while the ride was exhilarating. Baghdad fell quickly to the coalition forces, Saddam's statue was toppled before a crowd of ecstatic Iraqis and Bush was able to fly triumphantly onto the aircraft carrier USS *Abraham Lincoln* on 1 May 2003, where he addressed his troops under a 'Mission Accomplished' banner, like a conquering hero.[20]

But it soon became clear that the wave Bush was riding was not what it seemed. It was actually a tsunami capable of sweeping up everything in its path and leaving behind a wake of destruction. The war began deteriorating fast. The casualty count rose exponentially, both for civilians and coalition soldiers. Public looting became rampant and scenes of pillaged Iraqi museums were broadcast around the world. The bad news escalated month by month. It was now obvious that during the Bush administration's rush to war, there had been inadequate post-war planning, and some key decisions proved to be catastrophic, such as the dissolution of the Iraqi army, which had the effect of injecting thousands of trained soldiers into the growing ranks of the insurgency movement. Even the capture of Saddam Hussein provided only intermittent relief. Underlying all these problems was the fact that no weapons of mass destruction (WMD) had been found; neutralising them had been the stated reason for going to war in the first place. Worse still, the war appeared to be metastasising into a global recruiting ground and public relations campaign for the al-Qaeda movement, while it simultaneously fuelled anti-American sentiment, even among US allies. Meanwhile, many of Iraq's most highly trained people – its doctors, teachers, engineers and scientists – had been killed or left the country. Families were being torn apart. 'Violence has acquired a momentum of its own and is now self-sustaining,' Meghan O'Sullivan, deputy national security adviser, told President Bush during the summer of 2006.[21]

The more the situation deteriorated, however, the more resolute Bush and his team became in their public rhetoric. 'We will stay the course,' and 'Bring it on,' became the catch cries of the day. The cheerleader-in-chief was doing what he did best, cheering and maintaining the momentum as best he could, and ignoring the bad news. Bob Woodward in his book *The War Within* tells us that Secretary of State Condoleezza Rice never took her complaints about unduly positive military reports to Mr Bush because 'the president almost demanded optimism'. Bush's perpetually upbeat, rose-tinted view of the world wasn't the result of a lack of intelligence or insight.[22] According to Richard Haass, Bush was 'smarter, much smarter, than people generally understood. He also had a good fix on the attributes and weaknesses of those around him; Bush read people as well as you would expect from someone who succeeded in getting elected president. His fault was that he was quick to reach conclusions (be it about policy or people) and often viewed changing course as a sign of weakness, something a strong leader (to his way of thinking) would resist.'[23] Towards the end of his second term as president, however, all George Bush could do was try to hang on and foster the illusion that he still retained some control of the wave he was riding.

It is often said today that the Second Iraq War was a 'war of choice', meaning that it wasn't really necessary, and it is hard to refute this. But from the perspective of the momentum surfer, there is no real choice, there is just the flow. This is not to exonerate Bush's actions, but to highlight how difficult it can be for a momentum-driven leader to seriously consider alternative options that go against the prevailing direction. Once they commit to that direction, there is no turning back. Scott McClellan, Bush's press secretary, wrote in his book, *What Happened: Inside the Bush White House and Washington's Culture of Deception*, 'As I worked closely with President Bush, I would come to believe that sometimes he convinces himself to believe what suits his needs at the moment . . . Bush was not one to look back once a decision was made. Rather than suffer any sense of guilt and anguish, Bush chose not to go down the road of self-doubt or take on the difficult task of honest evaluation and reassessment.'[24]

Bush's tendency to go with the flow, and stay the course no matter what, was also evident in other dimensions of his administration. He eagerly rode the wave of financial deregulation that precipitated the global financial crisis; he was a steadfast cheerleader for the fossil-fuel industry despite increasing concerns about its environmental impact, and regularly appointed people to high office based on their loyalty rather than their competence. This is not to suggest that he was driven by malevolent intent or incompetence. By most accounts Bush truly believed that he was doing the right thing for America, and he was known to run an 'efficient and orderly' White House. Rather, I would argue that he had a particular outlook on the world that predisposed him to the influence of momentum, or Big Mo, but not to seriously question its direction. Over time, this momentum-driven outlook became self-reinforcing and generated a somewhat idiosyncratic version of reality, which flourished in the 'bubble' of the highly insulated White House environment. The investigative journalist Ron Suskind once questioned a senior Bush adviser about the need to face up to the reality of the situation in Iraq. The adviser responded by mocking the 'reality-based community', asserting: 'When we act, we create our own reality.'[25]

Much has been written about the influence of Bush's taciturn vice president Dick Cheney, and some have even suggested that Cheney was the real power behind the throne. But there is another way to look at this relationship. Momentum-driven leaders often prefer to have someone with gravitas in the background to counterbalance their lightness or more bubbly approach. Tony Blair, for example, had the heavyweight Gordon Brown behind him as chancellor of the exchequer (i.e. UK's treasurer). Brown is a brilliant, dour Scot who is the antithesis of the perpetually upbeat and charming Blair. The important point is, though, that these 'counterweights' don't slow down a momentum surfer, rather, they help to speed them up by legitimising their actions and making them appear more grounded. You could say they provide more ballast to the keel so the yacht can catch faster winds. This counterweighting role is far from being the only factor involved in what is usually a complex relationship, but its influence should not be underestimated. In the case of Bush, Cheney's enigmatic – some wags dubbed it 'Darth Vader-like' – presence imbued the presidency with a weightiness and influence it would otherwise not have had.

This influence also had a corrosive effect on the many people who were pulled into its sway. The Nobel Prize-winning economist Paul Krugman wrote in the *New York Times* on 20 July 2007:

> It's not clear that he [Bush] was ever in touch with reality . . . Yet, while Mr Bush no longer has many true believers, he still has plenty of enablers – people who understand the folly of his actions, but refuse to do anything to stop him . . . at this point I think we should stop blaming Mr Bush for the mess we're in. He is what he is, and everyone except a hard core of equally delusional loyalists knows it. Yet, Mr Bush keeps doing damage because many people who understand how his folly is endangering the nation's security still refuse, out of political caution and careerism, to do anything about it.[26]

Like good surfers, they all chose to ride the wave until the very end.

After George W Bush left office, it is perhaps somewhat telling that his first foray back into public life was to appear as a 'motivational speaker' at a seminar in Forth Worth, Texas, in October 2009. During his twenty-eight-minute speech he appeared to win over most of the eleven thousand attendees who had paid $250 a ticket to hear him speak. After years of declining popularity, the cheerleader was finally back on his home ground.[27]

CHAPTER 10

The Difficulty of Dissent

> Do I dare
> Disturb the universe?
>
> *T S Eliot*

One of the more troubling aspects of events like the Second Iraq War and the global financial crisis is why more people didn't speak up against what was happening. Why did so many people, even those in senior positions, appear to be so willing to 'go with the flow'? Why did a powerful general, an intelligence tsar and a prime minister become cheerleaders for a war based on such a dubious rationale? What caused experienced financial journalists and economists to become mute in the face of mounting evidence of an imminent global financial meltdown? More broadly, why is it so difficult to dissent from the crowd, even when an individual knows it is the right thing to do?

Behavioural momentum certainly plays a role in such self-censorship, for reasons discussed earlier (see pages 92–99). There is also the powerful influence of our upbringing. According to Stanley Greenspan, a clinical professor of psychiatry at George Washington University Medical School, from our earliest years we are conditioned to agree with those around us, particularly our parents. The groundwork for saying 'yes' and 'no' is laid in the first year of life, enabling us to communicate what we want. Whereas babies are very direct and honest about what they want and have no compunction about saying 'no' to the milk if they really want juice, by mid-adolescence reflective thinking sets in and children become aware of the need to fit in with the crowd to be accepted.[1] They also notice that when they conform, they are more likely to be rewarded by parents and teachers.

This presents a conundrum for any parent because, on the one hand, they want their child to stand up to the kind of peer-group pressure that leads to, say, negative behaviour such as drug taking, but, on the other hand, they don't want their children to stand up to them – to disobey them. Over time, however, as children grow out of the long years of teenage rebellion (*long* years for parents, that is), they tend to fall back into more compliant behaviour.

For many of us, this conditioning to comply stays with us for all our lives. Mostly it lies subconsciously dormant and does not constrain our ability to speak up. We are all likely to shout 'Fire! Run!' in a burning library, for instance, despite all the 'Keep Quiet' signs. But there are many environments that reinforce our conditioning not to speak up. The military is a case in point. Personnel are expected to be unfailingly obedient and 'Yes, sir!' is the standard response to a directive from a senior officer. When someone leaves the military after years of such training, it is little wonder they may have a problem disobeying a directive in civilian or government life, even if they know it is wrong.

One of the most famous military people to enter public life in recent years is General Colin Powell. He was the US secretary of state during the critical lead-up to the Second Iraq War. Powell was held in such high regard around the world that it was his speech to the United Nations on 5 February 2003 that helped persuade many people of the legitimacy of the case for war. Referring to intelligence about Saddam's weapons of mass destruction he said: 'Every statement I make today is backed up by sources, solid sources. These are not assertions. What we're giving you are facts and conclusions based on solid intelligence.'[2] Some years later, in July 2007, at the Aspen Ideas Festival in Colorado, Powell revealed that he had spent two and a half hours trying to persuade President George W Bush not to invade Iraq. 'I tried to avoid this war. I took him through the consequences of going into an Arab country and becoming the occupiers.'[3]

Imagine the personal moral dilemma that Powell found himself in during those months just prior to the war. He was a highly respected, decorated war veteran who had served his country valiantly for decades – and was an architect of the previous war under the first President Bush. At one time he was considered a viable presidential candidate. Now he was faced with the most difficult choice of his life: support a war he did not believe in or resist it. In the end, he did both – firstly, by actively trying to dissuade Bush from war and, having failed to do so, donning his proverbial soldier's uniform and carrying out his patriotic duty by doing what was asked of him, as all good soldiers are trained to do. Unbeknown to Powell, the evidence he presented to the United Nations turned out to be false, which further exacerbated his dilemma.

Germany's then foreign minister and vice-chancellor, Joschk Fischer, recalls that it was a difficult time for Powell. 'I spoke over and over and over with Colin Powell. He always looked, I don't know, not at me, but I could see the pain in his eyes.'[4] The example of Colin Powell is instructive, for it shows how even the most powerful and well-intentioned people, when faced with an overpowering momentum, can succumb to the flow.

Another global figure to put their legacy on the line for the Iraq War was British prime minister Tony Blair. At his first meeting with President Bush at his ranch in Crawford, Texas, in April 2002, it would have become clear to Blair that the war was inevitable. So, in order to bond with the new president and preserve the 'special relationship' between Britain and the United States, Blair probably believed he had no alternative but to go with the flow. The British ambassador to Washington at the time, Sir Christopher Meyer, described that Crawford ranch meeting as the moment when there might have been a *convergence* 'signed in blood' on the plan to go to war.[5] This 'convergence' dynamic is symptomatic of the momentum effect at work. It was also likely that Blair had reservations about the legitimacy of the war, notwithstanding his belief that Saddam Hussein was a threat to the region. For under international law, as defined by the UN Charter and various treaties, it is illegal to invade a sovereign state. Blair knew this – as a trained lawyer and politician – and he also knew how difficult it would be to persuade the UN to grant its authority to justify the war.*

Like Colin Powell, Blair too pushed for a diplomatic solution behind the scenes, but his efforts fell on deaf ears – even though he was President Bush's key ally. Kendall Myers, a senior analyst at the State Department, said he felt 'a little ashamed of' the way Blair had been treated and that his attempts to influence US policy were typically ignored. 'It was a done deal from the beginning, it was a one-sided relationship that was entered [into] with open eyes . . . There was nothing, no payback, no sense of reciprocity.'[6]

Blair couldn't change US policy, but at least he could try to gain the support of other countries and the United Nations to support the war. This prompted the ex-South African President and elder statesman Nelson Mandela to describe Blair as 'the US foreign minister'[7] and other, less charitable observers to label him as 'Bush's poodle'[8].

Spooky alignments

In retrospect, one of the least likely people to become swept up in the momentum for war was the CIA boss George Tenet, an affable and well-respected man at the time. Tenet sat at the apex of the powerful US intelligence community and was in a better

---

* In November 2002, the UN approved resolution 1441, giving Saddam Hussein a 'final opportunity' to comply with UN demands. This resolution was eventually used as a justification for the war, although its meaning was not clear-cut and there were ambiguities in how it could be interpreted.

position to know what was really going on with Iraq than perhaps anyone else on Earth, excluding Saddam Hussein. He also had the direct ear of the President through his daily briefing sessions. As such, Tenet was at the epicentre of influence and power.

Subsequently, Tenet has been intensely scrutinised over whether he did enough to warn of the dangers of going to war, and his role as a war 'cheerleader'. He purportedly said that the case for war against Iraq was 'a slam dunk'. This comment was often used by the administration to support its decision to invade Iraq. Tenet later revealed in his book *At the Centre of the Storm* that his 'slam dunk' comment was used out of context, and that the decision to go to war was made long before he uttered those words.[9]

Tenet's defence of his position generated much antagonism in the media. The columnist Charles Krauthammer of the *Washington Post* wrote, 'Tenet presents himself as a pathetic victim and scapegoat of an administration that was hell-bent on going to war, slam dunk or not.' Maureen Dowd of the *New York Times* wrote, 'If you have something deadly important to say, say it when it matters, or just shut up and slink off.'[10]

The most potent criticism came from Bob Woodward, the famed *Washington Post* journalist. Tenet had known Woodward for years and had sought his advice about his book. Nevertheless, in his review of Tenet's book in the *Washington Post* on 6 May 2007, Woodward suggested that Tenet had fundamentally misunderstood the relationship between the CIA director and the presidents he served. He said Tenet was 'hampered by a bureaucrat's view of the world, hobbled by the traditional chain of command', and that when he became concerned in July 2001 about the possibility of an imminent attack on the United States by al-Qaeda, he should have gone directly to the President instead of telling the national security adviser (Condoleezza Rice at the time).[11]

Tenet defended his actions to Scott Pelley on the CBS show *60 Minutes*, saying, 'The president is not the action officer. You bring the action to the national security adviser, and the people who set the table for the president decide on the policies they're going to implement.'[12]

Woodward would not buy the explanation. He said, 'President Bush told me that he didn't feel that sense of urgency, and that his blood was not boiling over before September 11. I would argue that Tenet's job was to boil the president's blood. That's why you show up on the president's doorstep.' He added, 'I'm raised in a culture where you don't observe the chain of command, you go around it.'

Woodward recounts how during the Watergate period he and his former *Post* colleague Carl Bernstein went to their boss Ben Bradley's house at two in the morning to tell him that their source, Mark Felt – the FBI official known as 'Deep Throat' – had said their lives were in danger. 'Sometimes there come points in your life when you have to make a decision about what you're going to do and they don't tell you in the morning that this is the day that one of those decisions is going to come. Do you break down the doors; do you break out of the system? This is the issue of courage.'[13]

By allowing his 'slam dunk' comment to be used so freely by the administration to justify the war and not speaking up about his concerns when it mattered most, it is clear that Tenet, the most powerful man in US intelligence, had become swept up in the momentum for war. But George Tenet wasn't the only member of the intelligence establishment to succumb to Big Mo during this period. The entire intelligence community did. Indeed, this spooky world provides a unique microcosm of how behavioural momentum operates in an organisational setting when the stakes are high and dissent is frowned upon. So let's take a peek behind the cloak and dagger.

The nature of intelligence work is opaque and often frustrating. Intelligence operatives are constantly trying to discern real threats from imaginary threats, usually with insufficient information and from within a constantly changing environment. These threats have become more dangerous in recent years, as a result of nuclear proliferation, biological warfare and virulent religious beliefs that foment violence. The greatest fear of the intelligence services is to miss something big. The trouble is that, even with the best information networks, the most sophisticated technology and resources, intelligence failures will happen.

The history of intelligence failures stretches back from ancient times, from the Trojan horse through to Pearl Harbor, the collapse of the Soviet Union and, more recently, the West's failure to anticipate the rise of fundamentalist Islamist-inspired threats.

By far the most cataclysmic intelligence oversight of recent times was the failure to anticipate the 9/11 attacks, despite warning signs such as the high number of Middle Eastern men taking flying lessons in the United States; al-Qaeda's known use of planes as weapons; an earlier attack on the World Trade Center, and the documented presence of terrorist suspects in America at the time.

Following 9/11, the stricken intelligence community was anxious not to repeat the mistake. The agencies became hypersensitive to any possible threat, particularly of a nuclear, biological or chemical nature. The Senate Intelligence Committee Report, which looked into the intelligence environment in the lead-up to the Second Iraq War, said that 'analysts were under tremendous pressure to make correct assessments to avoid missing a credible threat, and to avoid an intelligence failure on the scale of 9/11'.[14] In this pressure-cooker environment, it was perhaps understandable that when key members of the Bush administration expressed their concern about the possibility of Iraq having weapons of mass destruction, the intelligence community urgently focused on the issue. Although the CIA and other agencies had been monitoring Iraq for many years, they had had little success in discovering what was going on because of a lack of credible human intelligence (HUMINT) from within Saddam Hussein's regime. Now they redoubled their efforts.

It soon became evident that there were serious doubts about

the capacity of Saddam's regime to produce WMDs, especially following years of crippling UN sanctions and inspections by the Atomic Energy Agency Commission. It also appeared unlikely that there was a connection between Saddam's regime and al-Qaeda: secular Saddam's Ba'athist regime was opposed to the philosophy of al-Qaeda.[15] The integrity of the informants – with code names such as 'Curveball' – who had promoted an Iraq–al-Qaeda connection, was dubious.

This is where momentum emerges as a key factor. The intelligence community is staffed by intelligent, skilled and, by and large, ambitious people. The very nature of their work requires them to be highly tuned to the forces that operate around them. And because they operate within a bureaucracy, they are aware, too, that threats do not just emanate from external enemies, such as al-Qaeda, but can also come from within, in the form of internal political power plays. The bottom line: if some key players in the intelligence community discern there is an expectation for them to follow a particular path, they will do so. The critical point is they will not need to be directed to do this, they will have second-guessed everything because that is what they are trained to do: pick up on signals of intention, direction and momentum from their masters. They are also less likely to question or dissent from this direction.

David Kay, the former head of the Iraq Survey Group, spelled all this out to George W Bush during a briefing in the Oval Office:

The disease of the intelligence community is this over-focus on current intelligence . . . a good example is the President's Daily Briefing [PDB]. Do you understand that if you [i.e. the President] respond positively to anything in it, you're going to get nothing but that stuff for the next month or so? The president's expression of interest puts it at the top of the agenda in the intelligence community. George Tenet takes it back and drives it and it will keep appearing. They respond to it. Presidential interest suggests it is important and the intelligence flow just snowballs out of control.[16]

The combination of the 'snowballing process', the post-9/11 environment and the incessant warlike rhetoric from the Bush White House created an atmosphere within the intelligence community that encouraged analysts to interpret the available information in a way that was conducive to supporting a war with Iraq and to minimise evidence to the contrary.

It is perhaps not unduly surprising that people who work for the intelligence community could be swept up in the powerful momentum for war, given the dynamics at work in their organisations. Most of them probably also convinced themselves they were doing their patriotic duty. What is not so clear, though, is why people who had far less to lose, and every reason to speak up, were so willing to surrender to the flow. We are talking here about journalists: people who are paid to be professional cynics and challenge the status quo.

The first casualty of war

In the lead-up to the declaration of the Iraq War in early 2002, the media in the United States found themselves in a situation for which they were ill-prepared. Decades of corporatisation had undermined the news media's propensity and capacity to ask the hard questions. As discussed in chapter 7, they had been conditioned to toe the company line. So when the Bush administration signalled that they were considering taking pre-emptive military action against Iraq, the media response was largely predictable. They would continue their patriotic duty as cheerleaders, as they had done with the earlier strikes on Afghanistan in response to the 9/11 attacks.

But not everyone in the media was as gung-ho about attacking Iraq as they had been about Afghanistan. A handful of senior correspondents who had covered the Middle East for years grasped some truths that were not widely understood or appreciated by their colleagues, let alone the American public. They knew that Saddam Hussein and his Ba'athist regime were secularists – not particularly motivated by religion. In fact, Hussein was known to dislike Osama bin Laden and would not tolerate al-Qaeda people in his country. Therefore, it was unlikely he had had anything to do with 9/11. These journalists also believed that Saddam's weapons programme had been largely dismantled during the 1990s and there was little evidence that he had the capacity to start it up again, although the intention may have been there. As Colin Powell said in 2000, 'Saddam is contained.'[17]

However, these legitimate doubts about the administration's *casus belli* or rationale for the Iraq offensive did not garner much media coverage. They certainly didn't make the front page; they became buried within the storyline that had already gained traction with the mainstream news media and had now generated a powerful momentum. Any contradictory information would simply be subsumed by the media juggernaut.

There was another factor, too: fear. The administration made it clear that the stakes were too high during a time of war to brook any dissent or departure from the party line. To do otherwise would risk ostracism or retribution. Earlier, on 26 September 2001, the White House press secretary, Ari Fleischer, warned media commentators that they needed to watch what they said,[18] firmly setting the tone for the next few years. Reporters either conformed to the party line or paid the price. From the critical period of the lead-up to the war through to 2005, there was little overt or implied media criticism about the war, its rationale or even its progress. The general tone of coverage, in television and print, was either positive or neutral. To a large extent, the media had become the nation's most effective cheerleaders for the war.

Reflecting on the role of the media during this period, CNN's Christiane Amanpour said, 'I think the press was muzzled, and I think the press self-muzzled . . . I'm sorry to say, but certainly television – and perhaps to a certain extent, my station – was intimidated by the administration.'[19] This feeling of intimidation and coercion was echoed by many journalists. The *New York Times* columnist Paul Krugman wrote, 'After 9/11, if you were thinking of saying anything negative about the president . . . you had to expect right-wing pundits and publications to do all they could to ruin your reputation.'[20]

The concept of 'information and psychological warfare' has always been critical to a war effort, and the Iraq War was no exception. War planners need to get the public onside, and the media are often called upon to play their part. But there was something particularly disconcerting about the extent to which they acquiesced during this period, particularly in the United States. The US news media hail from a journalistic tradition whereby certain breaking stories have changed the world, or at least given it a vigorous shake-up. From the courageous exposés of Edward R Murrow about McCarthyism, to the revelations of Watergate by Woodward and Bernstein, and the My Lai massacre by Seymour Hersh, it has always seemed that no story is off-limits to the intrepid and resourceful newshound.

Now reporters found themselves reduced to being cheerleaders for a war for which many harboured great scepticism in terms of its legitimacy and conduct. Even at the height of the Abu Ghraib prisoner-abuse scandal – when it was suddenly starkly clear how mismanaged the war had become and how dubious its morality – the media were relatively muted in their response to the revelations. Dan Rather, a former CBS anchor, described the war atmosphere as stifling for journalists and added that it discouraged them from asking 'the toughest of the tough questions' because they feared being labelled unpatriotic.[21]

The US news media came to believe that if they didn't play their role in the war effort, they would automatically be perceived to be promoting terrorism and would face the consequences. The attorney general, Alberto Gonzales, went as far as to suggest that journalists could be prosecuted for publishing classified information.[22]

Notwithstanding the pressure to conform, there were some

outspoken critics who consistently pointed out contradictions in the war 'story'. But these individuals were largely confined to the Internet blogs, and even left-wing blogs exhibited a degree of self-censorship. The tragedy of the US news media during this period, and to a lesser extent the global media, is that they abrogated their responsibility to seek the truth and hold government to account for its actions.

From the outset, the case for war was built on a lie. Scott McClellan, the former White House press secretary during much of the war period, later revealed in his memoir that the Bush administration 'systematically deceived the American public about their reasons for going to war in Iraq' and inculcated a 'permanent campaign culture' designed to sell the war and maintain the momentum.[23] This revelation was reinforced in June 2008 by the release of the 170-page Senate committee report which concluded that President Bush and his aides built the public case for war against Iraq by exaggerating available intelligence and by ignoring disagreements among the agencies about Iraq's weapons programmes and Saddam Hussein's links to al-Qaeda.

The first casualty of this grand deception was dissent: people just did not speak up.

One person who has reflected deeply on the issue of dissent in public life, particularly in a high-pressure situation, is Richard Haass, who was the director of the State Department's policy-planning staff in the run-up to the war. Like Colin Powell, he found himself harbouring misgivings about the case for war in Iraq and made a number of attempts to bring about a change of direction, or at least a rethinking of it. He was unsuccessful, of course, because, despite his influential position, the war had built up such a powerful momentum that it had become unstoppable. He recounted some of these insights distilled from those experiences in a commencement address to graduates of his alma mater, Oberlin College, Ohio, in 2009.[24]

He began by pointing out to those students that they would inevitably find themselves disagreeing with their organisations sometimes, and that there are ways to register dissent, times to stay and fight, and times when it's more prudent to concede and move on. He described a meeting in early July 2002 with Condoleezza Rice, President Bush's national security adviser, in her West Wing office:

I began my meeting with Condi by noting that the administration seemed to be building momentum toward going to war with Iraq and that I harboured serious doubts about the wisdom of doing so . . . I asked her directly, 'Are you really sure you want to make Iraq the centerpiece of the administration's foreign policy?' I was about to follow up with other questions when Condi cut me off. 'You can save your breath, Richard. The president has already made up his mind on Iraq.' The way she said it made clear that he had decided to go to war. This was eight months before the March 2003 start of the conflict . . . Policy had gone much further than I had realized – and feared.

I did not argue at that moment, for several reasons. As in previous conversations when I had voiced my views on Iraq, Condi's response made it clear that any more conversation at that point would be a waste of time. It is always important to pick your moments to make an unwelcome case, and this did not appear to be a promising one. I figured as well that there would be additional opportunities to argue my stance, if not with Condi, then with others in a position to make a difference . . .

Haass reminded his audience that dissent has always held a special place in American life, and has long been hailed as noble and necessary. He quoted President Dwight Eisenhower, who said that Americans should 'never confuse honest dissent with disloyal subversion', and former Senator J. William Fulbright's words that 'in a democracy, dissent is an act of faith'.

'This is all well and good,' Haass continued, 'but in my experience, dissent tends to be more honoured in the abstract than in practice.' The reality, he explained, is that dissent is difficult and can present a real dilemma for people. The fact that he disagreed with the decision to attack Iraq was deeply troubling to him – personally and professionally – and he weighed up his options carefully:

> One option in principle that to me was not an option in practice was to leak my objections to the media or to try to otherwise undermine the policy. This is not dissent but disloyalty . . . dissent is not about breaking the law or infringing the rights of others . . . Another option was to continue to argue against the war in Iraq after a decision was all but made to go ahead. I did some of this but not a lot. While it may have made me and other sceptics feel better, it would have reduced any influence we might have had on planning for the war and its aftermath.
>
> Leaving (resigning) is in many ways the most dramatic form of dissent. Putting aside personal reasons (health, finances, family) there are two potentially valid, policy-related reasons for resigning . . . One reason to resign is because you disagree fundamentally with a major decision . . . the second set of grounds for resigning [is] a pattern of decisions that makes clear you have little in common with your colleagues . . . Resigning is not always the right answer, though you need to consider it if the differences are large in scale or number. Staying where you are and trying to influence decisions from the inside may be the best option, but be sure you are making a positive difference. Practice your right of dissent, but tolerate and encourage it for others, too.

Haass's address* may be seen by critics as self-justifying, given his senior role during the build-up to war, and there may be

---

*Can be read in full at http://new.oberlin.edu/events-activities/ commencement/haass-speech-2009remarks.dot

some truth to this. But he certainly deserves credit for airing an issue that most other senior officials have remained silent about – namely, the difficult balance between loyalty and dissent. As Haass points out, although our society appears to encourage our right to speak up, in reality there are few options for doing so. There is a significant gap between the rhetorical exhortations to protest and what is actually tolerated.

Whistleblowers

Faced with the difficulties outlined above, some people revert to drastic ways to express their dissent. One is to spread the word, or 'blow the whistle', about an issue that deeply concerns them, whether it be an issue of policy, behaviour, performance or ethics. The term 'whistleblowers' comes from English bobbies (policemen) blowing their whistles upon witnessing a crime to alert the public of the danger. Whistleblowers are not 'leakers', who, as Haass explained, can cross the line of legality. Rather, they take their case to the public openly, and usually only as a last resort, having exhausted every other avenue to have their concern addressed. They may have stated their case internally to their bosses and colleagues, but no one responded constructively. They may have cajoled and threatened, but to no avail. Finally, they have got to a point where they believe the only way to generate action is to go public.

However, as in all matters of dissent, there is a price to pay for whistleblowing – and always has been. When Martin Luther exposed the waste and abuse of the Catholic Church in 1517 by nailing a list of excesses called the *95 Theses* to the door of Castle Church in Wittenberg, Germany, his actions led to the Reformation, but he also faced the wrath of the Church and the public around him. Established institutions have always been highly self-protective, and remain so. The difference is that today the discrimination against dissenters and whistleblowers is more subtle. Before the energy company Enron collapsed in 2001 (the biggest corporate collapse in US history at the time), an Enron executive named Sherron Watkins alerted the chairman Ken Lay to accounting irregularities. Two days later she was shown an email from an in-house lawyer reminding executives that the law in Texas, where Enron was located, did not protect whistle-blowers. She also found herself demoted and relegated to a 'skanky office'.[25]

Dissenters and whistleblowers don't just face pressure from the organisations they expose; they often experience ongoing enmity from the public. Although people respect the courage involved in such a drastic step as whistleblowing, there is often an unspoken societal taboo against being a 'tattletale'. The pressures on whistleblowers are likely to be particularly intense in group-oriented societies like Japan, where loyalty to the group is paramount. When Kiroku Akahane, a seventy-two-year-old executive at the Japanese meat-processing company Meat Hope, revealed in mid-2008 that some of his company's 'pure beef' products actually contained pork, mutton and chicken, his life changed. He says he has been treated like an outcast in his local community of Tomakomai. He has been barred from joining in local religious festivals and shunned by relatives, and now attends a psychiatric hospital to deal with depression.[26] Even in a rather easy-going society like Australia, there is a reluctance to 'dob someone in' to the authorities for a misdemeanour. Some would suggest this reluctance can be traced back to Australia's past, when the early convict settlers deeply distrusted their colonial masters and tended to stick together. Even notorious bushrangers (outlaws), such as Ned Kelly, were often protected by the local community by a code of silence.

The taboo against dissent and whistleblowing is also preva-lent in academic and scientific circles – areas where most people probably expect there to be a higher degree of reverence for the truth. According to two researchers, Rhodes and Strain, 'The whistleblower is still presumed, by many with power-ful professional regulatory positions, to be a disaffected, anti-social, incompetent pariah, "not a team player", who fails to appreciate the damage [they are] causing to the hard-earned reputations of their professional colleagues and employer.' When Dr John Buse, a medical researcher at the University of North Carolina, suggested in 1999 in a presentation to the American Diabetes Association that a new diabetes drug called Avandia raised the risk of chest pain and heart attacks by 50 per cent, he says he was subject to intense pressure from the drug's maker, SmithKline Beecham (now part of GlaxoSmithKline).[27] 'There were a number of phone calls from SmithKline Beecham saying there were people in the company who felt my actions were scurrilous enough to attempt to hold me liable for a loss of market capitalisation.' Buse said the company also contacted his superior, Dr Fred Sparling, chairman at the University of North Carolina, in an effort to discredit him.

Pharmaceutical companies are not particularly receptive to research data that impedes the forward momentum of their drug-development programmes by querying the efficacy of their drug or by highlighting possible health dangers. This is because it costs around $1 billion to create a significant new drug. Every new product has to undergo exhaustive tests to comply with the health-and-safety criteria imposed by the US Federal Food and Drug Administration (FDA) and the European equivalent, the European Medicines Agency (EMEA). After all this effort and investment, and with so much at stake, pharmaceutical companies are keen to ensure that their drugs are approved and that they get a return for their investment. If they are lucky, the drug may become a 'blockbuster' – that is, a huge seller that is enormously profitable. Blockbuster drugs each generate over $1 billion in sales per year in the United States and develop such a powerful market momentum that they can remain at the top for many years. In marketing terms, they generate a lot of Big Mo.

The ways that pharmaceutical companies protect their

drugs, and tend to suppress potential whistleblowers, are usually more subtle than the example cited above of Dr Buse. It is more likely that research grants are suddenly withdrawn or are not renewed; controversial scientific papers are quietly ignored or shelved; and invitations to address forums stop coming or are cancelled – in an effort to reduce the dissenter's credibility and profile. It's rather like a 'preventative medicine' against whistleblowers.

Attitudes to whistleblowing vary considerably across professions and cultures. In March 2007, Ernst & Young, a major business consulting company, polled thirteen hundred senior executives in thirteen European countries – each of whom worked for multinationals that had promoted whistleblowing – to find out whether employees in their company felt free to report a case of suspected fraud. Across mainland Europe only 54 per cent said yes, while in the UK the figure was 86 per cent. In the United States, a CNN/*Time* poll suggested that six out of ten Americans see whistleblowers as heroes, but more than half – 57 per cent – also believe that whistleblowers face negative consequences at work most of the time. And they are rarely praised for their action.[28] Cynthia Cooper, who in June 2002 blew the whistle on a $4 billion fraud at WorldCom, was never thanked by her superiors for her revelation, even though she had properly taken her concerns directly to the company board's own auditing committee and had exposed one of the largest corporate frauds in US history.

Another deterrent to would-be whistleblowers is that their time in the public eye – which initially protects them – quickly fades. Then they face a lifetime of subtle discrimination by employers who are unwilling to hire a potential troublemaker, or by one-time friends and colleagues who feel uncomfortable with their notoriety.

*　　*　　*

Someone who knows a lot about the difficulties faced by dissenters, and particularly whistleblowers, is Dr Donald Soeken, who has spent many years counselling those who dare to speak out against wrongdoing in the workplace. In the late 1970s he worked as a mental-health counsellor at a United States Public Health outpatient clinic in Washington. Among other duties, Soeken was required to conduct 'psychiatric fitness-for-duty examinations' on certain federal employees. On interviewing the patients, he soon discovered that most of them did not have psychiatric problems, that many of them had spoken out about abuses in their workplace and that their superiors were using the exams as a pretext to get them fired.[29] Soeken recalls one such incident in 1978 that involved a secretary in the US Department of Transportation. 'Her name was Sally, and she had somehow found the courage to report overtime "padding" [payroll inflation] in her section. Because she had gone public with her whistleblowing, her boss was furious. They wanted me to certify her as "psychologically unfit for duty". For me, that's where the rubber hit the road. I spent several weeks thinking about Martin Luther and the Old Testament prophets . . . and I realised that I could not certify her as unfit.'

Soeken put some newspaper reporters in the Washington area in touch with Sally, which resulted in a front-page story that prompted a Maryland congresswoman (the late Gladys Spelman) to launch a congressional hearing into the practice of using psychological examinations to punish whistleblowers.

Soeken says, 'I am convinced that our whistleblowers are modern-day prophets. And they pay a huge price for speaking out against the abuses they observe. All too often their careers are destroyed. They lose their homes, and their families are torn apart. They need our help, because the laws that were meant to protect them simply aren't enforced in this country today.' According to Soeken, too often the response is to 'kill the messenger'. He warns that our society needs our whistleblowers: 'If we allow them to be silenced, we'll sooner or later pay a terrible price for it.'

One of the prices we are already paying is the development of a more 'conformist' society, one in which people are less willing to challenge the status quo and instead surrender to the flow – no matter how perilous its direction.

CHAPTER 11

A New Age of Conformity

We have seen how difficult it can be to speak up against the crowd, especially when there are powerful interests at stake. These forces are often adept at stifling dissent and keeping everyone in line. They have the capacity to coerce and intimidate. We have also seen how our conditioning encourages us to conform to authority from an early age and, after a brief period of teenage rebelliousness, continues to influence us throughout adulthood. But there is another, more subtle reason why we are so willing to surrender to the flow. This has to do with perceptual conditioning and how individuals interpret information in a group environment.

In the 1950s, a sociologist named Solomon Asch, of Swarthmore College in Pennsylvania, demonstrated through a series of experiments that people interpret information differently when they are in a group situation as opposed to when they are alone. When people were put in a room together, they tended to interpret information in the same way as those around them, even if it meant defying their own senses and judgements. To put it another way, once a certain proposition gains traction, or momentum, and everyone else in the room accepts it, an individual sitting there might conclude everyone else is probably right. Asch summed up: 'That we have found the tendency to conformity in our society so strong that reasonably intelligent and well-meaning young people are willing to call white black, is a matter of concern.'[1]

More recently, it has been observed that this type of conformity is universal and not specific to certain cultures: it has been demonstrated in numerous experiments around the world, including in Zaire, Germany, France, Japan, Norway, Lebanon and Kuwait. The finding is also supported by brain-imaging experiments that suggest that people in a group tend to see a situation as everyone else present does.[2] This tendency to conform is innate to us, and is not a new phenomenon.

What is different today, however, is that in terms of the Solomon Asch experiment, we are all sitting in a much bigger room surrounded by a much bigger group. This giant virtual room full of people is generated by the modern media, which expose us to viewpoints that appear to be commonly shared by millions of people. When we watch a news show, for example, the stories are presented in a way that presumes everyone watching agrees on certain values and codes of behaviour. This exerts subtle pressure on us to interpret news stories in a similar way to other viewers, even if this interpretation goes against our own judgements.

This was less likely to occur decades ago because the media provided a much greater diversity of opinion – particularly newspapers, whose editorial policies varied tremendously. There used to be competing social and political models on offer, each with its own way to interpret the world. Today there is primarily just one: the global corporatised model based on the accumulation of wealth and the adulation of celebrity. Whereas once politics was arrayed on a spectrum from left to right, today we focus on the political centre, where all the parties have converged. Ours is evolving into a 'monocular' society: a society of a billion eyes, all looking in the same direction at the same spot on the wall. Consider, for example, the Internet. Despite the millions of websites available, nearly everyone tends to visit the same small number of sites over and over. Search engines such as Google are deliberately designed to take us to the same sites as everyone else is visiting, ranked by popularity and relevance. The most popular news websites simply mirror the content of the top ten media organisations – the old guard, who magnify and reinforce the same storylines. These storylines are then repeated endlessly through the twenty-four-hour news cycle, as described in chapter 7, and generate a powerful, self-reinforcing momentum, until they become etched into the collective psyche – which further encourages us to surrender to the flow.

In effect, Asch's room has gone global.

This convergence of viewpoints has helped to usher in a new age of conformity, which is making our society more vulnerable to upheavals like the recent global financial crisis. The *New York Times* columnist David Brooks recently wrote:

> To me, the most interesting factor is the way instant communication has led to unconscious conformity. You'd think that with thousands of ideas flowing at light speed around the world, you'd get a diversity of viewpoints and expectations that would balance one another out. Instead, global communications seem to have led people in the financial subculture to adopt homogenous viewpoints. They made the same one-way bets at the same time.[3]

This behaviour is likely to be further exacerbated by the launch of new software programs from Bloomberg and Thomson Reuters that scan thousands of breaking news stories to provide 'high-frequency' traders with instant signals to buy and sell. This begs the question: if so many traders are receiving the same signals at the same time, how can they avoid conforming to the stampeding herd? It is already difficult enough for traders and fund managers to go against the prevailing flow. Research conducted by Judith Chevalier at Yale School of Management and Glenn Ellison at MIT suggests that when young fund managers deviated significantly from the strategies of their peers, they were more likely to lose their jobs, regardless of how well their funds performed. Twenty years ago, unconventional thinking in the investments markets was often rewarded – not so today.[4]

This growing tendency to conform also extends to professions where, most people would assume, there is a greater respect for objectivity. Consider, for example, the medical profession. Despite having access to extensive independent information on the Internet, most doctors tend to prescribe the drugs they see most heavily advertised and promoted – particularly the blockbuster drugs described in the last chapter. In Australia, a survey of 180 doctors by Australia's *Choice* magazine in August 2008 found that drug companies had a 'major influence' on what doctors prescribed. 'Doctors receive far more information from drug companies than from independent sources,' the report stated. Seventy-three per cent of the doctors referred to drug companies for information, and 65 per cent saw at least seven representatives from drug companies each month, while some saw twenty or more. 'Doctors are bombarded with marketing and promotions from drug companies,' according to the *Choice* report. Their prescribing habits conform to what they believe other doctors are prescribing. Again, the 'Asch's room' effect.

This tendency to fall in with the views and practices of everyone else is particularly prevalent in large organisations, such as corporations and governments. In large-scale environments, personnel are expected to align their behaviour with the organisational 'flow' and not challenge the status quo. Erika James, an associate professor at the University of Virginia's Darden School of Business, says that the way modern corporations enforce conformity can be very subtle. For example, a manager will often soften a direction with words like, 'Well, you would agree with . . .' or 'Don't you think that . . .'[5] The use of this kind of language contains a strong, albeit subtle, message to comply.

Another factor that encourages corporate conformity is the almost universal application of software tools like PowerPoint, which has the effect of making all presentations similar – not just in their look and style, but in the way thoughts are articulated.

Over time, staff members start to see the world in terms of bullet points and multicoloured pie charts. The medium becomes the message. So even emotionally disturbing presentations about, say, impending staff cuts convey an anodyne quality that serves to insulate the audience from the reality of the situation. It is interesting to note that at JPMorgan Chase, one of the few banks to survive the global financial crisis largely intact, the use of PowerPoint presentations is often discouraged – as part of a wider effort to encourage employees to retain a healthy scepticism about artificial ways of interpreting information.[6] In most companies it is the opposite. The in-house corporate-identity department will insist that every single presentation done by any employee, anywhere, has the same look and feel to ensure 'brand consistency'.

The use of PowerPoint has also crept, like an insurgency, into the US military, much to the chagrin of some senior officers. 'PowerPoint makes us stupid,' General James N Mattis of the Marine Corps, the Joint Forces commander, told a military conference in North Carolina. Another officer, Brigadier General H R McMaster, said that PowerPoint is 'dangerous because it can create the illusion of understanding and the illusion of control . . . some problems in the world are not bullet-izable'. McMaster, who banned the use of PowerPoint presentations when he led the successful effort to secure the northern Iraqi city of Tal Afar in 2005, said that PowerPoint's worst offence in a military context was the way it presented rigid lists of bullet points (in, say, a presentation on a conflict's causes) that took no account of interconnected political, economic and ethnic forces. 'If you divorce war from all of that, it becomes a targeting exercise,' General McMaster said. What particularly concerns many commanders is PowerPoint's capacity to stifle discussion, critical thinking and thoughtful decision-making. Notwithstanding these shortcomings, PowerPoint is unlikely to disappear any time soon from military or corporate environments, where conformity is the name of the game.[7]

In large organisations and corporations, compliance is further compounded by the fact that rewards and incentives usually go to those employees who do what they are told. No one would get this impression, however, by reading the human-resources literature of most modern corporations, which invariably extols the virtues of an open culture in which the individual is encouraged to challenge orthodox thinking. 'Our company thrives on innovation and creativity' is a common refrain.

The masters of such Orwellian communications are the banks, which have to tread a fine line between appearing innovative and dynamic, while at the same time appearing solid and reliable. This contradiction presents a difficult conundrum for the people who work in a bank's marketing department. I can shed some light on this, as one of my jobs at UBS was global head of advertising.

Striving for sameness

The most important objective of any advertising campaign is to stand out from the competitors in a positive way. It's all about differentiation. UBS's advertising had a catchy 'you and us' theme and was one of the most memorable and effective campaigns in the industry. But here's the strange thing. About a year after we launched our campaign, it was imitated by other banks – particularly the advertising style and imagery. Even the music sounded similar. It became increasingly difficult to differentiate a UBS commercial from, say, a Crédit Suisse one. They all began to blur into each other. In the same way the banks had slavishly imitated each others' risk models, portfolio-management tools, performance-management systems and investment processes, now the very thing that was supposed to differentiate them – their advertising – became part of the conformity cult that led the entire banking industry off a cliff.

In my experience, we can learn a lot about our increasingly conformist society from the advertising industry, because it acts as a kind of bellwether for societal norms. Advertising holds up a mirror to us, to reveal our aspirations and fears, and at its best can challenge or inspire us. But the industry has changed beyond recognition in recent years. Gone are the days of admen and women being brilliant, eccentric types with scant regard for political correctness. They belong to yesteryear – the people who were risk-takers, paid to challenge the status quo. Conformity was their mortal enemy. You can get a glimpse of such characters in *Mad Men*, the popular television series set in a 1960s Madison Avenue agency. Walk into any big agency today, however, and you could be excused for thinking you had walked into a typical corporate office – and you would not be wrong. In recent years the great agencies have been swallowed up by huge communications conglomerates like WPP and Interpublic, whose primary objective is to generate shareholder value. In the kind of bottom-line-driven environment they represent, it is often easier to retain a big lucrative client like a bank by giving them advertising that doesn't look too different from what their competitors are doing. After all, if their competitors are doing it, then it must be OK, right?

The other factor driving advertising to become more conformist is the growing influence of 'research' on the creative-development process. No creative idea is given the green light in a big advertising agency without it being thoroughly researched by a combination of qualitative and quantitative focus groups – where members of the general public sit around in a room and discuss the pros and cons of a creative idea. The irony is, of course, that these focus groups perfectly emulate the conditions of Asch's room, and are fertile grounds for group-think and conformist behaviour. Over the years, I have witnessed many a brilliant idea die the death of a thousand rhetorical cuts by focus-group members determined to show how insightful they are: British focus groups tend to be particularly scathing, whereas Americans are more polite and the Japanese too polite. Conversely, I have seen dumb ideas gather unwarranted positive traction (momentum) as everyone in the room falls in behind a particularly persuasive or dominant member.

The point is that too much research almost always has the effect of elevating the lowest common denominator, because the only idea that succeeds is the one that is least upsetting to the crowd. That is, the best-tolerated idea wins rather than the best-loved. This phenomenon doesn't just afflict advertising. The reason why most political campaign speeches and presentations today are so bland is that they have been so heavily researched that the life has been squeezed out of them for fear of upsetting marginal voting constituencies. The political process used to be about appealing to as many people as possible, but now it is about offending as few people as possible – which brings us to the befuddling issue of political correctness.

The politics of correctness

To say that in the West we live in a politically correct society is an understatement. It is becoming increasingly difficult to speak your mind without fear of offending someone or breaking some newly introduced anti-discrimination law. That said, it is vital that our society does not discriminate against people on the basis of their race, gender, sexual preference, or political or religious belief. But in doing so we must also preserve the right of free speech and not shy away from recognising a situation for what it is.

Sometimes, political correctness can take ludicrous forms, such as the recent recommendation by Britain's Professional Association of Teachers to replace the term 'failed' with 'deferred success' for exam results, in order to avoid stigmatising students,[8] and the replacement of common terms like 'patient' with 'client', on the grounds that patients should not be patronised by medical staff. In recent years, the English language has been quietly and systematically overhauled by various well-meaning groups to remove any expressions that could give offence. The process extends to preschool literature, such as fairy tales, which have been purged of anything that remotely implies stereotyping, sexism or any deviation from accepted social norms. For example, a government-funded books project in Britain recently changed the words of the popular children's rhyme 'What shall we do with the drunken sailor?' to 'What shall we do with the grumpy pirate?'. 'Baa baa, black sheep' was changed to 'Baa baa, rainbow sheep', and a book about the 'three little pigs' was banned because it might upset some religious groups.

While tampering with the language like this may seem relatively trivial and inconsequential, it is evidence of a deeper malaise and, for reasons we shall explore, is a symptom of a momentum-driven society.

The purpose of language is to convey meaning – accurately, concisely and clearly; it is not designed to insulate anyone from real-life experiences by painting rose-tinted views of the world. It is supposed to bring individuals into contact with the world as it actually is. To achieve this purpose language sometimes has to be robust and direct, especially in the context of human relations. It is far better to be honest with your neighbour, no matter what their creed, race or gender, than tiptoe around them behind a veil of politically correct language while suppressing what you really need to say. It's possible to be direct without being rude.

Baroness James, better known as P D James, the best-selling author of books like *Children of God*, recently addressed a packed audience at the Palace of Westminster in London: 'We are bedevilled by political correctness . . . If in speaking to minorities we have to weigh every word in advance in case inadvertently we give offence, how can we be at ease with each other, how can we celebrate our common humanity, our shared anxieties and aspirations, both for ourselves and for those whom we love?' James, who is a former senior civil servant in the criminal-policy department of the Home Office, added, '[Political correctness] is a pernicious if risible authoritarian attempt at linguistic and social control.'[9]

In Britain, this control also extends to areas like sport, where the fear of upsetting children prompted the Education Department to adopt a 'medals for all' policy, so that no child would be faced with 'losing' in a competitive event. Dame Kelly Holmes, who won two gold medals at the 2004 Athens Olympics, was moved to comment that the culture of political correctness had made 'competitiveness' a dirty word and had led to the decline of competitive sport in schools. 'I was surprised by how many schools I came across where sports day had been abandoned. It's very important to learn how to lose . . . What you should do is pick yourself up, dust yourself down and start all over again. If everyone gets a prize, where on earth is the incentive to push yourself to do better next time?'[10] After London won the right to host the 2012 Olympics the Labour government promised to end the 'medals for all' culture which had led to the decline of competitive sport in the United Kingdom.

Across the Atlantic, the Americans have been grappling with the growing impact of political correctness for decades. The historian and educator Diane Ravitch tells how she was asked to review some proposed educational texts for children for the US Education Department.[11]

After I had read about a dozen such passages, a combination of fiction and non-fiction, I realized that the readings themselves had a cumulative subtext: the hero was never a white boy. Instead, the leading character – the one who was most competent, successful, and sympathetic – was invariably either a girl (of any race) or a non-white boy. Almost without exception, white boys were portrayed as weak and dependent. In one story, a white boy in a difficult situation weeps and says plaintively, 'If only my big sister were here, I would know what to do' . . . The passages, I discovered, had been edited to eliminate anything that might be perceived by anyone as a source of bias.

When Ravitch enquired why so few reading passages were drawn from classic children's literature, the publisher explained that it was 'a well-accepted principle in educational publishing that everything written before 1970 was rife with racism and sexism. Only stories written after that date were likely to have acceptable language and appropriate multicultural sensitivity.'

Ravitch says that one of the strangest examples of political correctness she came across concerned the true story of a heroic young blind man who hiked to the top of Mount McKinley, the highest peak in North America. The story described the dangers of hiking up an icy mountain trail, especially for a blind person. The publisher's 'Bias and Sensitivity Panel' voted 12–11 to eliminate this inspiring story because the story contained 'regional bias', as it was about hiking and mountain-climbing, which favours students who live in regions where those activities are common. Secondly, they rejected the story because it suggested that people who are blind are somehow at a disadvantage compared to people who have normal sight, that they are 'worse off' and have a more difficult time facing dangers than those who are not blind.

> By institutionalizing this extreme sensitivity to anything that offends anyone, publishers of both textbooks and tests have been turning their products into inoffensive pap for the past generation [Ravitch says]. The result is that in these books, the real world is replaced by a politically correct fairy-tale land in which it is acceptable to censor *Romeo and Juliet* or *Macbeth* so ninth graders aren't exposed to wicked concepts – as if they don't consume any on TV.

So what does all this have to do with momentum? Perhaps more than we think.

The rise of political correctness in the 1980s and 1990s coincided with the first major steps toward a momentum-driven society. This was when the media, communications, technology, legal systems and financial markets first began to rapidly integrate and accelerate the pace of perceptual and real change. It was the birth of the 'surrender to the flow' mentality, that now permeates our world. Political correctness is, in many ways, a manifestation of this mentality for it discourages people to go against the accepted norms or to challenge the status quo. It is an extension of the desire to create a 'frictionless' world, in which all abrasiveness is systematically removed from the system, thus smoothing over superficial problems while covering up the real ones. We have already seen how dangerous this frictionless environment can be in the global financial system. It's interesting to note that the most politically correct environments are often corporate environments (such as large banks) that are most susceptible to Big Mo.

Without doubt, the proponents of political correctness will argue vehemently that it came about to protect against discrimination and ensure greater equality and fairness. And there is obviously a lot of truth to this – at least there was in the beginning. But as we have seen throughout this book, certain attitudes and ways of thinking soon develop their own momentum, which becomes self-perpetuating and eventually spirals out of control. The political-correctness movement is no exception. It may have started off with noble intentions, but it has now devolved into a form of 'tyranny with manners'.

By stripping language of its robustness and replacing it with anodyne alternatives we are also undermining our capacity to confront threats in a direct and timely manner. One of the most notorious examples of this constraint was an incident at a US military base in Fort Hood, Texas, in November 2009, when an army psychiatrist named Nidal Malik Hasan shot dead thirteen of his companions.[12] Although the major, who was a Muslim, was known to harbour and express violent Islamist views and condone suicide bombing, no one ever challenged him on them for fear this would be seen to be discriminatory in light of his religion. Whether his murderous act was inspired by Islamic extremism or not is beside the point. He could just as well have been a Christian or a Jew or an atheist. What is concerning is that he was not assertively challenged about his views before the crime was committed – for reasons of political correctness. Although this is an extreme and tragic example, it highlights the law of unintended consequences. For by attempting to harmonise relations through political correctness the tensions were driven underground until such time as they surfaced again with deadly effect.

More broadly, by constraining our instinctive need to speak

plainly and candidly with each other, political correctness is conditioning us to be less able to speak out on other issues of importance. It makes us more likely to surrender to the flow rather than say or do anything that might offend someone.

Part 3

The Faces of Big Mo

CHAPTER 12

The Momentum-Driven Company

So far we have focused on the factors that have increased the level of momentum in our world and on why individuals and organisations are so susceptible to its influence. These include environmental factors like the rapid integration of communications, technology, media and financial markets, all of which accelerate the speed of events. We have also explored some of the false assumptions that enable momentum to spiral out of control, such as our misplaced faith in equilibrium to restore balance and our reverence for efficiency, speed and dangerous theoretical models. We have analysed the behavioural factors that make people so susceptible to Big Mo and the spooky quantum forces that seem to drive them. We have also looked at why it is so difficult to speak up against the status quo in today's world and how the combination of the Asch's room effect and political correctness help bring about an alignment in our thinking and behaviour to produce a conformist society.

The picture that emerges is of a momentum-driven society, one in which we are increasingly compelled to go with the flow, no matter what the consequences: a society in which no one is really accountable for what happens – *because it just happens*.

Like any powerful force, however, momentum operates in

different ways in different circumstances. As we shall see in Part 3, Big Mo has many faces.

We learned in chapter 5 how big companies can be particularly vulnerable to the forces of momentum, because their internal efficiency and scale create the conditions for momentum to occur. In effect, the very qualities that enabled these companies to grow so large begin to work against them. This internal dynamic is further compounded by the rise of 'momentum surfers' into senior executive positions (see chapter 9) and the increasing level of conformity in the workplace (see chapter 11). The interplay of these factors means that the contemporary company is often no longer driven by a genuine strategic outlook, but rather by momentum. It is a 'go with the flow' company.

As previously discussed, this is what happened with many of the big banks in the lead-up to the global financial crisis: they lost their strategic perspective and ignored critical risk factors. They were swept up in a competition among themselves to achieve quick profits by diving deeper into the pool of toxic-derivatives debt. By doing so, they brought the world financial system to the brink of collapse. When later asked to explain the reason for this collective myopia, the bankers' rationale was, in essence, 'Everyone else was doing it, why shouldn't we?' Indeed, one of the telltale signs that a company is caught in a momentum trap is when it measures its performance primarily on how well it is doing against its competitors, rather than against more fundamental benchmarks. Imagine a swimmer who is caught in a fast-flowing river heading for the falls, saying, 'Don't worry. I'm in a better position than the person swimming next to me.' Their only meaningful measure in reality would be their position relative to the riverbank.

The rise of the momentum-driven company has transformed the way analysts view large corporations. Up until quite recently, analysts would draw a clear line between the big blue-chip companies and their smaller, more volatile siblings; now all companies are regarded as having similar vulnerabilities. No longer can anyone count on a blue-chip company to generate stable revenues and investment returns year after year. Thanks to the momentum dynamic, their performance can be just as volatile as that of a start-up company, perhaps even more so, because when a big company gets it wrong, it really gets it wrong. Big companies are more prone to 'systemic risk'. One senior equities analyst in London told me, 'There is no such thing as a blue-chip company any more – not in the way we used to think of them. If General Electric, General Motors and some megabanks can go down so quickly, like they did during the financial crisis, anyone can go down. They're all in the same boat now.'[1]

This increased volatility among global companies has significant implications for the world's economic infrastructure. Some of these companies are so staggeringly large that they generate annual revenues that exceed the gross domestic product of a medium-sized country. They employ hundreds of thousands of people in dozens of countries, and serve millions of people with vital products and services such as food, manufactured goods, resources and energy. Society counts on them to be relatively stable and to do their job.

This more volatile corporate environment didn't just happen overnight. It can be traced back decades to when businesses became obsessed with efficiency and integration, and to a more marketing-focused, or opportunistic, outlook. But it wasn't until the turn of the twenty-first century that the first truly momentum-driven company operating at hyper speed on a very large scale emerged. This company was Enron. Although a few years have passed since this story unfolded, it is just as relevant today as it was then, perhaps more so.

The company that fell for Big Mo

The story of Enron is that of the biggest corporate collapse in US history at the time. It showed how quickly and dramatically the mightiest companies can fail and, as such, gave a foretaste of the global financial crisis that was soon to come. In 2000,

Enron was the leading energy-trading company in the world and was valued at over $100 billion. Within a year its share price fell from $95 to $1, and its 19,000 employees lost their jobs and company retirement savings.[2] The shock of Enron was so great, not just because of its scale, but because the people running the company had been considered the best and brightest of their generation. Handpicked, carefully screened graduates from Harvard and Yale, they were the brightest in their class, stellar performers.

Enron started life as a regional gas-pipeline company, which resulted from a merger between Houston Natural Gas and Internorth in 1985. It owned lots of pipes that carried gas to homes and businesses, for which it charged a fee. Its collection of pipes grew and grew until Enron owned more pipes than any other company in history, and transported 17.5 per cent of all the gas in the United States. It was a solid, straightforward business. As one former Houston Natural Gas executive said of the pipes, 'All they do is make money. It's boring, but it's dependable.'[3]

When ex-McKinsey management consultant Jeff Skilling arrived on the Enron scene in the early 1990s, he recognised the value of the 'pipe business' but thought it wasn't 'sexy' – certainly not for a man of his capabilities and intelligence. Once, during an interview with Harvard Business School, when asked whether he was smart, he famously responded: 'I'm fucking smart.'[4]

Skilling also recognised that the energy industry was about to change fundamentally. For decades it had been heavily regulated by federal authorities who oversaw pricing, distribution arrangements, ownership structures and standards. By the early 1990s, the government began to deregulate the industry by allowing more customer choice and dropping barriers to enable the energy suppliers to operate more freely across different energy sectors such as gas, oil and electricity, and across different state markets.

Deregulation presented a golden opportunity to Skilling and his cohorts, an opportunity to surf the wave of change. In this looser, new environment they set about transforming Enron's conservative pipe business into an energy-'trading' business, which would be a lot more exciting to work for and potentially far more profitable. This transformation was based on a big idea: 'Best energy everywhere and cheaper'. By 1999, Enron was involved in a quarter of all natural-gas and electricity deals in the world, including major operations in developing countries, such as Brazil and India. Enron became a darling of Wall Street for bringing hi-tech and complex finance to the traditionally dull business of supplying energy. Enron also led the way in trading energy over the Internet through the establishment of Enron Online, which enabled it to trade over eight hundred different products, covering electricity, gas, oil and even metals. According to one media commentator, with this new model, 'Enron didn't just own the casino, on any given deal, Enron could be the house, the dealer, the odds maker and the guy across the table you're trying to beat in diesel futures, gas futures, or the California electricity market.'[5]

Enron's biggest transformation, however, was not about pipes or diesel futures or electricity. It was about culture. The 'old' Enron had had an engineering mindset, as befitting a pipeline business, and this mindset permeated everything it did. It was methodical, careful and constantly checking for flaws. The 'new' Enron, under Skilling, soon developed what could be described as a momentum-driven mindset, which was fast moving and opportunistic. It was all about pushing the machine forward, faster and faster, and not looking back or asking too many questions. Skilling and his chairman, Ken Lay, ran employee meetings like political rallies and used their consummate skills as cheerleaders to build the momentum. During one hour-long intra-company communications video they announced Enron's vision to be not just the world's leading energy company but the world's leading company, full stop. Their favourite words were 'awesome' and 'outstanding', which, coincidentally, are words commonly used by the surfing community. In fact, Skilling proved to be the consummate momentum surfer and rode the wave of energy deregulation for all it was worth. However, he studiously avoided explaining how

Enron actually made money, describing the company's financial statements as a 'black box' that could not be understood by outsiders. But 'It's a good black box,' he would say, 'because Enron's businesses are growing.'[6] In a scene from the award-winning documentary *Enron: The Smartest Guys in the Room*, Skilling enthusiastically implores Enron employees to put all their retirement savings into Enron stock.

By the late 1990s, to the outside world, Enron was not just riding a wave, it was the wave. It was seen as a cash-generating machine. But Enron's senior management knew differently, because there was a problem with the business model. Unlike other online trading places like eBay, which matches buyers and sellers for a fee, Enron was the principal in every transaction. This meant it had to have enormous amounts of capital to fund its various trading positions, and it had to pay interest on that capital. Each day that Enron held on to a substantial position in a commodity, it had to pay interest on the money it borrowed to take that position. It was an expensive enterprise. It had become too big for the good old pipe business to be able to provide enough nickel-and-dime cash flow for their needs. And they couldn't borrow any more money from the banks because this would lower their credit rating and increase the interest they were being charged. It seemed the Big Idea that was Enron was not so big.

They had to find a new way to feed the cash-hungry beast. Enron's chief financial officer, Andrew Fastow, soon came up with an idea. He could create special purpose entities (SPEs) which would, in effect, enable Enron to strip much of the risk out of the business by keeping it off the balance sheet. Fastow, who once bragged that he could 'strip out any risk', set about creating a labyrinthine network of interlocking SPEs that transformed Enron's balance sheet by keeping the cash flowing in, or at least the illusion of cash.[7] This financial 'innovation' bought Enron time. Skilling kept on hyping the momentum. As late as June 2000 he told the *Financial Times* that Enron's business model would enable it to 'intermediate everything, commoditise everything. We believe that markets are the best way to order or organise an industrial enterprise. You are going to see the de-integration of the business systems we have all grown up with.'[8]

The share price kept going up. The media played along and *Fortune* magazine continued to label Enron as one of America's most admired companies.[9] Meanwhile, company insiders who were familiar with Enron's mounting cash crisis preferred to look the other way. In such a situation, 'A lot of people don't want to hear the straight truth,' says Thomas Donaldson, a business ethics professor at the University of Pennsylvania's Wharton School. 'Investors don't want the CEO to say something negative that will drop the stock, even for the short term. There's a culture of puffery, a culture of winking.'[10]

But then some curious journalists began to ask uncomfortable questions. Enron's response was one of vigorous denial, as is typical of an organisation caught in a momentum flow and determined to keep things moving forward at any cost.

It wasn't long before the cracks appeared in the Enron façade. 'The signs were there for anyone who cared to look,' wrote Richard Lambert, editor of the *Financial Times* from 1991 to 2001.[11] 'The fact that Enron executives had for some time been selling shares for all they were worth was public information. So were the company's links with the obscure off-balance-sheet partnerships that were subsequently to trigger its downfall.'

According to Alexander Dyck and Luigi Zingales, who wrote 'The Bubble and the Media',

Three important lessons emerge from the media's coverage of Enron. First, that while many transactions were concealed, there was enough public information available to raise serious doubts about the credibility of Enron's earnings. Second, that instead of scrutinising Enron's accounts, the media acted as a cheerleader all the way to the end. Thirdly, journalists who question the existing optimistic consensus incur constant harassment from the target company.[12]

Another early warning signal about Enron that went largely unnoticed was the fact that it had paid no tax in the five years leading up to its collapse. This was because the US Internal Revenue Service did not recognise the market-to-market accounting process used by Enron to claim its profits, and therefore, as far as they were concerned, Enron was simply not making any money to be taxed.

Malcolm Gladwell, writing in the *New Yorker*, told a remarkable story of how in the spring of 1998, six business-school students from Cornell University did a project on Enron. 'It was for an advanced financial-statement-analysis class taught by a guy at Cornell called Charles Lee, who is pretty famous in financial circles,' recalls Jay Krueger, a member of the project team.

The students chose Enron because one of the team had a summer internship interview there, and he was interested in the energy sector. Six weeks later the team came back with their analysis. They had scrutinised every piece of information they could find out about Enron, examined the various businesses, how their performance compared to other competitors, and so on. 'They used statistical tools designed to find patterns in a company's performance – the Beneish model, the Lev and Thiagarajan indicators, the Edwards-Bell-Ohlsen analysis – and made their way through pages and pages of footnotes,' Gladwell wrote. 'The students' conclusions were straightforward. Enron was pursuing a far riskier strategy than its competitors. There were clear signs that Enron may have been manipulating its earnings.' The twenty-three-page report was posted on the website of Cornell University, where it remains to this day. The students' recommendation was on the first page, in bold-faced type: 'Sell.'[13]

It is ironic that Enron, a company whose fortunes were built on pipes designed to keep energy flowing, was ultimately undone by the perils of the flow. It became a victim of the momentum dynamic. The seeds of Enron's demise were sown by a group of people who exhibited all the characteristics of momentum surfers; they were leaders whose prime concern was to keep riding the wave and keep things moving forward at any cost. When problems surfaced, they reacted by suppressing dissent and redoubling their bets, thus further amplifying the mistakes and accelerating the momentum – until eventually, the whole enterprise spiralled out of control and could no longer be held together by the dizzying delusions that had sustained it.

In January 2002, *Newsweek* ran a major story about Enron, subtitled 'It's the Scariest Type of Scandal: a Total System Failure. Executives, Lenders, Auditors and Regulators All Managed to Look the Other Way . . .' Sound familiar? Enron was the first momentum-driven company of the twenty-first century to be swept away in its own Big Mo, but it would certainly not be the last.

CHAPTER 13

Celebrity Mo

The rather frumpy, middle-aged woman strutted to the centre of the stage, then squinted into the lights towards the thousands of people in the audience. Cameras zoomed in on her face, framed by tousled hair and thick eyebrows, beaming the image to millions of viewers. The woman was not used to this sort of thing, not by a long shot. Rarely had she ventured beyond her small Scottish village where, for the past decades, she had taken care of her ailing mum and her beloved cat, Pebbles. Her life had revolved around a few friends, the local pub and church, and some singing. But something inside her had driven her to compete in this talent show. She gripped the microphone and a rather cocksure man on the adjudicating panel invited her to introduce herself. As she spoke, the man rolled his eyes, barely containing his mirth at the woman's brazenness. For this was not just any talent show; it was *Britain's Got Talent*, the number one programme of its kind in the country. Titters rippled throughout the hall as the incredulous audience waited for what was surely going to be a cringingly gauche performance.

Then the woman sang.

It took only a few seconds – just the opening lyrics of her song – before the audience fell drop-jawed into a state of shock and disbelief. The woman's voice was so beautiful, so virtuous and so downright surprising, that it was difficult to comprehend. Her song, 'I Dreamed a Dream' from *Les Miserables*, rang out with a majestic joyfulness that reverberated throughout the hall. By the end of her rendition, everyone who'd witnessed it had fallen under the spell of this forty-seven-year-old self-confessed virgin.

The story of Susan Boyle's meteoric rise to fame is now the stuff of legend. Within a few weeks, millions of people had seen her performance on television, and tens of millions more had watched her on YouTube. She was front-page news for weeks on all major media. By month's end she was a household name. By the end of the year, Boyle's debut album, *I Dreamed a Dream*, topped the charts in America, the United Kingdom, Australia and New Zealand and became one of the fastest-selling albums in history.[1] She was now a global celebrity.

Although Susan Boyle is not the first person to have experienced a meteoric rise to stardom, her case is one of the most instructive, for it exemplifies the momentum-driven nature of the world in which we are now immersed. Consider for a moment what would have happened if Susan Boyle had delivered her remarkable performance a decade earlier. Certainly she would have surprised many people, but without the viral-like support of YouTube and a host of social-network sites like Facebook and Twitter, it is unlikely that she would have been catapulted to such stratospheric stardom so quickly – if at all. To do so then would have taken a lot of hard work by record companies and their publicists to build and sustain the momentum. It would also have cost a lot of money, which they might not have been willing to invest in promoting a middle-aged 'unknown'. In fact, Susan Boyle had performed in public ten years earlier, when she recorded 'Cry Me a River' for a charity. Some critics say that the quality of her singing in this rendition is as good as, if not better than, her performance on *Britain's Got Talent*. But only a thousand copies of the record were made, and Susan Boyle was not heard of again beyond her local village for another decade.

It would take an entirely new media environment to emerge before Susan Boyle could find her place in the limelight – an environment in which a dormant talent, combined with the element of surprise and novelty, could be discovered, magnified and canonised to an extent that was inconceivable just a few years ago. This is celebrity-manufacturing on the Big Mo scale, where it is possible to achieve greater mass (mass audience) moving at instantaneous speed (acceleration) to generate momentous levels of adulation and fame. According to Visible Measures, an American company that computes viewership of Internet videos, Susan Boyle's YouTube video had already been watched 310 million times in all of its forms by late 2009. 'What we're really seeing with Susan Boyle in a very powerful way is the power of "spreadability",' said Henry Jenkins, co-director of MIT's Comparative Media Studies programme and author of the book *Convergence Culture: Where Old and New Media Collide*. 'Consumers in their own online communities are making conscious choices to spread Susan Boyle around online.'[2] This 'spreadability' is facilitated by the unprecedented developments in digital technologies and multimedia convergence.

This new media environment, however, isn't just about technological advances and star-making; it's as much about a profound change in the way we measure the status of a person in our society. All civilisations have, over the millennia, developed their own ways of estimating a person's status. These estimations are usually based on a combination of a person's achievements, wealth, power, position, family ties, creativity and so on. What's unique about our society is that status is increasingly based on how well known a person is – their fame – rather than what they actually do. We have moved well beyond Andy Warhol's prediction that in the future 'everyone will be famous for fifteen minutes'.[3] On the web, everyone can be famous to fifteen people – or to half a million people – through social networking sites like Facebook, YouTube and Twitter. Those who crave fame no longer have to rely on the ephemeral nature of the mass media to put them in the spotlight and keep them there. They can make their own spotlight.

Consider the bizarre case of the 'balloon boy', who, for a

week in October 2009, riveted the attention of the American public and many others around the world. A six-year-old boy named Falcon was reported to have been trapped inside the basket of a hot-air balloon which had escaped its mooring and was being blown across America. It was the kind of perilous, hair-raising story that is every parent's nightmare and every television news producer's dream come true. The broadcasting networks jumped onto the story, and some even dumped a live broadcast of President Obama in New Orleans to track the balloon floating over Colorado. Millions of people tuned in – doubling the TV ratings for that day.

But the balloon-boy story came crashing to earth almost as soon as it took off. It turned out to be a hoax concocted by the boy's father, Richard Heene, who, having once tasted fame on a television reality TV show called *Wife Swap*, now wanted more. So he created his own script and cast himself as a central character. His moment in the spotlight cost him a prison sentence. Frank Rich, writing in the *New York Times* on 24 October 2009, says we should be careful about being self-righteous in our condemnation of the father's deception.

> Richard Heene is the inevitable product of this reigning culture, where 'news', 'reality' television and reality itself are hopelessly scrambled and the warp-speed imperatives of cable-internet competition allow no time for fact checking . . . None of this absolves Heene of blame for the damage he may have inflicted on the children he grotesquely used as a supporting cast in his schemes. But stupid he's not. He knew how easy it would be to float 'balloon boy' when the demarcation between truth and fiction has been obliterated.[4]

Rich says there's also some poignancy in the father's determination to grab what he and many others see as among the 'last accessible scraps of the American dream'. Heene had found difficulty in getting work in a depressed construction industry and was becoming increasingly desperate to turn things around:

> Once his appetite had been whetted by two histrionic appearances on *Wife Swap*, an ABC reality program, it's easy to see why Heene would turn his life and that of his family into a nonstop audition for more turns in the big tent of the reality media circus. That circus is among the country's last dependable job engines. More than a quarter of prime-time broadcast television is devoted to reality programs. Heene is a direct descendant of those Americans of the Great Depression who fantasized, usually in vain, that they might find financial salvation if only they could grab a spotlight in show business. Some aspired to the 'American Idol' of the day – 'Major Bowes Amateur Hour', a hugely popular weekly talent contest on network radio. Others travelled the seedy dance marathon circuit, entering 24/7 endurance contests that promised food and prize money in exchange for freak-show degradation and physical punishment. Horace McCoy's 1935 novel memorializing this Depression milieu was aptly titled *They Shoot Horses, Don't They?* . . . The role models for today's desperate fame seekers are *Jon & Kate Plus 8*, not Gable and Lombard. But even if they catch a break, as Heene did on *Wife Swap*, they still may end up betrayed by a stacked system . . . Many reality shows are as cruel as the old dance marathons. The usual Hollywood workplace rules allowing breaks for rest or meals often don't apply. Nor, sometimes, does the minimum wage. Let 'em eat fame.

We have entered an era in which the most sought-after attribute a person can possess is broad appeal, which encourages some people to go to extraordinary lengths to attract the public spotlight. Perhaps this is what happens when mass media drive democracy; it has the paradoxical effect of exalting the lowest common dominator. It crowns popularism. It transforms democracy into a 'media-ocracy'.

This is not to suggest that genuine talents like Susan Boyle do not deserve their place in the sun. The more talented and hard-working people are recognised the better. But increasingly, celebrity status is achieved through notoriety rather than through someone's talent or their contribution to society. Like the balloon boy's father, many contemporary celebrities seek fame for fame's sake. So what's the harm in this, you may ask? Surely it's just entertainment, isn't it?

Perhaps not. The popular fascination with celebrity has gone way beyond entertainment and appears to have pushed weightier issues to the back of people's minds. Audiences would rather be titillated than informed. This trend is reinforced by the news media which devote an increasing proportion of airtime to celebrity news and gossip rather than more consequential and newsworthy events.

A milestone on the path towards this celebritisation culture occurred in the States in 1997 when the trial of a former football star named OJ Simpson generated round-the-clock coverage by all the major news networks, week after week, pushing aside all other significant news stories. Celebritisation has since escalated to such an extent that the *priority* of news stories often bears little relation to their importance. In 2007, for example, in America one of the major news stories of the year, as measured by airtime, concerned the celebrity Paris Hilton and her problems with a traffic fine. These celebrity-driven news stories are then rehashed and magnified through the numerous cable talk shows and Internet blogs that have sprung up in recent years, which, in turn, perpetuate the sense that everything a celebrity thinks, does or says is somehow worthy of news coverage.

By far the biggest news story of 2009 was the death of the pop singer Michael Jackson, which, at one point, eclipsed the combined news coverage of the global financial crisis, climate change and the wars in Iraq and Afghanistan. So relentlessly intense was the coverage that it was impossible to turn on a television set without being interrupted by the latest update on the funeral arrangements, or a screening of one of his music videos. While there is no doubt that the King of Pop was the most influential musician of his generation, and hugely loved and admired by his fans, it is difficult to justify the priority assigned to his death by the news media. Compare his life achievements to, say, someone like Martin Luther King, or Nelson Mandela, who spent twenty-seven years in a prison on a matter of principle. It is also inconceivable that one day we will see the same news priority assigned to the death of Neil Armstrong, the first person to ever set foot on another world (and who really did do the 'moon walk'), or James Watson, co-discoverer of the genetic code, or Muhammad Yunus, who alleviated the poverty of millions through micro-banking. Why? Because, despite their monumental achievements, they are not A-list celebrities. They have a lower rank, according to the strange rules that govern the celebritised world, and are just minor gods in a pantheon of deities dominated by football players, TV stars and models.

A-list celebrities not only enjoy a higher status, they are often perceived to have more authority, even when it comes to subject matters about which they have little or no knowledge. That's why celebrities are widely used to promote products and claims that can often be misleading. An editorial in *The Lancet* medical journal suggests that celebrity endorsement of junk food is contributing to high rates of obesity. 'One of the most invidious techniques used by junk food advertisers is to pay sports and pop celebrities to endorse foods. This is especially bizarre since sports celebrities need a properly balanced diet to achieve fitness. Such celebrities should be ashamed,' the editorial said.[5]

The corrosive effect that celebritisation has on status and societal values now extends into the darkest corners of our world. Jo Chandler, a writer for Melbourne's *The Age* newspaper, tells the story of a photojournalist named John working in Kinshasa, in the Congo. After years of covering wars and the harshness of African life, John 'moves stiffly on legs damaged by landmines in Angola . . . He tells me he earned the equivalent of a handsome year's pay for a single, long-lens picture of a pregnant Angelina Jolie in Namibia ... While news organisations are increasingly reluctant to pay the price of capturing the grim reality that was once his trade, Angelina delivered the mother lode. John lights another cigarette and shakes his head, as if appalled by his own anecdote.'[6]

Closer to home, we see the effects of celebritisation on our children, where school vocational surveys reveal that a large proportion of children nominate as their ambition 'to be famous'. Not famous for anything in particular, just famous. This perspective of fame as a legitimate career choice is reinforced by reality shows such as *Big Brother*, where it appears that ordinary people, doing essentially ordinary things, can evolve into celebrities earning huge incomes and even launch their own brand of perfume. Such celebrities are worshipped for their very ordinariness and ability to embody the common person. Jade Goody, the British reality TV star who died in 2009 of cervical cancer aged just twenty-seven, was such a celebrity. She was brought up on an impoverished housing estate, became familiar with drugs and crime as a child and was barely educated. To many people she personified a rags-to-riches ideal, but to others, such as the legendary interviewer Sir Michael Parkinson, she represented 'all that is paltry and wretched about Britain. Jade Goody has her own place in the history of television, and, while it's significant, it's nothing to be proud of,' Parkinson said. 'Her death is as sad as the death of any young person, but it's not the passing of a martyr or a saint or, God help us, Princess Di ... She was projected to celebrity by *Big Brother* and became a media chattel to be exploited till the day she died.'[7]

Reality TV shows like *Big Brother* don't merely speed up the celebrity-manufacturing process by launching people to overnight stardom, or incite stunts by attention-seekers like the balloon boy's father. They also heighten the sense that life is moving faster by compressing the drama into hourly chunks of viewing time. *Big Brother* is where reality TV meets Big Mo. In this fast-moving pseudo-world, celebrity culture has reached its apotheosis.

Some celebrities, like Susan Boyle, are discovered and find themselves swept up in the media juggernaut. Others are more deliberate and calculating in their ambition. They behave more like a momentum surfer who seeks out to ride the wave of public opinion. They willingly feed the media's voracious appetite for every snippet of their quotidian existence, and do whatever it takes to attract the public eye – and keep it. To such celebrities the new media, like Internet blogs and Twitter, are a godsend, for they enable them to drip-feed fans with constant updates about what they are doing, thereby enabling their fans to vicariously 'share' their world in real time. The King of Twitter is the Hollywood actor Ashton Kutcher, who, in April 2009, became the first celebrity to gather one million followers on Twitter.[8]

By living vicariously, especially through the lives of celebrities, and relating to their ups and downs as if they were our own, we tend to push our own authentic experience aside and ignore the basic, everyday needs of those closest to us. Perhaps this is the real danger of the cult of celebrity: it distracts us from where our focus and attention are sorely needed.

More broadly, the cult of celebrity transforms our news media, through which we view and interpret the world, into a paparazzo's lens, so that important, consequential stories are ignored in favour of the glamorous and the sensational. It is not dissimilar to how the games in the Roman Coliseum once distracted their audience from the decaying empire beyond its walls.

The veteran American journalist and media commentator Bill Moyers said, 'The next time you're at a newsstand, look at the celebrities staring back at you. In-depth coverage on anything, let alone the bleak facts of power and powerlessness that shape the lives of ordinary people, is as scarce as sex, violence and voyeurism are pervasive.'[9]

CHAPTER 14

Techno Mo

There is a scene at the beginning of Stanley Kubrick's classic film *2001: A Space Odyssey* in which some early hominid apes realise the potential of using bones as tools. However, their playful delight at the discovery soon turns to menace as they learn of the destructive potential of these tools and begin to attack each other with them. We then see a bone spinning slowly in the air, which gradually morphs into a revolving space station, as the film shifts forward in time by millions of years. In just a few cinematic moments, Kubrick articulated a conundrum that has confronted our civilisation from the outset. How do we ensure that technology continues to serve us rather than threaten us?

There is no doubt that we live in a techno-centric age. Practically everything we do is enabled by some sort of gadget, whether it be the latest computer, phone, GPS navigation system, 3D flat-screen TV or home appliance. Such technologies empower us to accomplish tasks with less effort and more speed. More generally, they help us to build better cities, improve our transport systems, develop new vaccines and reach for the stars. Such advances are the culmination of centuries of technological progress that has underpinned our civilisation's survival and development.

Over the past few decades, however, there has been a distinct shift in the way technology is evolving. Traditionally, advances in technologies have tended to occur within specific industries or fields of activity. For example, a new invention for processing wool tended to remain within the textile industry. Similarly, innovations developed by locomotive builders tended to be applied primarily within the railway industry. The principle held for shipbuilders, car manufacturers, pharmaceutical companies and so on. Different disciplines tended to operate within their boxes. Although there has always been some sharing (spillover) of technologies between different industries, generally speaking, technological innovation has been relatively focused and industry-specific.

Today, it is the opposite. Each new innovation is like a piece of Lego that can be readily transposed from one industry to another and recombined in any number of ways to create whole new products. This is called technological 'convergence'. A prime example of this convergence process is the modern 'smart phone', such as the iPhone or BlackBerry. These ubiquitous devices incorporate a vast array of technologies that were originally developed for other industries. They offer features such as computer systems, GPS systems, Internet services, music and video players, cameras, alarm clocks, games, bar code readers, touch screens, radios, telephony and an infinite number of application programs. Multi-function phones have become so popular and sophisticated that they have attained an exalted status in our society. When the iPhone was launched a few years ago, it was dubbed the 'God phone' by its fans, bedazzled by its ability to perform so many complex tasks with miraculous simplicity. It became the talisman for the digital age, and *Time* magazine named it 'Invention of the Year' for 2007. Then in 2010 the Apple iPad became the new king of convergence.

Technological convergence is now the name of the game. The quest is to combine as many different Lego-esque technologies into a single device, in order to create as much functionality as possible in a slick package. This convergence ethos doesn't just dominate the communications and consumer-goods markets; it permeates almost every industry. Cars, planes and ships are now showcases of digital and engineering convergence, as are the latest skyscrapers. Cutting-edge military systems converge a lethal array of ballistics, robotics, computers, sensors and communications into weapons like the Predator drone, a combat system so advanced that it would have been considered to be in the realm of science fiction until just a few years ago. This is the sharp end of the convergence revolution. The next wave of technological convergence, however, is likely to be even more impactful as nano-technology – atom-sized versions of Lego blocks – promises to do for the material sciences what digital technology has done for communications.

Technological convergence doesn't simply optimise the ways in which innovations can be used; it is also a powerful agent of change. This is because, by making various applications work together synergistically, it encourages individual technologies to spur each other on to greater innovation – accelerating the speed of progress. Convergence is a force multiplier and accelerator. Simultaneously, the industries involved in developing each technology recognise that their commercial interests coincide, and so they harmonise their efforts and march in lockstep with each other.

As you can imagine, this mighty convergence of forces produces a powerful technological momentum, or Techno Mo, which feeds on its own innovative energy. It creates a juggernaut effect. Over time, this juggernaut can become highly self-protective. This behaviour has, for many years, been exemplified by large interconnected enterprises such as the so-called 'military industrial complex', which is renowned for aggressively protecting and enhancing its interests. More recently, however, the influence of Techno Mo has begun to permeate many other aspects of our society as more industries become swept up in the technological revolution.

To better understand just how powerful Techno Mo can be, let's take a closer look at that iconic and ubiquitous symbol of twenty-first-century life, the mobile phone.

Wireless wonderland

Over 4 billion people now use mobile phones through a global communications network that spans 90 per cent of the Earth's surface.[1] The backbone of this network is a vast array of high-speed broadband connections which operates like the world's digital nervous system, and which helps underpin much of our technological infrastructure. So vast and complex is this network that it must rank as one of the world's greatest engineering achievements of all time.

The remarkable thing, however, is that this global technological transformation has occurred so rapidly, and with so little fanfare. It just seemed to happen. Suddenly, millions of mobile-phone antennae began to pop up everywhere – on the tops of apartment buildings, on schools, hospitals, churches, anywhere. Meanwhile, the number of mobile-phone users went from zero barely two decades ago to billions today. What is even more remarkable still, is that there appears to have been very little research conducted into the consequences of such a massive technological transformation, particularly in terms of its potential impact on public health.

The last time the public was subjected to such a major technological revolution was on the introduction of pesticides into the food chain. These pesticides, such as organochlorides and organophosphates, eliminated crop-destroying bugs and diseases and enabled farmers to significantly increase both their output and the shelf life of their produce. As a consequence, food became cheaper and more abundant, particularly in the industrialised countries. Over time, however, it became clear that some of these pesticides could cause long-term environmental and health problems, including birth defects and serious illnesses.[2] The consumer backlash against them eventually led to regulatory changes and the creation of the organic-food industry, but only after a long hard battle.

The lesson of the pesticide industry is that the application of innovations can run ahead of the precautionary science. The unforeseen consequences of an innovation can remain undetected for decades; meanwhile, even tiny amounts of exposure can be having a negative impact on public health and the natural environment. For example, in the case of some pesticides, concentration levels as low as 0.1 parts per billion can induce dangerous, widespread and persistent effects.[3] This time lag often makes it difficult to establish safe guidelines for innovations because there is insufficient information on which to base them. So, by default, the public are being used as guinea pigs in large collective experiments, until such time as the results become conclusive.

The mobile-phone 'experiment' currently has over four billion guinea pigs. The sheer scale of the wireless revolution means that many of us now live, work and even sleep in an invisible 'soup of electromagnetic radiation', which is many times stronger than the natural fields in which living cells have developed over the past 3.8 billion years.[4] More problematic, however, is the fact that the safety guidelines for this global experiment were set decades ago and are based on what many scientists believe is an outdated concept of what constitutes a health hazard with regard to mobile phones. This concept is known as the 'thermal effect' – the degree to which a phone heats up human tissue sufficiently to cause a health problem. The basic idea is that if the heat doesn't cook you, it can't hurt you. A lot of us can feel this heating effect around our ears when we have been using our phone for a long period. It is called 'dielectric heating' and operates in a similar way to a microwave oven, but at a much lower power. Current mobile-phone legislation is designed to ensure that this heating effect is not too strong by setting a maximum rate at which a mobile phone can emit radiation that is absorbed by the body. For example, the Specific Absorption Rate (SAR) in the United States is set at 1.6 W/Kg, averaged over a volume of 1 gram of tissue, while in Europe the rate is set at 2 W/kg, averaged over a volume of 10 grams of tissue.[5]

This emphasis on the thermal effect can be traced back to 1947, when the US military faced questions about the health effects of radar systems and power lines, following anecdotal reports of internal bleeding and other ailments among its workers. The government assigned to the case a German scientist named Herman Schwan, who had been brought to America after World War II. Over the next few decades, Schwan was instrumental in promoting the idea that only the thermal effect mattered with regard to the impact of electromagnetic radiation on public health.[6] He discounted contradictory evidence from researchers in other countries showing a 'non-thermal' effect, because it went against his a priori calculation based on the 'known laws of physics'. Schwan's insistence that we only need to worry about radiation heating things up earned him the eternal support of the electronics and power industry, who continue to benefit from his unyielding views, even to this day. The widespread acceptance of the thermal-effect theory also enabled phone companies to launch their mobile phones in the 1980s without pre-market safety testing, because the devices were deemed by the industry to be low-power devices incapable of creating harm.

According to a growing number of scientists, however, the real danger of mobile phones is not the thermal effect but the more subtle and long-term non-thermal effects. Exactly how these effects might work is not clear, although there are various theories.

Dr George Carlo, an epidemiologist and medical scientist who has studied this problem for decades, believes that mobile-phone radiation may cause human cells to defend themselves by hardening the cell membranes, and in so doing prevent nutrients and waste products from circulating freely. As these waste products accumulate inside the cells, they create free radicals which disrupt the DNA-repair process. This causes damaged material to leak into the fluid between the cells (interstitial fluid), where it is free to replicate and proliferate, and possibly result in cancer.[7]

Another non-thermal effect that electromagnetic radiation may have on the body is to interfere with the natural communication between cells. This seems plausible because the body uses its own electromagnetic signals of different frequencies to communicate internally. If mobile phones can affect less sensitive devices such as pacemakers or telecommunication systems on airplanes, which are shielded against radiation, it stands to reason they could affect the body's more sensitive and unprotected electrical fields. This interference with intra-cellular communication may trigger various maladies, among them neurodegenerative disease, attention-deficit disorder and behavioural problems such as sleep disorder by, for example, interfering with the pineal gland's ability to produce melatonin, on which sleep depends.

But, of course, these are only theories at this stage. What is more worrying to health professionals is the growing number of research surveys which suggest a correlation between mobile-phone use and health problems. This has prompted some health professionals to take no chances.

Alarm bells

In July 2008, three prominent neurosurgeons told the CNN interviewer Larry King that they had resolved not to hold cellphones to their ears ever again. They were responding to the news that Dr Ronald Herberman, director of the University of Pittsburgh Cancer Institute, had written to the institute's three thousand staff advising that they should limit the use of the mobile devices because of the risk of cancer.[8] This was the first time that the director of a major research centre had issued an alert which contradicted the longstanding guidance from most health authorities that mobile phones are safe. Herberman's memo, which was peer-reviewed by an international panel of experts prior to its release, conceded that the evidence was inconclusive and was based partly on 'early unpublished data' from ongoing research reports. But the memo made clear that he had become convinced that there was sufficient information to 'warrant issuing an advisory to share some precautionary advice on cellphone use'. Herberman was particularly concerned about the use of mobile phones by children, who, he warned, should only use them for emergencies, because their growing brain tissue would be more sensitive to the electromagnetic radiation emitted by mobile phones.[9]

Another study, carried out in January 2008 by the blue-chip Karolinska Institute and Uppsala University in Sweden and the Wayne State University in Michigan, USA, demonstrated that radiation from mobile phones delays and reduces sleep, and causes headaches and confusion.[10] The research, which was sponsored by the major manufacturers of phone handsets, showed that when people used handsets shortly before bed they took longer to reach the deeper stages of sleep and spent less time in these stages, which interfered with the body's capacity to repair damage suffered during the day. The failure to get sufficient sleep led to mood and personality changes, ADHD-like symptoms, depression, lack of concentration and poor performance.

The phone manufacturers were embarrassed by the findings and tried to play them down, insisting that, contrary to the published conclusion, the results were 'inconclusive' and that the researchers did not claim that exposure to mobile phones caused sleep disturbance. However, the professor who led the study, Bengt Arnetz, said, 'We did find an effect from exposure scenarios to mobile phone that were realistic. This suggests they have a measurable effect on the brain.' He explained that the radiation may activate the brain's stress system, making people more alert and more focused and decreasing their ability to wind down and fall asleep. The research findings complemented another study, which monitored 1,656 Belgian teenagers for a year and demonstrated that those who used their mobile phones at least once a week, particularly around bedtime, were more than three times more likely to be 'very tired'.[11] The director of the Edinburgh Sleep Centre, Dr Chris Idzikowski, says, 'There is now more than sufficient evidence, from a large number of reputable investigators, who are finding that mobile phone exposure an hour before sleep adversely affects deep sleep.'[12]

More ominously, other research points to more life-threatening risks. A study led by Dr Siegal Sadetzki, a cancer specialist at Tel Aviv University, suggests that frequent users of mobile phones are 50 per cent more likely to develop mouth cancer than those who don't use them at all. The study also found an increased risk of cancer for heavy users who lived in rural areas. Because there are fewer antennae, mobile phones in rural areas need to emit more radiation to communicate effectively. Dr Sadetzki predicts that, over time, the most pronounced effects will be found in heavy users and children. This research is considered significant because it was conducted on the Israeli population, who were among the first to widely adopt mobile phone technology.[13] Another study carried out by Professor Kjell Hansson Mild of Unea University in Sweden and Professor Lennart Hardell of the University Hospital in Orebro, Sweden, suggests that people who use their phones for a decade or more are 30 per cent more likely to be diagnosed with malignant gliomas (the type of cancer that killed US Senator Edward Kennedy in 2009).[14] Professor Mild said, 'I find it quite strange to see so many official presentations saying there is no risk. There are strong indications that something happens after 10 years . . . and 10 years is the minimum period needed for cancer to develop, and they normally take much longer.'

A report released in August 2009 by the International Electromagnetic Field (EMF) Collaborative, which was endorsed by more than forty scientists and officials from fourteen countries, concluded that there is a 'significant' risk of brain tumours resulting from mobile-phone use, particularly in children. It said that the EMF exposure limits advocated by industry and used by governments are based on a false premise that a cellphone's electromagnetic radiation has no biological effects except for heating. The lead author of the report, Lloyd Morgan, noted that studies independent of industry funding have more consistently found higher risks for brain tumours when exposure was ten or more years, adding, 'Even some industry-funded studies show that there is a connection between cellphone use and the risk of brain tumours.'

Apart from the physiological effects of electromagnetic radiation, there are growing concerns about the psychological impact of mobile phones, particularly on young people. A survey conducted among hundreds of eighteen- to twenty-five-year-old mobile-phone users by Francisca López Torrecillas, a professor at the University of Granada, in Spain, suggests that 40 per cent of the group exhibited addiction tendencies to their phone. Torrecillas says that mobile addicts tend to neglect important obligations, such as their job or studies, and drift apart from friends and close family. 'These people can become totally upset when deprived of their mobile phones for some time, regardless of the reason,' Torrecillas says. 'Switching off their phones causes them anxiety, irritability, sleep disorders or sleeplessness, and even shivering and digestive problems.'[15]

Given the relatively high cost of making a call on a mobile phone, most teenagers use their mobiles primarily for text-messaging rather than for chatting. In the United States, for example, thirteen- to seventeen-year-olds account for a large proportion of the 75 billion text messages sent each month. Teens with mobile phones average well over 1,000 text messages a month, compared with 203 calls, according to Neilson Co.[16] The upside of so much text messaging is that teenagers are not holding the phone close to the head and so are avoiding potential health problems. The downside is that hard-core texters find it difficult to be 'in the moment' because their minds are constantly being interrupted by messages from friends. They are rarely focused on one thing at a time. This kind of constant multi-tasking causes a 'kind of mental brownout', according to David E Meyer, a psychology professor at the University of Michigan. He says that if 'a teenager is reading Shakespeare when a text message interrupts, Hamlet's going to fade in and out in a ghostly fog'. The addictive nature of phone text messaging and Internet-related activities has prompted concerns in the medical community. In 2008 the *American Journal of Psychiatry* published an editorial by psychiatrist Jerald J Block suggesting that addiction to the Internet and text messaging should be recognised in the diagnostic manual for mental illnesses.[17] But his suggestion would result in a lot of patients. In April 2010, a Pew Internet &

American Life Project study revealed that most US teenagers would rather text their friends than talk to them face to face.[18]

It's not just young people who become addicted to the digital flow. An increasing number of adults spend their lives tethered to their BlackBerrys in a 24/7 world with no downtime. The professor and author David W Orr, says, 'Our conversations, thought patterns, and institutional speed are increasingly shaped to fit the imperatives of technology. Not surprisingly, more and more people feel overloaded by the demands of incessant communication. But to say so publicly is to run afoul of the technological fundamentalism that now dominates virtually everywhere.'[19]

The juggernaut

Given the growing concerns about the health impact of wireless technologies, both behaviourally and physiologically, a reasonable person might expect that the telecommunications industry, and the public, would adopt a more cautious approach to their usage. But this is certainly not the case. The public's voracious appetite for wireless technologies shows no signs of waning, and the telecommunications juggernaut has no plans to slow down. It is business as usual. In response to health concerns, the industry argues that because the scientific evidence on the issue is 'inconclusive' there is no reason to change course. A similar argument was used by the tobacco companies for many decades on the issue of carcinogens, and more recently by the oil companies in the context of the climate-change debate.

The reality is that this issue is less about the science and more about the dynamics driving it. For over the past few decades, the wireless-technology business has developed an enormously powerful momentum. We are not just talking about one industry here, but dozens of industries that depend on wireless technologies, all working together to produce convergent products, all pushing in the same direction with the same interests at heart. This is Techno Mo at work on a grand scale. The wireless-and-telecommunications industry is now one of the largest and most powerful businesses on the planet. It generates hundreds of billions of dollars in sales each year, employs millions of people and accounts for a significant portion of the global economy. This exponential growth has been facilitated and encouraged by governments, which derive billions of dollars in revenue through the sale of wireless bandwidths. In return for these huge fees to operate in a bandwidth spectrum, mobile-phone companies are often allowed to fund their costly wireless infrastructure (antennae) by making a down payment – usually around 10 per cent – and have their mobile-phone customers pay off the rest of the debt. [20] This helps explain why mobile-phone marketing is so aggressive: it's because the companies often have large debts to pay off.

This combination of convergent technologies, innovation, consumer demand, corporate ambition, government incentives and debt has created an environment that is propelling the wireless juggernaut forward with a powerful momentum. In such an environment, it is understandable that many people may become so swept up in the flow that they ignore or downplay warning signs of potential problems (much like the bankers did in the lead-up to the global financial crisis). Imagine for a moment that you are a senior telecommunications-company executive and are involved in an industry-sponsored research project designed to look at the health effects of your mobile phones. You are surrounded by like-minded executives whose livelihoods depend on the wireless-technology boom continuing. The research findings turn out to be inconclusive and rather ambiguous, but they do highlight some anomalies that may indicate a potential health risk and should be pursued further. Given these findings, however, you could be justified in declaring that 'the research, as it stands, demonstrates no clear health risk: mobile phones are safe'. By omitting what is inconclusive, you tilt the argument in your favour.

As with the pre-Iraq War intelligence covered earlier, momentum can exert a subtle yet powerful influence on the way information is interpreted, particularly when it is ambiguous or inconclusive. A review of three hundred surveys on mobile-phone safety completed in the past six years showed that those funded by the telecommunications industry are six times more likely to find 'nothing wrong' than the studies that are funded independently.[21] Research can be interpreted in divergent ways when strong vested interests are involved. For example, the Interphone project is a vast research effort designed to understand the risks of radio-frequency radiation emitted by mobile phones. It cost $30 million and covered 13 countries, and was partly funded by the mobile phone industry.[22] When the long-awaited results were published in May 2010, they generated wildly differing interpretations.

Perhaps not surprisingly, The Global System for Mobile Communications (GSMA), which represents the interests of the worldwide mobile communications industry, said in their press release that, 'An increased risk of brain cancer is not established from the data from Interphone.'

Other groups saw the results quite differently. Dr Lennart Hardell, professor in oncology and cancer epidemiology at Orebro University, Sweden, concluded, 'The final Interphone results support findings of several research groups, including our own, that continuing use of a mobile phone increases risk of brain cancer.'[23] The media's response to the Interphone results was equally polarised. To cite just a few examples, London's *Daily Telegraph* ran the headline, 'Mobile Phone Study Reveals Cancer "Concerns" Over Heavy Users'[24] whereas the BBC interpreted the same research as saying there was 'No Proof of Mobile Cancer Risk'.[25] Louis Slesin, the editor of *Microwave News*, who has been following this issue for years, said that despite the playing down of the results, 'at the very least, the risks are greater than many believed only a few years ago'. He said that a number of the members of the Interphone project told *Microwave News* that they now see the risk among long-term users as being larger than when the study began. Some think the risk warrants serious attention. The person who leads the Interphone project, Elisabeth

Cardis, said, 'To me, there's certainly smoke there ... Overall, my opinion is that the results show a real effect.'[26] One of the problems with such research programmes is that cancer usually takes at least ten to fifteen years to develop, whereas the available surveys cover only a limited timeframe, which is not sufficient to answer questions about long-term exposures. 'The great cosmic joke', pondered Maureen Dowd in the *New York Times*, 'would be to find out definitively that the advances we thought were blessings – such as (sic) the fancy phones people wait in line for all night – are really time bombs. Just as parents now tell their kids that, believe it or not, there was a time when nobody knew that cigarettes and tanning were bad for you, those kids may grow up to tell their kids that, believe it or not, there was a time when nobody knew how dangerous it was to hold your phone right next to your head and chat away for hours.'[27]

In the absence of definitive proof whether wireless technologies are causing long-term harm, many scientists are calling for the adoption of the 'precautionary principle'. This is a risk-management policy which, according to the World Health Organisation (WHO), is 'applied in circumstances with a high degree of scientific uncertainty, reflecting the need to take action for a potentially serious risk without awaiting the results of scientific research'.[28] This principle addresses the concern that even if the individual risk of using a mobile phone turns out to be relatively low, with 3 billion users in the world, even a tiny risk would translate into a major public-health problem. Governments already apply the precautionary principle to risks like nuclear terrorism, where, even though the threat is extremely low, the consequences are so serious that no chances can be taken. After revelations that a Pakistani nuclear scientist was surreptitiously offering nuclear-weapons expertise to outsiders, the then US vice president Dick Cheney declared, 'If there's a 1 per cent chance that Pakistani scientists are helping al-Qaeda build or develop a nuclear weapon, we have to treat it as a certainty in terms of our response.' This became known as 'the 1 per cent doctrine', and describes the need to confront a new type of threat: a 'low probability, high impact' event. Yet, governments have been extremely reluctant to apply the doctrine to non-military threats.

Meanwhile, certain groups around the world are not waiting for government intervention. They are already implementing the precautionary principle by resisting the unconstrained rollout of wireless technologies, particularly wireless broadband networks (WiFi). The University of Lakehead, in Ontario, Canada, which has 7,400 students, has largely eliminated WiFi from the campus, preferring to use optical-fibre cable where possible. Fred Gilbert, the vice chancellor of the university, said the WiFi was removed because of 'the weight of evidence demonstrating behavioural effects and physiological impacts at the tissue, cellular and cell level'.[29] The Ministry of the Environment in Germany indicated, on 20 July 2007, that a cable system would be given preference over WiFi and advised schools and teaching centres to avoid WiFi when possible.[30] In Paris, France, the city council deactivated WiFi installations in six of the city's public libraries after workers complained about health problems.[31] In Britain, where there are about seventy thousand mobile base stations and a similar number of WiFi hotspots, local groups have protested against the implementation of wireless networks in schools and city centres such as Glastonbury. They have challenged local planning rules that instruct councils to 'respond positively' to phone companies' plans and that prevent councils from objecting to antennae on health grounds.[32]

Community activism of this nature, however, is unlikely to have much impact on the wireless juggernaut. The forces of Techno Mo are enormously powerful and resistant to threats – even legal ones. Currently, there are seven pending class actions in the United States against the mobile-phone industry, claiming that phones have damaged people's health or killed them. If even one of these cases is successful, it is likely to set a legal precedent that would shake the industry to its foundations. For this reason, insurance companies have largely withdrawn their cover for mobile-phone companies against potential class actions such as this.[33] But given the size of the wireless industry and its relative importance to the stock market and the economy, it is unlikely that any government would be keen for such a legal precedent to be set. The irony, it seems, is that, although the wireless-communications industry empowers billions of voices to be heard every day, it can be very effective in stifling dissenting voices that perhaps should be heard.

The industry also makes it difficult for consumers to know how much radiation they are being exposed to. Radiation levels are rarely (if ever) displayed on mobile phones or their packaging. This lack of transparency prompted legislators in the US city of San Francisco to force phone manufacturers to clearly display the radiation-absorption levels of their phones and to warn pregnant women and children against using them near their heads and bodies. It is doubtful, however, whether such warnings will affect consumer behaviour. As Maureen Dowd observed, 'We don't yet really know the physical and psychological impact of being slaves to technology. We just know that technology is a narcotic. We're living in the cloud, in the force field, so afraid of being disconnected and plunged into a world of silence and stillness, that even if scientists told us our computers would make our arms fall off, we'd probably keep typing.'[34] Meanwhile, the safety limits for radiation for wireless devices remain virtually the same as they were decades ago and continue to be based on the thermal effect rather than the potentially more damaging non-thermal effects.

I must stress that it is not my intention to persuade you either way on this contentious issue or to cause undue alarm. Remember that the jury is still out on the long-term health impact of mobile phones and wireless technologies. If, however, you do wish to further explore this topic, the relevant sources can be found in the Notes section, see pages 321–2. Rather, my intention is to highlight the nature of technological momentum, or Techno Mo, and the enormous influence it now exerts in our world. The evolution of the wireless industry provides just one example of how this influence works, by ensuring that the precautionary principle takes a back seat to technological progress and convenience. Other examples include the technologies used by the oil industry to drill deep below the sea bed, the high-frequency computer trading programs used in the financial industry, and the complex software systems that increasingly run our infrastructure. When such hi-tech systems go wrong in our highly interconnected world, the price of failure can be catastrophic. Such is the nature of Techno Mo.

CHAPTER 15

When Big Mo
Finds God

One of the most momentous developments of our time, and yet one that has occurred largely under the radar, is the resurgence of religion as a global force. The last few centuries of scientific advancement, democratic reform and post-Enlightenment thought, had lulled a lot of people, particularly in the West, into believing that religion was in terminal decline. For many, the foundations of religion had been demolished by Darwin, Freud and the luminaries of rationalism. Governments had largely relegated religion to the sidelines, even in developing nations, some of which came to see secularism as indivisible from modernism. In place of religion rose the shiny new gods of capitalism and the marketplace. In 1966 a *Time* magazine cover story asked 'Is God Dead?', and three years later man walked on the Moon, as if symbolising the conquest of the heavens. [1]

During the 1970s, however, there was a sudden and unexpected upturn in the growth rates of the four major religions – Christianity, Islam, Hinduism and Buddhism – which has continued to this day. Christian religious groups now exert significant influence over numerous governments, including that of the United States, where the President starts each cabinet meeting with a prayer. The British Houses of Parliament sittings commence with a prayer too. In countries that have been secular for decades, such as Turkey, Islamic interests have assumed power; they have also gained a stronger hold throughout the Middle East and Asia. Israel, which was founded largely as a secular state, is now riven by internal religious conflict. Hindus in India have a large stake in national politics these days. In South Korea, which hosts five of the world's biggest 'mega-Christian churches', the national parliament holds monthly prayer meetings. Post-communist countries have rediscovered religion too, including Russia, where the FSB, the successor to the anti-religious KGB, now has its own Orthodox church located near its headquarters.

This global religious renaissance has been triggered by various factors. In the West, the counter-revolution of the 1960s and 1970s tapped into strong spiritual and naturalist yearnings that were not being satisfied by the established order, with its emphasis on materialism. These frustrations were exacerbated by the excesses of the Cold War and the Vietnam War, which eroded faith in Western governments, especially among young people. In Eastern-bloc countries, and many others under Soviet influence, Godless Marxism was appearing less omnipotent with each new political or military setback. In the developing nations of the Middle East and Asia, many communities discovered there was a price to be paid for rising material prosperity, in the form of weakening cultural values.

The combination of these factors created a climate in which religion seemed appealing, by offering a balm for the anxieties of the age and a framework for accommodating moral and spiritual aspirations. It brought reassurance to societies undergoing rapid modernisation and comfort to those mired in poverty or oppression. Religious organisations were increasingly at the forefront of charitable and humanistic enterprises and acted as strident voices against social injustice and iniquity – thus helping them to gain new-found respect in many communities. The advent of global mass media during the 1970s and 1980s enabled religions to reach out to their followers and attract new ones. The burgeoning television evangelistic movement – televangelism – in the United States spread its Christian message worldwide through the Trinity Broadcasting Network and the God Channel. Meanwhile, radio and television stations in developing countries began to offer more local content including religious programming, helping to rekindle long-dormant religious aspirations in communities from Asia to the Middle East.

By the beginning of the 1980s, the global religious landscape had transformed dramatically. The Islamic scholar the Ayatollah Khomeini, had been swept to power in Iran, a born-again Christian, Jimmy Carter, was now president of the United States, and Jerry Falwell's Christian-based Moral Majority movement was in the ascendant. This upward trend of religious influence has continued to this day.

More recently, however, it has taken a different turn. Religious assertiveness has begun to manifest in more extreme forms – which is the dark end of the spectrum of the religious renaissance. From the Middle East to the Balkans, to Asia and beyond, religiously motivated extremism and violence have ignited a series of conflicts and wars, culminating in the Islamist-inspired 9/11 attacks in the United States in 2001. The 9/11 attacks were the global wake-up call for how dangerous – and serious – extremist religions can be. One consequence is that for the first time since the days of Oliver Cromwell in the mid-seventeenth century, any act of terrorism is now automatically assumed to have a religious link. By contrast, a few decades ago, most terrorism was associated with Maoist guerrillas, anarchistic middle-class Germans or Italians, or the Palestine Liberation Movement, which was then primarily a secular organisation predominantly led by Marxists.[2]

It scarcely needs stating that religion also has a positive side, and for the majority of followers it offers a path to salvation and redemption. Indeed, religion has often been a force for good in the world and a civilising influence. The great religious texts provide the basis for many of our laws and customs, and all religious denominations espouse the virtues of compassion, forgiveness and charity. But for some reason, when religion does turn bad, it can turn really bad.

What is it about religious beliefs that make them potentially so much more deadly than, say, beliefs about science, nature, arts or economics? Why are the consequences often so devastating? Why does religion 'drive men to such heights of evil', as Lucretius exclaimed in *De Rerum Natura*.[3] What prompts Catholic priests in Argentina to help torture people, Buddhist monks to lead murderous attacks in Sri Lanka, or Sunni and Shia militiamen in Iraq to wipe out entire families – all in the name of their religion?[4] And why has the 'dark side' of religion re-emerged today with such a vengeance?

Hot and bothered

One reason why religions sometimes veer towards extremism today is that they are particularly susceptible to the growing forces of momentum in our society. The underlying dynamics are remarkably similar. Most religions start off with a central idea or experience that is magnified over time to such an extent that it becomes a self-perpetuating, self-reinforcing 'truth'. Unlike a scientific or economic truth, a spiritual belief cannot be rigorously tested or disproved, so there is no negative feedback to keep it in a state of relative equilibrium. It can continue to develop unhindered, clothing itself in more dogma and ritual, which in turn enhances its capacity to inspire awe among believers. Over time, the self-reinforcing momentum of a religion can become so powerful, and reverberate so strongly, that it elevates the core beliefs to the status of 'super-sacred' – that is, they become sacralised. These beliefs can no longer be doubted or challenged and require absolute adherence by the faithful. The 'sacrifice of the intellect to God' (*'Dei sacrificium intellectus'*), as Ignatius Loyola, the founder of the Jesuits, put it.[5]

As this faith-based momentum continues to build, the religion – or factions within it – may evolve by adopting a fundamentalist, or even extremist, position. Certain aspects of the religion become greatly magnified and generate a fierce intensity or metaphorical heat. These 'hot' manifestations of religions have, over the years, included the Christian Pentecostalists, the Church of Latter-Day Saints and the Islamic Wahhabists, who maintain a strict interpretation of the Koran which stresses jihad as a key pillar of Islam. Paradoxically, the less hierarchical a religion, the more likely it is to generate extreme interpretations of its core text over time, because, in the absence of hierarchy, there is less authority to slow the internal momentum. In physics terms, there is less friction or negative feedback to maintain the 'narrative equilibrium'. A feature of such 'hot' religions or radical offshoots is that they become highly focused and energetic, are often intolerant of dissent and seek to impose their views on non-believers. As a result, they are more likely to come into conflict with other religions, or with the wider community. It is the 'hot' religions that are having the biggest impact on the world today. They are also generating a lot of momentum, or Big Mo, even though they comprise a relatively small proportion of total religious communities.

It used to be assumed that the more leisurely and accommodating brands of religions would flourish over time because they could coexist with secular governments and the rise of scientific rationalism. But the hot religions provide a psychological level of 'certainty' that their followers appear to find attractive, especially compared to the more watered-down, 'wishy-washy' versions. Hot versions articulate a clearer sense of identity, which can easily resonate among dispersed minorities, such as Muslim communities scattered throughout Europe, particularly among the young.[6] For young people from moderately religious homes who may be looking for ways to rebel, a hard-line religion can place a powerful – and empowering – means to do so at their disposal. This can manifest, for example, in the determination of a Parisian schoolgirl of Moroccan descent to wear the headscarf that her mother discarded decades ago, or that of a young Pakistani man in London to prove his religious superiority over his businessman father by adopting a very strict version of Wahhabism.

Christian movements, too, are developing hotter forms, such

as the Alpha Course for Christians, which preaches a charismatic version of the religion and is helping to trigger a growth spurt among church congregations – even in Western Europe and Britain, which have lagged behind the religious revival occurring elsewhere.

Hot religions generally have a big influence on demographics because – bucking the trend of the wider Western world – their followers tend to marry young and have big families, whether they be Orthodox Jews, fundamentalist Christians, Hindus or Muslims, whereas, according to Ronald Inglehart, director of the World Values Survey, which studies religions in eighty countries, secular people go forth and multiply much more modestly than do their religious brethren.[7] He says that secularisation is its own long-term demographic 'gravedigger'. Hot religions now exert a strong, albeit subtle influence over many aspects of our lives, including issues such as globalisation, labour laws, fair-trade agreements, climate change and legal systems. Even science, long regarded as a no-go area for religious interference, is being increasingly confronted by religious-inspired initiatives. One notable example has been attempts by certain religious organisations to introduce into schools a new version of creationism called 'intelligent design', which directly challenges Darwin's theory of evolution. A new Christian museum in Kentucky, sympathetic to the new creationism, shows huge dinosaurs walking alongside humans around 4000 BC and explains how Noah fitted a sample of all the world's animals into a boat 135 metres long.

Perhaps the most emotive issue, however, has to do with the attempt by Christian groups in the United States and parts of Western Europe to prohibit research into stem-cell technology on the grounds that it interferes with God's plan. Christian groups have also had a say on sex education in schools, insisting that curricula promote abstinence and teach that 'sexual activity outside of the context of marriage is likely to have harmful psychological and physical effects'. A 2004 report commissioned by a Democratic congressman, Henry A Waxman, revealed that

80 per cent of the curricula contained false or misleading information, such as greatly exaggerating the risk of pregnancy or HIV transmission when condoms are used.[8] According to James Wagoner, president of Advocates for Youth in Washington DC, 'You could almost see the abstinence-only movement as the sexual health equivalent of creationism.' [9] Meanwhile, every day in the United States some ten thousand young people are diagnosed with a sexually transmissible infection, two thousand become pregnant and fifty-five contract HIV.

The influence of evangelical Christian groups is magnified by the enormous financial resources available to them, which are gathered from followers through donations or a modern version of tithing, whereby they give 10 per cent of their gross income to the Church. Many devout Christian are so committed to tithing that during the recent global financial crisis they decided to give up their homes rather than stop paying their tithes. Ozell Brooklin, a director of Acorn Housing in Atlanta, Georgia, which offers foreclosure counselling, says, 'I've had home owners who face foreclosure sitting in front of me saying, "I'll do anything, anything to keep my home." But after we've gone through their monthly expenses and the only thing left to cut is their tithe, they say, "I guess this home is not for me," and they walk away.' According to Dr Roger Oldham, a member of the 16 million-strong Southern Baptist Convention, tithing is a compelling personal commitment. 'For those people, a contract with God is worth more than their home.'[10]

Perversely, religion may have played a role in the global financial crisis by preaching the 'prosperity gospel' to people who could not afford to get into debt and who ended up taking out subprime loans to buy a house. The prosperity gospel, also known as the prosperity doctrine or the health-and-wealth gospel, is centred on the notion that God provides material prosperity for those he favours, and that 'Jesus blesses believers with riches'. Jonathan Walton, a professor of religious studies at the University of California at Riverside, warned in 2008, in the online magazine *Religion Dispatches*, how evangelistic (hot) Christian churches preached unrealistic ideas about money to their followers:

> Narratives of how 'God blessed me with my first house despite my credit' were common . . . Sermons declaring 'It's your season of overflow' supplanted messages of economic sobriety and disinterested sacrifice. Yet as folks were testifying about 'what God can do', little attention was paid to a predatory subprime-mortgage industry, relaxed credit standards, or the dangers of using one's home equity as an ATM . . . I would hear consistent testimonies about how 'once I was renting and now God let me own my own home', or 'I was afraid of the loan officer, but God directed him to ignore my bad credit and blessed me with my first home' . . . This trope was so common in these churches that I just became immune to it. Only later did I connect it to this disaster.

Walton says that those areas that were hardest hit by the subprime-mortgage foreclosures were also those areas where the prosperity gospel was preached most vigorously. They included the Sun Belt, particularly in California, Florida and Arizona, where the lion's share of the new prosperity-gospel churches were built during the 1990s and early 2000s. Kate Bowler is a doctoral candidate at Duke University, North Carolina, USA, and an expert in the gospel. While researching a book, she spent a lot of time attending the 'financial empowerment' seminars that are common at prosperity churches. She recalls that advisers would pay lip service to 'sound financial practices', but overall they would send the opposite message by adorning the churches with seminar posters featuring big houses in the background and ensuring the parking spots closest to the church were reserved for luxury cars. What mattered, she deduced, was to promote the dream, not the means of achieving it.[11]

In the Islamic world, the relationship between money and

religious influence is more complicated. This is because it's impossible to draw clear dividing lines between the religion, the state and an individual's way of life: Islam, which means 'submission', provides an entire system of rules for people to live by known as sharia law. This fusion of religion and state derives from Islam's founder, Mohammad, who (unlike Jesus) was a merchant, rule-maker, warrior and lawmaker.

Sharia law is gaining traction or being reinstituted in many countries, even in fast-developing nations such as Malaysia and Dubai. While most interpretations of sharia law are moderate, there is an increasing tendency for more extremist versions to gain hold, as is the case in Taliban-controlled parts of Afghanistan, where, for example, girls are not allowed to attend school and women are stoned to death for adultery.

There are those who would argue that the burgeoning influence of religion in our world is a good thing – particularly when it suits their particular beliefs. And no doubt there are many positive examples of religious influence that reflect and uphold the time-honoured traditions of compassion, tolerance and charity. But there is one aspect of the religious renaissance that is almost universally condemned. This is the rise of religious-inspired violence. Yet, oddly, our society, and particularly our politicians, don't like to talk about this issue directly. They prefer to talk around it.

British biologist, and author of *The God Delusion*, Richard Dawkins says that Western politicians avoid suggesting that religion is a cause of violence, preferring instead to characterise their battle as a war against terror, 'as though terror was some kind of spirit or force with a will and mind of its own, motivated by pure evil'.[12] He believes that, however misguided we may think Islamic terrorists are, 'they are motivated, like Christian murderers of abortion doctors, by what they perceive to be righteousness, faithfully pursuing what their religion tells them . . . They have been brought up from the cradle to have total and unquestioning faith.'

The reluctance to discuss openly the nature of religious violence is somewhat understandable, given its potential to stigmatise certain religions. But as discussed earlier on pages 152–7, when a society avoids confronting issues directly for reasons of political correctness, the problems usually get worse, not better. In the context of religious violence, it is the underlying belief systems that must be engaged with and challenged as much as the destructive behaviour that emanates from them. Unfortunately, these virulent beliefs have been given a free rein in recent years and are rarely challenged by the clergy or clerics within their own religion, let alone people outside it. In this 'frictionless' environment, such beliefs have developed a powerful momentum – or Big Mo – which, as we shall see, has been facilitated by the communications revolution.

Digital crusaders

One of the most paradoxical aspects of hot religions is that, although they often have medieval connotations, they are very effective at exploiting the modern media. Their uncompromising messages resonate with a media that favours a simple black-and-white view of the world – one which clearly delineates between good and bad, rather than the relatively ambiguous messages of the more laid-back religions. Hot religions have become particularly adept at using online media to reach out to their followers through Internet chat rooms, and to congregate virtually, en masse, and commune through cyberspace.

But it wasn't really until the events of 9/11 and the Second Iraq War that this digital savvy was put to the test and evolved into a potent force. Suddenly chat rooms became virtual recruiting halls, which enticed followers of hot religions, particularly Islamist versions, to leave their homelands and fight to defend their faith in faraway places like Kashmir, Iraq, Chechnya, Somalia, Afghanistan or Mozambique. The jihad went digital. Thousands became swept up in the ensuing violence. Many ended up in places like Guantanamo Bay, countless thousands of others have died, and many more continue their struggle, periodically wreaking havoc from Bali to London – anywhere their enemies gather. This digital recruiting drive shows no signs of slowing down. On 13 December 2009, the *Washington Post* published this report:

> 'Online recruiting has exponentially increased, with Facebook, YouTube and the increasing sophistication of people online,' a high-ranking Department of Homeland Security official said. 'Increasingly, recruiters are taking less prominent roles in mosques and community centers because places like that are under scrutiny. So what these guys are doing is turning to the internet,' said Evan Kohlmann, a senior analyst with the US-based NEFA Foundation, a private group that monitors extremist web sites.[13]

Every action taken by the extremists is then magnified by the global media, whose voracious appetite for sensationalism ensures that the perpetrators' efforts will not go unnoticed. Religious conflict has gone global and has generated a powerful self-perpetuating momentum. This religious form of Big Mo can exert a powerfully seductive pull over people.

Maajid Nawaz is a seventeen-year-old British Asian Muslim from a professional family in Essex who joined the extremist Hizb ut-Tahrir group and eventually became one of its leaders. He recalls that the group 'provided me with a sense of identity and purpose, a way to worship God through our political activities and create a new world order. My activities soon brought me into conflict with my parents and other Muslims. I thought my parents had misunderstood their ideology.' [14]

Even though Islam's sacred text, the Koran, denounces violence and says that, whoever kills an innocent, it is as if he killed all mankind, some people choose to make the ultimate sacrifice for their belief by becoming martyrs. Shortly after the 9/11 attacks, the *New Yorker* magazine carried an interview with a failed suicide bomber, a polite young Palestinian aged twenty-seven. When asked by the interviewer, Nasra Hassan, what the attraction of martyrdom was, he responded:

> The power of the spirit pulls us upward, while the power of the material pulls us downward. Someone bent on martyrdom becomes immune to the material pull . . . Even if the operation fails, we still get to meet the Prophet and his companions, *inshallah*. We were floating, swimming, in the feeling that we were about to enter eternity. We had no doubts. We made an oath to the Koran, in the presence of Allah – a pledge not to waver. This jihad pledge is called *bayt al-ridwan*, after the garden in Paradise that is reserved for prophets and the martyrs. I know that there are other ways to do jihad. But this one is sweet – the sweetest. All martyrdom operations, if done for Allah's sake, hurt less than a gnat's bite.[15]

It is, perhaps, insensitive to draw a parallel between the emotions of a tragic would-be suicide bomber and the feelings of people caught in a momentum flow in less dire circumstances. But it's impossible to ignore the similarities – 'Pulls us upwards . . . We were floating, swimming . . . We had no doubts . . . a pledge not to waver.' These phrases could just as easily be used to describe many other situations where people become swept up along a perilous path and cause destruction to those around them.

Another way in which strongly held religious beliefs can foment violence is by exacerbating an existing dispute. Many of the current struggles in the Middle East were not initially about religion but about land, which can be divided, or power, which can be shared. The Israeli–Palestinian conflict began four decades ago as a dispute over land between two tribes who were rather secular at the time. But 'If you believe that God granted you the West Bank, compromise is not really possible,' as a writer in *The Economist* observed.[16] The dispute is now about non-negotiable absolutes, in which each side's claim and counterclaim exacerbates the other's, encouraging both parties to become more hysterical and extreme. This same process also encourages religious sectarianism, whereby various factions of the same religion compete for ownership of the 'holy truth'. Christopher Hitchens, author of *God is Not Great*, cites the example of Northern Ireland, where 'sectarianism is conveniently self-generating and can always be counted upon to evoke a reciprocal sectarianism'.[17] As each party in a dispute becomes more certain and assertive of their rights – whether Catholic or Protestant, Jew or Muslim, Shia or Sunni – they encourage their opponent to become equally assertive, in the process reinforcing the religious belief on which their claim is based. Sometimes these claims can degenerate into outright lies. As Sigmund Freud once observed, 'Where questions of religion are concerned, people are guilty of every possible sort of dishonesty and intellectual misdemeanour.'[18]

Meanwhile, in every corner of the world, religious influence is growing and continues to have a profound impact on the course of events. It is anticipated that by 2050 the proportion of people in the world who are attached to one of the four major global religions will increase from 73 per cent to 80 per cent.[19]

I would argue, however, that it is not so much the outright numbers that are significant, but rather the proportion of people within each religion who evolve from passive participants to more fundamentalist or 'hot' participants, because these segments are highly susceptible to the forces of momentum, and particularly Big Mo. As such, they are inherently unstable and volatile, and likely to initiate or exacerbate conflict in our world. Dangerous religions are like the investment banks of the financial world: highly focused, very 'hot', and full of zealous people – but also capable of wreaking mass destruction for the rest of us.

It is likely that religion will become as significant to the new century as political ideology was to the last. One of America's leading scholars on religion, Philip Jenkins, believes that when historians look back on the twenty-first century, they will probably see religion as the 'prime animating and destructive force in human affairs, guiding attitudes to political liberty and obligation, concepts of nationhood and, of course, conflicts and wars.'[20] In the context of momentum, however, and its power to generate, reinforce and perpetuate religion over time, perhaps the last word should go to Oscar Wilde, who said, 'Truth, in matters of religion, is simply the opinion that has survived.'[21]

Now let's turn our attention to an issue where the 'truth' appears to be particularly elusive, and is largely affected by the forces of momentum. This is the issue of climate change.

CHAPTER 16

Enviro Mo

Few global issues are more debated than climate change. On one side, the sceptics tell us that global warming is a naturally occurring cyclical phenomenon over which we have little control and which we should not be too concerned about. The other side warns of an impending global catastrophe precipitated by greenhouse gases caused by human activity.

Public opinion on the matter is understandably polarised and has been remarkably volatile. A decade ago, a relatively small percentage of people in developed countries were concerned about climate change. By 2007 it was the hot issue in the media and among politicians, and was on everyone's lips. It had generated a lot of Big Mo very quickly. However, in the absence of a consensus and decisive leadership, the issue of climate change is slipping down the priority list of people's concerns. Polls by the Pew Research Center and Zogby International in 2010 showed a sharp decline in the percentage of Americans who say there is solid evidence that global temperatures are rising, and fewer see global warming as a serious problem.[1] This trend is also reflected in recent polls conducted in other countries. Even the much awaited – albeit inconclusive – Copenhagen Climate Change Summit in December 2009 generated only temporary interest.

So what's going on here? Why does sentiment on this important issue swing so wildly? Why is it so difficult to form a convergent and consistent perspective on a matter of such global consequence?

To find answers to these questions, perhaps a good place to start is with an examination of the context in which the climate-change issue is unfolding. Firstly, we are dealing with an issue where there is a lot at stake – not just in terms of our ability to survive as a species but also in terms of the huge commercial and economic interests involved, particularly the oil industry.

Big Oil is not just another industry; its products have been the basis for our economic progress over the past 150 years. The burning of coal, oil and other fossil-fuels to support industrialisation has enabled Western nations in particular to become successful and dominant. It is not surprising that governments view access to fossil fuels, particularly oil, as a strategic imperative. This belief in the sanctity of fossil fuels has helped ensure that the interests and infrastructure associated with the fossil-fuel industry have been empowered through generous subsidies and tax advantages. It has also spawned a network of influential lobbyists, such as public-relations firms, who not only promote the interests of the oil industry but are also paid to protect it from threats. Such intense lobbying has also resulted in governments making it easier for oil companies to exploit natural resources by, for example, allowing them to drill deeply offshore with minimum safety oversight. This has sometimes led to environmental disasters, such as the massive BP spill in the Gulf of Mexico in 2010.

Notwithstanding the impact of such disasters, the greatest long-term threat to Big Oil in recent years has come from climate scientists who argue that fossil-fuel emissions cause global warming, which, in turn, is likely to have catastrophic consequences for humanity. This has not been good news for the oil companies such as ExxonMobil, which is the world's most profitable corporation and generates sales of over $1 billion a day.[2] Something had to be done to counter this negativity. However, the industry strategists are sophisticated enough to know there was little point in the industry defending itself, because it would be seen as self-serving. They needed a different strategy.

They turned to the experience of the tobacco industry, which decades earlier had fought battles over the health effects of smoking. Big Tobacco learned it was more effective to challenge the science of its detractors by sowing seeds of doubt about the evidence suggesting that cigarettes caused cancer. They did this by funding so-called 'independent' studies which highlighted anomalies in scientific evidence, which were then magnified to cast doubt over the whole issue. In this way, they branded the scientific health concerns as junk science. They established grass-roots organisations which seemed to spring up from the community to warn against the government interfering in personal freedoms, such as the right to smoke. These campaigns were highly effective and helped delay serious government sanctions against the tobacco industry for many years.[3]

The same basic model has been used by Big Oil for climate change – that is, portray the evidence that suggests climate change is caused by man-made emissions as contradictory or inconclusive junk science. The oil companies, led by ExxonMobil, funded sympathetic organisations such as the Centre for the Study of Carbon Dioxide and Global Change, the Heartland Institute, TechCentral Station and the Cato Institute, which promoted studies that cast doubt over the scientific consensus.[4] In 2005, Britain's premier scientific body, the Royal Society, found that in 2005 Exxon distributed nearly $3 million to thirty-nine groups that 'misrepresented the science of climate change by outright denial of the evidence that greenhouse gases are driving climate change'. In Australia, which is particularly vulnerable to climate change, as demonstrated by the frequent bushfires, the main body that tries to undermine the science of global warming is the Lavoisier Group, whose website has links to the Exxon-funded Competitive Enterprise Institute.[5] Oil-industry lobbyists also argued that the evidence against fossil fuels would not meet the legal test for liability in a civil suit because it fell short of the 'beyond reasonable doubt' test of guilt.

This activity shows no sign of abating. A 2009 report by the International Consortium of Investigative Journalists examined the climate lobby in eight countries: the United States, Canada, Australia, India, Japan, China, Belgium and Brazil.[6] The report revealed that in the United States alone there are over 2,800 climate lobbyists, five for every member of Congress, an increase of more than 400 per cent over the past six years. Their main message is that unless governments weaken their commitments to combat climate change by cutting greenhouse emissions, there will be widespread job losses, power blackouts and severe economic hardship. The report found that the voices of the environmental groups 'can barely be heard above the clamour of the older, well-capitalised and deeply entrenched industries that have been lobbying on climate change for more than 20 years'.

Governments have also played their role in defending the industry. When the NASA scientist and climate expert James E Hansen addressed the American Geophysical Union, setting out how 2005 had been the warmest year on record, he was promptly prevented by the US government from communicating with the media again. 'We were also forced to remove all our data about the latest temperature rises from the NASA website', he says.

Tactics of this kind enabled the fossil-fuel industry to delay intervention on climate change for decades and conditioned the public to ignore the issue. A survey conducted in 1997 by the Gallup organisation and Pew Research Center showed that the percentage of people in America who were concerned about global warming actually dropped from 35 per cent in 1989 to 24 per cent by the late 1990s. Other surveys at the time suggested the majority of people in Western economies viewed climate change as a marginal issue and ranked it relatively low on their list of priorities.

Although there have been vocal 'eco warriors' in many countries for decades, their protests have usually been intermittent and issue-specific, and would quickly fade from the public consciousness. Up until the turn of the twenty-first century, there was no general sense of a threat to the planet.

But it wasn't just the cheerleaders of the fossil-fuel industry who were blinding us to the threat of climate change. Other, more subtle factors have been at work. Heading the list, as previously discussed, is our persistent and misplaced belief in the power of equilibrium to correct any imbalance in a system. However, as the world learned to its cost, this belief can be highly dangerous when applied to a large global system like the global financial industry; a system so complex and integrated that it can – and briefly did – spin completely out of control. Yet the most complex system we know is the natural environment. So when things go wrong in the environment, they can really go wrong.

It is difficult for most of us ordinary citizens to comprehend the possibility of a total environmental collapse because of the way we are conditioned to perceive the world. Particularly in the developed countries of the West, we tend to split the world into different dimensions, or disciplines, such as biology, chemistry, arts, religion, physics, astronomy, economics, zoology and so on. This split can be traced back nearly four centuries to when the leading scientists of the day, led by René Descartes, agreed with the Church that they would stop meddling in 'internal' science, such as spiritual or mental phenomena, and concentrate on the 'external' sciences.[7] This Cartesian split continues to affect science to this day and has fostered a fragmented view of the world in which there is little overlap between disciplines. Consequently, at the unconscious level, we tend to perceive the environment as separate from other dimensions such as economics, physics and technology. We don't automatically connect one with the other or see them as part of a seamless whole. The reality is, though, that the world is one 'unbroken wholeness', as described by the physicist David Bohm.[8]

This split view of the world conditions us to accept the fossil-fuel industry's line that there is no linkage between one discipline (i.e. climate) and another discipline (i.e. industry). We can barely perceive this conditioning effect because it is so much a part of our collective consciousness, or rather subconscious. So even though logically we may agree with the evidence supporting man-made climate change and be disturbed about it, at the unconscious level we may not join the dots between the two issues. Few people see the irony of having a 'Save the Rainforest' sticker on their petrol-guzzling SUV car, because centuries ago René Descartes drew a dividing line between their car and the rain-forest. They exist in quite different, unconnected dimensions.

The Cartesian view of the world has been further compounded by frequent distortions of scientific facts. In 2005, for example, the broadcaster David Bellamy, who is a climate sceptic, told the *New Scientist* that most glaciers in the world are growing, not shrinking. He said his evidence came from the World Glacier Monitoring Service in Switzerland, a reputable body. The moni-toring service responded by saying that the Bellamy claim was 'complete bullshit'. Glaciers are retreating. By the time such errors are pointed out, it is usually too late, because in terms of public opinion the damage is already done. Mud sticks. The media's constant striving for a 'balanced view' on the climate-change issue doesn't help either. According to Kim McKay, a consultant to the National Geographic Society and co-founder of the United Nations-supported environmental programme Clean Up the World, 'Media balance means that if you have a hundred scien-tists all agreeing on the causes of climate change, and one who disagrees, the media will give the dissenting scientist equal time,' she told me. 'This inadvertently creates the impression that both sides of the argument have equal merit. It is the opposite of media balance. It just creates unjustifiable doubt. And let's face it: doubt is an easy product to sell.' [9] David Michaels, a scien-tist and a former government health regulator under the Clinton administration, says that various industries 'manufacture un-certainty' to delay legislation that may affect their products.

Whatever the story – global warming, sugar and obesity, second-hand smoke – scientists in what I call the 'product defence industry' prepare for the release of unfavourable studies even before those studies are published. Public relations experts feed these for-hire scientists contrarian sound bites that play well with reporters, who are mired in the trap of believing there must be two sides to every story. Maybe there are two sides – and maybe one has been bought and paid for.

Michaels cites the example of a memo that a Republican political consultant, Frank Luntz, delivered to his clients in early 2003. In 'Winning the Global Warming Debate', Luntz wrote the following:

> Voters believe that there is *no consensus* about global warming within the scientific community. Should the public come to believe that the scientific issues are settled, their views about global warming will change accordingly. Therefore, *you need to continue to make the lack of scientific certainty a primary issue in the debate . . . The scientific debate is* closing [against us] but not yet closed. There is still a window of opportunity to challenge the science [emphasis in original].[10] (In January 2010, Frank Luntz used similar tactics to delay much-needed reforms to the financial system by linking them to contentious bank bail-outs.)[11]

The combination of powerful vested interests protecting Big Oil, our split (Cartesian) view of the world, the use of uncertainty tactics to challenge the science and media distortion have created what the Australian scientist Dr Tim Flannery calls 'a lethal complacency'. This complacency has, for a long time, made it extremely difficult to summon up the support necessary to take meaningful action on climate change. It's fair to say that the momentum has been firmly on the side of Big Oil.

A turning point

Around the turn of the twenty-first century, there was a distinct shift in the way that the public began to view climate change.

People began to see it more in global terms. They began to notice changes in their immediate environments that hinted at wider, more serious implications, whether it was a balmy 21-degree Celsius (70-degree Fahrenheit) winter in New York, torrential floods in India or devastating cyclones such as Hurricane Katrina. On their televisions they watched huge chunks of ice breaking off the Antarctic shelf and crashing into the sea, the melting of the Greenland ice cap, whole islands sinking under water, lakes and riverbeds drying up and glaciers receding for the first time in thousands of years. They learned that the average global temperature for the past eleven out of twelve years had been the warmest on record. Something was definitely going awry with the environment, and it was affecting people in a way that was real, immediate and personal. It has no longer a distant threat or an abstract idea.

Meanwhile, there was growing scientific evidence that these environmental changes were not just part of a natural cycle or the result of solar activity, as the oil industry was suggesting.[12] The evidence pointed to greenhouse gases such as carbon dioxide (CO_2) and methane (CH_4), which were causing a greenhouse effect by warming the planet's atmosphere. The scientists learned that, according to information extracted from ice cores, the levels of CO_2 had increased by 149 per cent since pre-industrial times in 1750 and were higher than at any time during the past 650,000 years.[13] Other geological evidence suggested that current CO_2 levels were the highest they had been for 20 million years.

Yet, despite this disturbing new scientific evidence and the dramatic visible changes in the environment, the climate debate was precariously balanced and could have quite easily faded again from the public consciousness, as it had done many times before.

Fortunately, over the next few years, three critical things happened which had the effect of energising the climate-change debate and kick-starting momentum for action. For starters, in 2006 an influential report by the economist Sir Nicolas Stern, a former chief economist of the World Bank, put forward for the first time a coherent economic case for the need to urgently deal with climate change.[14] The Stern review predicted that climate change would have such a serious impact on economic growth that it could create a recession worth up to 20 per cent of GDP, and that we needed to make an investment of at least 1 per cent of global GDP to mitigate the effects of climate change. The report was corroborated by analysis from the insurance industry which showed that 35–40 per cent of the worst recent catastrophes around the globe have been climate-change-related and that over the past three decades the proportion of the world's population that has been affected by weather-related disasters has doubled from 2 per cent to 4 per cent. The significance of the Stern review was that it helped to overcome the Cartesian (or split) view of the world by drawing a direct link between one discipline, economics, and another discipline, the environment.

Secondly, in 2007 the Intergovernmental Panel on Climate Change (IPCC) published their report, which concluded it was 90 per cent to 99 per cent likely that emissions of heat-trapping greenhouses gases like carbon dioxide, generated by anthropogenic (human) activity, were the main cause of global warming over the past fifty years.[15] In a slap in the face to the oil industry, the report said that although natural phenomena such as volcanoes and solar variation probably had a small warming effect from pre-industrial times to 1950, since then they have had a small cooling effect. These conclusions were endorsed by over thirty academies of science and scientific societies, including all the academies of science of the major industrialised countries. The only scientific organisation to reject the conclusions was the American Association of Petroleum Geologists.

The details of the report were disturbing. By the year 2100, global surface temperatures were likely to rise by 1.1 degree to 6.4 degrees Celsius (2.0 to 11.5 degrees Fahrenheit), and sea levels to rise by 110 to 770 millimetres (0.36 to 2.5 feet). These increases would have major repercussions for agriculture, weather conditions, and the spread of diseases such as malaria and dengue fever. It predicted that 18–35 per cent of a sample of 1,103 animal and plant species would be extinct by 2050. The increased amounts of CO_2 would cause the oceans to become more acid with a lower pH value, which as stated on page 66 would kill many aquatic organisms and seriously disrupt the food chain, leading to food shortages. Although ocean acidification is known as 'the other CO_2 problem', its impact may be even greater that the CO_2 effect on the atmosphere. Ominously, the IPCC predicted that CO_2 levels would rise from the current 386 parts per million (ppm) to 541 to 970 ppm by the year 2100, which is way above the maximum level of 450 ppm recommended by most climate scientists. Meanwhile, the world's population is forecast to grow from 6.7 billion to 9.2 billion people between 2010 and 2050, which will further exacerbate other environmental problems such as the overfishing of the seas, massive deforestation and general pollution. In effect, the report said that the metabolism of the fossil-fuel economy was on a collision with the metabolism of Earth.

The combination of the Stern report and the IPPC report had a powerful impact. The trouble was, however, that they were reports – and reports tend to be filed away and rapidly fade from public view.

But then a third factor came into play. While the scientists and economists were busily finalising their drafts, a remarkable documentary film that conveyed essentially the same climate message in a graphically more entertaining form was being shown in cinemas around the world. This documentary, called *An Inconvenient Truth*, was so influential that it won an Academy Award and helped its producer, the ex-US vice president Al Gore, win the Nobel Prize. The documentary's most persuasive feature was an animated graph that correlated the rise in average global temperatures with the rise in carbon emissions in the atmosphere. Gore, a long-time climate activist, had been presenting the same information for many years, but it was only by bringing the story together through the magic of cinematography that his message captured the public imagination.

After decades of inertia on climate change, it appeared that the momentum was finally shifting towards constructive action. However, it is unlikely that this shift would have occurred without the synergistic combination of the Gore film, the Stern report and the IPCC report – all working together and creating sufficient impetus to kick-start the issue. This is not to diminish, of course, the tireless efforts by countless people and activists around the world who have worked on the climate issue for years and whose efforts paved the way for change. But no amount of incremental climate activism was capable of fundamentally altering the equation – the vested interests of the oil industry together with a widespread public apathy were too entrenched.

The change had to occur at the quantum level by realigning the field, or coherent domain, in which the climate debate was occurring. This meant introducing a compelling combination of facts and arguments into the public consciousness, in a way that engaged the mind and heart simultaneously and made clear the threat that climate change posed to humanity. It meant shaking up the kaleidoscope and seeing the pieces form a whole new shape. This is what Gore, Stern and the IPCC achieved.

As borne out by recent developments, however, there is no guarantee that this constructive momentum will be maintained or that it will lead to the necessary action on greenhouse gases. In December 2009, representatives of most of the world's nations met in Copenhagen to hammer out a binding international climate treaty for the first time in history. The best that could be achieved, however, was an in-principle agreement by some major countries to limit greenhouses gases – but it was neither legally binding nor comprehensive. Apart from the political obstacles of reaching a consensus among so many constituents, there is little doubt that other considerations undermined the agreement.[16] A series of emails from the Climatic Research Unit at the University of East Anglia that were leaked just before the Copenhagen conference suggested that some UK climate scientists had manipulated data to support their case. Shortly thereafter a number of errors were revealed in the IPCC report that suggested a lack of scientific rigour. Although these revelations did not challenge the overall legitimacy or findings of the climate-change report, they were given so much media attention that they fostered doubt among an increasingly sceptical public.[17] This doubt was reinforced by extremely cold temperatures in the northern hemisphere during early 2010, which seemed to contradict the global-warming argument – even though such extremes of weather are actually symptoms of long-term global warming, as are hotter summers, wetter wet seasons and more violent storms. In other words, the weather becomes more weird.

These developments, together with the continued behind-the-scenes lobbying of the oil industry, have further complicated efforts to make the necessary changes at the political level. Al Gore has lamented that it is 'extremely difficult to move the political system when it is beset by well-financed and well-organised interest groups'.[18] Although many of these groups may now appear more receptive to the winds of change, it is unlikely that their self-protective interests have diminished. Not even the massive BP oil spill in the Gulf of Mexico in 2010, the largest environmental disaster in US history, could derail the forward momentum of the fossil-fuel industry. Meanwhile, public sentiment on the issue is precariously fickle, at a time when Mother Nature desperately needs some Big Mo on her side.

CHAPTER 17

Political Mo

A few short years ago, a relatively unknown black man with an Islamic-sounding middle name, Hussein, decided to run for president of the United States. No majority-white country had ever elected a black leader. He faced not only the seemingly insurmountable barrier of racism, but his mixed cultural background made him appear like an outsider at a time when the American public had become increasingly xenophobic in its outlook, following years of external terrorist threats. Consequently, he was confronted with formidable opposition, both from within and from outside his own political party. By any reasonable calculation, this man's chances of success seemed remote.

Yet, against all the odds, after a long and arduous campaign, Barack Hussein Obama eventually succeeded in his quest to become the forty-fourth president of the United States. On a chilly 20 January 2009, nearly two million people spilled into Washington Mall to witness his inauguration. Millions more people around the world watched on television to welcome his ascent to the most powerful position on Earth. It was an event of monumental and historic proportion, the kind of sea change that occurs only once every few generations. During his acceptance speech, Obama did not dwell on the personal obstacles he had faced along the way but did allude to them subtly in passing: 'A man whose father less than sixty years ago might not have been served at a local restaurant can now stand before you to take the most sacred oath.'[1]

Obama's remarkable feat in capturing the presidency has already become the stuff of legend and is considered to be the best-run political campaign of all time. It has generated exhaustive analysis by political pundits keen to understand how his team triumphed against such odds. Of the many contributory factors, some were obvious, others less so. There was clearly an appetite for change among the American public after the disappointments of the Bush era. Obama, unlike his presidential rivals, had opposed the deeply unpopular Iraq War. He was also a brilliant orator, able to articulate his ideas in a way that resonated with voters across the spectrum. He was young, telegenic and intelligent, and carried himself with a reassuring humility. Unlike many other black American leaders, there was no hint of the firebrand activist. Obama was cool, calm, measured. And his ability to raise funds from supporters – so crucial for an American election – proved to be phenomenal, particularly during the important closing stages of the campaign. Yet these factors in themselves were not decisive. A candidate can have many things going for them, and still not get across the line on polling day. There is another critical factor involved: momentum.

Politics is all about momentum. In the lead-up to the British general election in May 2010, James Forsyth wrote in the *Spectator*, 'In a campaign, momentum matters. It is, for good or ill, the prism through which the media report things.' Forsyth told me that momentum has become a more powerful factor in UK politics in recent years because voters are now less tied to political parties; they are less tribal. So they are more likely to join the bandwagon of the 'next big thing' and become swept up in the momentum as it gathers traction.

The Americans have known about the impact of political momentum for a long time. As discussed on pages 114–5, when George Bush senior was seeking the Republican nomination for president in 1980 and had won the Iowa caucuses, he believed his campaign had the early momentum. He even said, 'We will look forward to Big Mo being on our side, as they say in athletics.' [2] Unfortunately for Bush, the Big Mo eventually favoured Ronald

Reagan, who won the Republican nomination and then the presidency.

A quarter of a century later, another aspiring presidential candidate, John Kerry, would also learn about the fickle nature of political momentum. Kerry was tall, rich and patrician; the Democrat senator from Massachusetts, and a Vietnam War veteran who had been awarded the Silver Star for bravery. His campaign started off well and gained early traction. But it was soon derailed by a group of Vietnam veterans, some of whom served with Kerry on the Swift Boats that patrolled Vietnam's river-estuary systems during the war. The veterans vociferously attacked Kerry's character and loyalty through a series of TV commercials and a highly effective viral Internet campaign. The 'Swift Boat' campaign generated so much negative momentum that it soon turned public opinion against Kerry. His campaign manager at the time, Tad Devine, said that although many of the claims by the veterans were dubious or inaccurate, they 'played into a narrative that already existed about Kerry – that he was somehow a person who might shift with the wind, might not be enough of a leader or whatever'.[3] The irony was that here was a decorated war veteran who, unlike the sitting president, had actually seen real combat, yet he was portrayed as being unfit for the role of US commander-in-chief.

By the time Kerry responded to the Swift Boat campaign it was too late; the negative momentum had already gained a stronghold. During political campaigning, 180-degree shifts in momentum are not unusual. To avoid being 'swift-boated' during his 2008 presidential campaign, Barrack Obama and his team responded to any such attack immediately. They established a website called 'Fight the Smears', which enabled supporters who received a smear about Obama to immediately send a factual rebuttal to the source of the smear – in other words, to nip the momentum in the bud before it could take hold. The net-savvy Obama campaign operated like an Internet start-up and spread with viral intensity. It was a momentum-building machine. The user-friendliness of the Obama website, supported by extensive social-networking activities, helped to activate a huge supporter base that raised millions of dollars from over 1.2 million donors. In the month of February 2008 alone, Obama raised $55 million, of which $45 million came via the Internet. This funding enabled him to run expensive television campaigns to drive home his mantra of 'Change'. The culmination was a thirty-minute info-mercial about his policies that was simulcast on nearly all the major networks at 8 p.m. EST on 29 October 2008 and was reinforced through online activities.

The Obama campaign also benefited from some influential voices in the blogosphere, such as the *Huffington Post* website, which posts blogs (commentary) by like-minded liberals as well as sympathetic news items. The founder of the *Huffington Post*, Arianna Huffington, also set up a related blog dubbed 'OffTheBus', in which citizens could sound off on the 2008 pres-idential campaign and challenge the momentum of the mighty Republican media machine, which included powerful voices like Fox News. 'We've already seen example after example of what happens when reporters hop on board the same bus, and the "conventional wisdom" gets passed around like a joint at a Grateful Dead concert,' Huffington wrote, referring to the media's treatment of John Kerry eight years earlier. The antidote, she says, is 'crowd sourcing' – that is, channelling the wisdom of the masses to challenge the status quo.[4]

It is not merely well-funded campaign activity, however, that influences the direction of political momentum. A shift in Big Mo can also occur because of something the candidate says or does in a high-pressure situation. The way they handle so-called crossroads moments can reveal much about their character, which the public responds to at a visceral level. Though seemingly inconsequential, these moments can reset the direction for the rest of the campaign, by altering the 'coherent domain', as discussed in chapter 8.

For Obama, this crossroads moment happened in July 2007, barely a few months after he announced his candidature for the presidency. During a debate sponsored by YouTube and CNN, Obama was asked, 'Would you be willing to meet separately, without preconditions, during the first year of your administration, in Washington or anywhere else, with the leaders of Iran, Syria, Venezuela, Cuba and North Korea, in order to bridge the gap that divides our countries?' Obama answered, 'Yes, I would.'

His response was immediately seized upon by his rival for the democratic nomination, Hillary Clinton, as evidence of Obama's naivety and lack of foreign-policy experience, and therefore his unsuitability to be president. Obama's response directly contradicted the long-established maxim that the US Administration unconditionally does not deal with states that sponsor terrorism.

It was the kind of gaffe that Clinton's team was a master at turning to their advantage. They were regarded as the best political operatives in Washington and knew how to exploit the media. Their legacy stretched back to the 1992 election, when the Democratic strategists James Carville and George Stephanopolous helped propel Bill Clinton to the White House, having elevated political communications to a potent new level. Obama's strategy team was relatively young and inexperienced, comprising mostly people in their twenties and thirties who operated in a closely knit environment.

The morning after the debate they all knew that the full force of the legendary Clinton machine was about to be unleashed, thereby reinforcing perceptions of Obama's inexperience. What could they do about it? Dan Pfeiffer, Obama's communications director, recalled the morning conference with the team.

> We knew this was going to be the issue of the day . . . and we're all trying to figure out how to get out of it, how not to talk about it. Then Obama took the telephone from an aide and said words to the effect, 'This is ridiculous. We met Stalin. We met with Mao. The idea that we can't meet with Ahmadinejad [president of Iran] is ridiculous. This is a bunch of Washington-insider conventional wisdom that makes no sense. We should not run from this debate. We should have it.' [5]

The impact of Obama's words on his team was profound. It boosted their confidence and shifted their strategic posture 180 degrees. 'Instead of writing a memo explaining away our position to reporters, we changed our memo and wrote an aggressive defence of our position and went on the offense,' Pfeiffer said. The episode taught the young Obama team that they could take on the feared Clinton machine, Pfeiffer said. 'It was like we had taken our first punch and kept on going.'

This was not the only turning point of Obama's campaign, nor was it the most dramatic or momentous, but in many ways it was probably the most consequential. It shifted the directional momentum of the Obama campaign in a way that would reverberate right through to polling day. Obama could easily have said, 'OK, guys, I misspoke, let's fall back into line with US policy here. The last thing I want people to think is that I'm some sort of peacenik willing to have fireside chats with dictators and terrorists on their terms. How about we avoid the word "pre-conditions" and say there will be some basic ground rules, etc. . . .' But Obama did not do this. He refused to go with the flow on an issue where it seemed all the forces were lined up against him. By successfully taking that stand, he signalled that he was willing to challenge the fundamental orthodoxies that governed not only the thinking of the Republican opposition but also of his own Democratic Party. It was a transcendent moment.

The incident also demonstrated that Obama's perceived weakness (i.e. inexperience) was actually his strength, because he could look at things afresh without the baggage of the past. Perhaps more importantly, it sent a clear and unequivocal signal to his team that their message of 'Change' was not purely a campaign slogan but a promise that his administration would alter the way things were done.

This was reinforced a few months later when Obama overturned another longstanding orthodoxy: he acknowledged the impact made by the Republican president Ronald Reagan. This also triggered harsh criticism from the Hillary Clinton campaign team, who implied he was supporting the Republican movement.

Obama responded, 'Ronald Reagan, I think, shifted our politics in a fundamental way. You know, I was criticised by the Clintons for saying that, but it's just a fact that there was a realignment, and the conservative framework for thinking about issues has dominated for the last twenty-five years. I think we are in a place where we can start changing that.'[6]

A decade earlier, in the United Kingdom, a young Tony Blair faced a crossroads of his own. His rise through the Labour Party had been meteoric. He too, like Obama, was intelligent, well educated, telegenic and a gifted orator. After he was elected leader of the Labour Party in July 1994, he set about transforming his party in order to make it more electable, following years in the political wilderness. A significant hurdle was a section of the Labour Party's constitution, Clause IV, part 4, which called for the 'common ownership of the means of production, distribution and exchange'. It read like a page out of Karl Marx's Communist Manifesto. This clause was considered by Labour die-hards to express the philosophical soul of their movement and was strongly embraced by the trade unions, which were a powerful force in Labour politics.

Blair could simply continue to ignore this clause and pretend it wasn't there, as recent Labour leaders had done, in order to avoid a confrontation with the party idealists and unions. Instead, he decided to confront the issue head-on and make a case for updating the party's constitution to make it more relevant to a globalised world. The ensuing debates were highly charged and polarised the party and its followers, but eventually Blair succeeded in overturning Labour's seventy-seven-year-old commitment to common ownership. The upshot was that he shifted the momentum towards modernisation and the creation of the 'New Labour' Party.[7] The *New York Times* described Blair's feat in glowing terms: 'Tony Blair took full command of the Labour Party today, charting a course that would eliminate the last traces of Karl Marx and move the party unabashedly to the centre, where Britain's middle class resides. Abandoned will be Labour's image as a leftist, union-dominated party.'[8] So pivotal was this event that the term 'Clause IV moment' has become shorthand in Britain for any significant turning point faced by a leader, in which they have the opportunity to set a new direction.

The permanent campaign

It's one thing to make changes when in opposition, as Blair did with Clause IV, or to promise change, as Obama did during his campaign. It is quite another thing to deliver change when that person is in office and has to deal with the realities of government bureaucracy and the enormous pressures involved. Like every president before him, Obama soon discovered that even the most powerful man on Earth is constrained in what he can do. By the end of his first year in office, beset by political stalemates over health care, climate-change policy, costly wars and rising unemployment, Obama rated himself only a B plus for his efforts. A president does not have unilateral power to make things happen, nor do they start with a clean slate. They invariably inherit policies and problems that have been worked on by a thousand hands – many of which seem intractable and bogged down in inertia.

To overcome bureaucratic inertia of this kind, politicians have long recognised the importance of building momentum for their cause. It is considered a vital tool for getting things done in a democratic government. Lately, however, there has been a growing tendency by politicians to view momentum not just as a tool but as an end in itself. Some even appear to become addicted to it, and it is not hard to understand why. Momentum can create a buoyant feeling – of being swept forward; of getting somewhere – which can be a rare experience for a politician. So they become obsessed with generating as much positive momentum as possible. Their governments develop the type of 'permanent campaign culture', that Scott McClellan, the former White House press secretary, observed in the Bush administration.[9] While this behaviour is somewhat excusable during the hype of an election campaign, which only last a few months, it can have destructive consequences when in office. Because, as we have seen throughout this book, once momentum gains traction it can be difficult to control and tends to develop a life of its own. When politicians are seduced by its flow, they are likely to lose sight of their bearings. Government becomes all about moving forward, keeping up the pace, regardless of the directional consequences. It's government by tempo.

This behaviour is exacerbated by the frenetic twenty-four-hour news cycle of the modern media, which has a voracious appetite for political news. If the media beast is not fed regularly, it grumbles that the government is not doing enough. So governments feel compelled to constantly conjure up newsworthy initiatives to keep pace with the momentum-driven media. Also, to ensure that each new initiative is well received, governments devote an inordinate amount of effort to ensure the message is correctly 'spun' and is designed to have maximum impact on that holy grail of modern politics, the public-opinion poll.

A vociferous critic of this process in the United States is *The Daily Show* host Jon Stewart, who believes that US politics is largely in the hands of the marketing people and what he calls the polishers – people who are more interested in polishing the image, creating the sound bite, manufacturing the illusion. 'We are just not used to unvarnished rhetoric . . . talented journalists spend their entire lives trying to get into the White House press corps, and suddenly find out they're dictation machines where the White House tells them what to say. I can't tell you how many times I've run into a journalist who says, "Boy, I wish I could be saying what you say [on *The Daily Show*], and I always think, "Well, why don't you?"' [10]

The increasingly momentum-driven and media-centric nature of modern politics has a corrosive effect on the political process. It pushes politicians to become more extreme in their political views than they would otherwise be, in order to make them more 'interesting' to the media and therefore more acceptable to the public. The more controversial the better. Yet, paradoxically, politicians are expected to be balanced in their personal lives without a hint of extreme behaviour or eccentricity. The only way many politicians cope with such contradictory expectations is to develop different personas for their public and private worlds. When the gap between the two personas grows too vast, the result can be devastating, as we saw with the political demise of John Edwards, who was once considered a presidential hopeful for the Democrats until his infidelities and cover-ups were revealed.

Modern politicians are also expected to 'mirror' the moods and feelings of their electorate. So, for example, when the extent of the BP oil spill catastrophe in the Gulf of Mexico became apparent, there was a mighty clamour for President Obama to 'emote' and express his feelings on the issue. He was accused of being too 'cool-headed' which, ironically, was one of the main reasons he was elected. His handling of the event reminded many people of the way his predecessor George Bush responded to Hurricane Katrina and which deeply wounded the Bush presidency. Now Obama faced his own presidential crossroads event in the Gulf of Mexico. Whether or not the criticisms of his performance were justified, they generated a lot of negative momentum that damaged his reputation.

Further distorting the political process, particularly in the United States, is the growing influence of corporations. In January 2010, the US Supreme Court overturned a longstanding restriction on the ability of corporations to fund political campaigns, arguing that corporations are just like people and entitled to the same First Amendment rights. Notwithstanding the dubious nature of this argument, the ruling does not take into account the enormous momentum, or Big Mo, that large corporations can generate in support of their candidate. If major corporations, such as banks, can fund candidates who are committed to deregulating their industries, the effects can be highly destabilising – as we saw in the lead-up to the global financial crisis.

It is extremely difficult for a politician, no matter how clever, strong or values-driven they are, to resist the new orthodoxies that govern political life. Consider, for a moment, how someone like Sir Winston Churchill would fare in today's political system. He was a man who drank and smoked copiously and was prone to eccentricities. He was crumpled in appearance and gruff of manner. Not what one would call a telegenic person. By modern standards, Churchill was a flawed character and would be excoriated by today's media. Not that he would care much, as he wasn't that interested in day-to-day fluctuations in public opinion; he was more concerned with the bigger picture. Could anyone imagine Churchill chatting with his 'spin doctor', poring over the opinion polls to divine the latest popular fad or whim in order to figure out what to do next? Not by any stretch of the imagination. When one of his advisers recommended that he keep his ear close to the ground, he responded that the public would find it hard to look up to leaders detected in that position. Churchill believed that a leader who is too anxious to please loses the respect of those he or she seeks to please. At a time of crisis, he offered the public blood, toil, tears and sweat – hardly the sort of message you hear today from political spin doctors.[11] Churchill was the antithesis of a momentum surfer; and for this reason, it is highly unlikely he would survive in today's political environment – despite being what many historians regard as the greatest leader of the past century.

In truth, the political environment has changed so much in the past twenty-five years it's doubtful whether even 'the Great Communicator', former president Ronald Reagan, would have succeeded today. This is because Reagan personified an America of old-time values and aspirations. His perspective seemed almost static, as if drawn from a Norman Rockwell painting. He was certainly not a frenetic, ephemeral politician and, as such, may have been out of pace with the tempo of the modern news cycle. Yet it was precisely Reagan's aura of enduring stability and inner certainty that helped inspire a renewal of American confidence and global leadership that eventually paved the way for the end of the Cold War and led to major reductions in the nuclear arsenals of the United States and the Soviet Union. Reagan was often lampooned during his presidency for being intellectually shallow, but the publication of his personal diaries and the historical resonance of his decisions reveal a man who was deeply serious about his politics.

The irony is that although government is becoming an increasingly serious business, it is attracting less seriously minded people. For the process that selects and anoints aspiring politicians now resembles the selection process for a reality TV show, in which only the most opportunistic and media-savvy types survive. These are masters of the autocue and ten-second sound bite, who can detect the tiniest seismic shift in public opinion: people who are willing to surf the political momentum, wherever it may lead, regardless of the consequences. There are exceptions, of course, but the trend is clear. Marshall McLuhan warned decades ago that, 'Politics will eventually be replaced by imagery. The politician will be only too happy to abdicate in favour of his image, because the image will be much more powerful than he could ever be.'[12] We have now arrived at that place.

CHAPTER 18

Geopolitical Momentum

Some years ago, I was attending a meeting at the headquarters of the World Economic Forum (WEF) in Geneva, Switzerland.[1] It was one of those gloriously beautiful days that frequently bless this lakeside city. There was not a hint of cloud in the sky and I could see for many kilometres through the still air. Around mid-morning everyone took a break from the meeting and milled around outside chatting with Klaus Schwab, the venerable founder of the WEF, who showed us around the small Japanese garden that his wife had designed and which imbued the area with an elegant serenity. He then pointed across the lake to the building that had housed the old League of Nations, the precursor to the United Nations, and explained how this grand 1920s edifice had meant to symbolise the world's commitment to preventing wars, following the catastrophe of World War I. The building looked so beautiful and tranquil, nestled on the foreshore of Lake Geneva, as if signi-fying it had fulfilled its utopian promise that all would be well in the world.

But it wasn't. For this was 20 March 2003, the first day of the Second Iraq War. Halfway across the world, people were dying under barrages of smart bombs, at the outset of a long, bloody conflict that would see hundreds of thousands of people lose their lives.

Earlier, in chapter 9, we explored the critical role momentum played in this war and how it swept up everyone in its path, even the most powerful people in the world. Some of them were all too willing to ride the lethal Big Mo. Apart from causing so much death and destruction, costing trillions of dollars and diverting resources away from the pursuit of the real perpetrators of 9/11, this war is significant for another reason. It signalled the beginning of the end of US geopolitical primacy in the world, by vividly demonstrating the limits of hard (military) power while undermining America's credentials as an upholder of international law. The United States suddenly no longer seemed to be the omnipotent guardian of the global order that it had worked so hard to construct since the end of World War II.

This perception of weakness was soon reinforced by America's woeful response to the destruction wrought by Hurricane Katrina in New Orleans, which appeared to be managed with all the competency of a moribund Third World country. Then came the global financial crisis, which was perceived as emanating from the excesses of Wall Street. This was followed by yet another crisis in 2010 in the form of a massive oil spill in the Gulf of Mexico that the US seemed powerless to stop. The cumulative impact of these events, coming so close together, has damaged America's reputation in the world.

In short, the United States is increasingly seen as falling back relative to other nations – economically, culturally, politically and socially. It has lost its glow. According to the Global Powerhouse Barometer (GPB), published by the *Washington Post*, 'US influence is in steep decline . . . The US is still the military superpower but it's already sharing the global influence stage with the emerging powers that can move global events as well or better. A dramatic global realignment appears to be in progress (and quickening).'[2]

This relative decline is reflected across a number of indicators. For example, according to a 2009 Boston Consulting Group Study, the United States has fallen to eighth place in terms of global innovation. Although America still wins more Nobel prizes each year than any other country, these are mostly awarded to people in the twilight of their careers, and therefore this measure does not necessarily reflect where the breakthroughs are being made today. Nobel Prizes are a trailing indicator, not a predictive one. The Education Trust says that the US is the only indus-tralised country in which young people are less likely than their parents to graduate from high school. The focus of education is changing too; in recent years, more people graduated in the United States with sports-exercise degrees than electrical engin-eering. The Puritan ethic of delayed gratification appears to have given way to a leisure- and pleasure-obsessed society. The United States now spends more on litigation than on research and devel-opment. In September 2010, *Newsweek* ranked America as 11th in the world – not even in the top ten – in terms of education, health, quality of life, economic competitiveness and political environment.[3] More broadly, the 'American dream' now casts less of a spell over the rest of the globe. As Richard Haass, the president of the Council on Foreign Relations, explained, we have moved from a unipolar world dominated by America to a 'non-polar world'.[4]

It is disconcerting to think that just a few short years ago, at the turn of the twenty-first century, the United States wasn't just a superpower, it was, in the words of former French president, Jacques Chirac, a hyper-power – so dominant was its position economically, militarily, culturally, scientifically and education-ally. Given these advantages, the American empire was expected to consolidate its dominance well into the twenty-first century. It was also widely assumed that the destiny of the American empire would follow the time-worn path of other great empires – such as those of the Romans, Ottomans, Hapsburgs, Romanovs, Bourbons, Great Britain and the Ming dynasty – in that its rise and fall would be a drawn-out process. It would reflect the view of imperial decline espoused by historians of the French Annales school which emphasises *la longue durée* – the long term – in which empires follow a gradual and predictable life cycle.

But America's relative decline has not been gradual; it has

been sudden and unexpected. It is difficult to reconcile with the cyclical view of history.

Of course, it would be unwise to bet against America's capacity to reinvent and renew itself – it is a most resilient and resourceful nation, and it may yet reverse the trend. The prophets of American decline have been proved wrong many times before.

There are, however, factors at work today that will make it more difficult for America to regain and retain its pre-eminent position. Firstly, other nations such as China and India are catching up to America – a phenomenon that Fareed Zakaria, in his excellent book *The Post-American World*, calls 'the rise of the rest'. This 'catch-up' process is inevitable in a globalised world as more nations gain access to similar technologies and develop their skill sets. Another factor is the fiscal profligacy of recent US administrations, which has saddled America with a huge and growing national debt, which will be compounded by the skyrocketing costs of Medicare and Social Security as the baby-boom generation becomes eligible for these entitlements.

But these factors, important as they are, don't fully explain America's recent predicament. I would argue that there is another more subtle dynamic at work that relates to the increasing interconnectedness and complexity of American society.

Recall in chapter 5, 'The Paradox of the Strong', how it was those banks with the most sophisticated and interconnected systems that were most vulnerable to the global financial crisis. Their internal efficiency generated a powerful negative momentum that became self-perpetuating and spiralled out of control. This dynamic spread like a contagion throughout the entire financial system and threatened to destroy it. Similarly, over the past decades, the United States has become much more interconnected and complex in terms of its financial, economic, military and communications infrastructure. This interconnectedness has created a highly strung society that is more likely to overreact to stimuli and threats, and therefore is more vulnerable to negative momentum or Big Mo. In other words, the structural and technological 'efficiency' that propelled America to the top now threatens to work against it.

It's somewhat akin to the example of the 1918 flu pandemic, whereby it was those with the most *efficient* immune systems that were most affected by the disease: the young and healthy. Their highly efficient immune systems overreacted and generated a destructive internal momentum that lethally compromised their internal systems.

When America was attacked on 9/11, its immune system went into hyper-drive. All the cogs in the mighty US machine began to whirr with startling synchronicity. The government unleashed a massive global military response at a cost of trillions of dollars. Simultaneously, in order to keep the economy humming along, it opened the floodgates of easy credit, which spiralled out of control in the highly lubricated, frictionless world of the US financial system – and laid the foundations for the global financial crisis. Meanwhile, the government fostered a political and media environment in which it was difficult to question the prevailing direction. Everyone was required to lock step with each other – like those people on the ill-fated Millennium Bridge in London we discussed on pages 15–6 – whose synchronised actions upset the dynamic equilibrium of the bridge.

Unfortunately, as we learned in chapter 2, when the equilibrium of a complex system is upset it doesn't automatically return to a state of balance. Neither, it seems, do great empires, as the Scottish historian Niall Ferguson explained in an article in *Foreign Affairs* magazine. 'Great powers and empires are,' he suggested, 'complex systems, made up of a very large number of interacting components that are asymmetrically organized, which means their construction more resembles a termite hill than an Egyptian pyramid. They operate somewhere between order and disorder – on "the edge of chaos", in the phrase of the computer scientist Christopher Langton. Such systems can appear to operate quite stably for some time; they seem to be in equilibrium but are, in fact, constantly adapting. But there comes a moment when complex systems "go critical". A very small trigger can set off a "phase transition" from a benign equilibrium to a crisis – a single grain of sand causes a whole pile to collapse.'[4]

It is too early to tell, in historical terms, whether the events of 9/11 triggered such a phase transition in the US. What is clear, though, is that they set off a chain reaction that magnified any perturbations in the US system to such an extent it pushed the country into a state of disequilibrium, which is now reflected in the increasingly partisan and polarising nature of the US political process. This instability has been exacerbated by the growing complexity and interconnectedness of US society, which, like the banking system, has made it acutely vulnerable to negative momentum and Big Mo. This environment fosters a feeling of helplessness among the citizens, because they fear that their individual efforts amount to little in the face of the Big Mo forces driving their society. As Bob Herbert opined in the *New York Times*, during the BP oil spill crisis in 2010, 'As a nation, we are becoming more and more accustomed to a sense of helplessness. We no longer rise to the great challenges before us. It's not just that we can't plug the oil leak, which is the perfect metaphor for what we've become. We can't seem to do much of anything . . . Meanwhile, the greatness of the United States, which so many have taken for granted for so long, is steadily slipping away.'[6]

It seems that America is now dealing with a new type of 'systemic threat' – borne of complexity and Big Mo events – which it has never faced before. This threat might not be automatically corrected by the safeguards built into the US political and social system, and which have ensured American renewal over the past few centuries. Those safeguards were created for a simpler time.

To test this theory, let's consider what would have happened if the 9/11 attacks had happened 30 years earlier, in 1971. Certainly there would have been a massive military response, but it is unlikely it would have metastasised into a powerful internal dynamic that swept up everyone in its path. Why? Because despite its awesome military and economic might at the time, America during the seventies was a less integrated, automated and complex society than it is today. Its economy was more decentralised and pluralistic; markets were more fragmented; the banking system was still highly regulated; journalists more questioning; student campuses and activists were more outspoken and influential; communications were less interconnected. Even the vaunted US military had yet to fully integrate its capabilities within the Air–Land–Sea joint doctrine. This national diversity was reflected in the American political system, which incorporated a broad spectrum of viewpoints — unlike the narrow polarised structure we see today.

This diversity and fragmentation meant there would have been less of a domino effect, because the pieces were less connected. There were so many natural friction points in the society that it would have been difficult for negative Big Mo to gain traction – even though this was at the height of the Cold War, when America faced a far more existential threat than the recent threat of terrorism.

Put another way, America's immune system at the time was less efficient and therefore less likely to overreact to threats – internal or external. It would be a few more decades before America evolved into the highly strung, fully interconnected system – or monoculture – that we see today, and which, perversely, has made it so vulnerable to the forces of Big Mo.

This recent experience of America highlights one of the great conundrums of our technological age: we are so conditioned to see efficiency and integration as a good thing that we cannot comprehend that it can work against us by making our systems vulnerable to dangerous internal dynamics; whereas if we paid closer attention to the natural world we would see that the most important guarantee of a species' survival is diversity, not homogeneity. Indeed, the entire ecosystem is really a conglomeration of friction points, calibrated to ensure that there is a natural balance between the vast arrays of life forms that live within it. Any attempt to centralise the ecosystem by, say, integrating various functions into fewer and larger control nodes, would ultimately destroy it. Yet this is precisely what we do with the systems that underpin our civilisation. We try to centralise and homogenise them and, by doing so, make them more vulnerable to dangerous dynamics like momentum. This, in effect, is what has accelerated America's imperial decline. It is not the only factor involved of course; but it is certainly the least understood one, and perhaps one of the more influential.

Big Mo speeds up history.

A geopolitical vacuum

The sudden decline of US influence is not just a concern for Americans. For over half a century American primacy has been a stabilising and inspiring influence around the globe. America has been the 'indispensable' nation. Many countries regarded America as the 'shining light on the hill', the proof that things can and will get better. They saw, in this bubbling crucible of democracy and innovation, their own future. America's story became the world's story.

But now many of those countries that traditionally looked to America for direction are becoming disillusioned. Even the American brand of capitalism, which once inspired millions and was emulated around the world, has been seriously damaged by the global financial crisis. It was the Scottish historian Niall Ferguson who prophetically wrote in his book *The Ascent of Money* that it might well be 'a financial crisis that signals the twilight of American global primacy'.[7] 'The United States has been a model for China,' says Yu Yongding, a prominent economist in Beijing. 'Now that it has created such a big mess, of course we have to think twice.' Chinese vice premier Wang Qishan put it more diplomatically: 'The teachers now have some problems.'[8]

The end of the American story, which was really the global story, means there is no longer a coherent way of making sense of how all the international pieces fit together. There is a geopolitical vacuum, or, more precisely, a narrative vacuum.

This has serious consequences, because wars don't begin with a clash of guns but with a clash of narratives. That is, two parties begin to see the world through very different narrative prisms – it is their stories that clash. In today's geopolitical vaccum, when such stories emerge, they are likely to gain momentum and traction disturbingly quickly, because there is less friction to slow them down. They can develop a lot of Big Mo.

This process is now well under way. Emerging powerhouses, such as China, India and a resurgent Russia, are radically rethinking their allegiances and how they fit in globally. Ironically, the world was more stable during the Cold War, when interrelationships between countries were clearly defined within the context of the East–West divide. Not so these days. Without a 'global story' to provide a contextual framework for international relations, things are in a state of flux and there is an 'every nation for itself' attitude. Many countries are challenging the national stories imposed on them by their former colonial masters, which were promulgated by the Western media. As Fareed Zakaria wrote in *The Post-American World*, 'Where once there were only the narratives laid out by the *New York Times*, *Time*, *Newsweek*, the BBC and CNN, there are now dozens of indigenous networks and channels from Al Jazeera to New Delhi's NDTV to Latin America's Telesaur. The result is that the "rest" (the newly emerging powerhouses) are now dissecting the assumptions and narratives of the West and providing alternative views.'[9]

These emerging storylines will generate, over time, a stronger sense of national identity and a powerful cultural momentum. For some countries, this will mean assertively distancing themselves from the imperialist umbrella under which they operated for decades, perhaps centuries. Much like an adolescent moving away from the shadow of their parent, they may feel an urge to rebel, especially if there has been a history of abuse or neglect in the old relationship. The influential *Financial Times* columnist Gideon Rachman wrote on 4 January 2010:

> Brazil, South Africa, Turkey and India are all countries
> whose identities as democracies are now being balanced –
> or even trumped – by their identities as developing nations
> that are not part of the white, rich, Western world. All
> four countries have ruling parties that see themselves as

champions of social justice at home and a more equitable global order overseas. Brazil's Workers' Party, India's Congress Party, Turkey's AKP and South Africa's African National Congress have all adapted to globalisation – but they all retain traces of the old suspicions of global capitalism and of the US.[10]

Sometimes, if a national story is fuelled by ethnic tensions, religious conflict (particularly involving hot religions, as discussed in chapter 15) or historical falsehoods, they can have dangerous consequences, as we have witnessed in places like the Balkans. The French philosopher Voltaire said long ago, 'Those who can make you believe absurdities can make you commit atrocities.'[11]

Indeed, it is difficult to overstate the influence that a nation's narrative can have on its destiny. For example, America's evolution into a global superpower can be directly traced to the transcendent ideas and values embodied in its national story. It has been a tale of revolutionary zeal, perpetual reinvention and an eternal search for a better way. Above all, it has been a story about the freedoms and rights of the individual rather than the collective. Although America celebrates community and teamwork, it is really about John Wayne, not the posse. This highly individualistic view permeates every aspect of American society, from its legal system to education to sport and business. This idea has been successfully exported around the world over the past half-century, as an integral part of the American dream and the capitalist model. Francis Fukuyama, professor of international political economy at the John Hopkins School of Advanced International Studies in Maryland, says that America has long championed a particular vision of capitalism, 'underpinned by ideas of freedom, innovation, low taxes and small government'.[12] This vision is sometimes referred to as the 'Washington Consensus'.

However, we are now seeing the development of some alternative national narratives in the world, ones that are much less individualistic and freedom-based than the American model. Consider, for example, the story of modern China. This is not just a straightforward tale of modernisation but one of an alternative path to modernisation. Although it has adopted the trappings of Western capitalism, China's version is more authoritarian and less democratic. It emphasises social order over the rights of the individual. It is a society orientated towards the collective, which extols the Confucian values of harmony above all else. Dramatic glimpses into this alternate narrative were given during the opening and closing ceremonies of the Beijing Olympics in 2008, when thousands of Chinese performed with an unnerving degree of synchronised precision. Not a movement out of place. Perhaps no other nation on Earth could have staged such a spectacle.

A few months earlier, the world witnessed China's newfound willingness to defend its national story, when it denounced Western media for focusing so much attention on its crackdown on Tibetan monks. It wasn't only the Chinese government, however, that was so defensive. The great diaspora of Chinese communities around the world was also uncharacteristically outspoken and pro-China on this sensitive issue. Thousands of Chinese students took to the streets in the United States to protest against critical Chinese coverage by news networks such as CNN. Internet chat rooms were overwhelmed by Chinese people defending their country's right to crack down on Tibet. This response was a 180-degree turnaround from the late 1980s, when Chinese students protested against their own government following the Tiananmen Square crackdown. It is clear that China's new national story has gained a lot of momentum in a very short time.

This story is challenging the long-established Washington Consensus because, as Katrin Bennhold reported in the *International Herald Tribune*, developing countries everywhere are looking for 'a recipe for faster growth and greater stability than that offered by the now tattered "Washington Consensus" of open markets, floating currencies and free elections.' And as they do, 'There is growing talk about a "Beijing Consensus".'[13] Bennhold explained that China's hybrid model of Confucianism–

Communism–Capitalism under the umbrella of a one-party state, with a lot of government guidance, strictly controlled capital markets and an authoritarian decision-making process, enables a country to make tough choices and long-term investments without having to heed daily public polls. For example, the Chinese government has been able to increase funding for scientific research at a level far above the rate of inflation, which has resulted in the strongest growth in scientific research of any nation. Jonathan Adams, research-evaluation director at Thomson Reuters, believes that if China continues on its trajectory, it will be the largest producer of scientific knowledge by 2020 – the same year as China's economy is expected to become the largest on Earth, according to the consulting firm PriceWaterhouseCoopers.[14]

It was assumed until quite recently that as China became more successful economically, it would naturally become less authoritarian and more liberal. When President Clinton visited China in 1998, he proclaimed, 'In this global information age, when economic success is built on ideas, personal freedom is essential to the greatness of any nation.' His successor, President George W Bush, made the same point a year later, saying, 'Economic freedom creates habits of liberty. And habits of liberty create expectations of democracy . . . Trade freely with the Chinese and time is on our side.'[16] The trajectory of the China story, however, appears to be heading in the opposite direction as the government exerts more control over the press and political freedom.

Russia, too, is reinterpreting capitalism within a more authoritarian framework, in which the rights of the individual are subordinate to the state. Interestingly, it is also seeking to imbue its national story with the illustrious overtones of Tsarist Russia and the Byzantine Empire of the fifteenth century. All over Russia today the Byzantine symbol of the double-headed eagle is as commonplace as the Red Star was under the Communists.

Further south, India's emerging narrative still resembles a patchwork quilt, which is not surprising, given the complexity of its cultural fabric. But the new India story is becoming increasingly coherent and is rapidly developing its own momentum, fuelled by its commercial and technical success, and by a burgeoning media and film industry which helps to synthesise the vagaries of Indian life and culture into a more seamless whole.

One of the most powerful narratives to emerge in recent years is not so much a national one as a cultural and religious one. It is the storyline that the West has declared war on: Islam. This perspective has gathered so much momentum that it now permeates numerous regional communities, not just in the Middle East but in parts of Asia and Africa, and even in pockets in the West. According to a Jordanian-born counterterrorism expert, 'This narrative is now omnipresent in Arab and Muslim communities in the region and in migrant communities around the world ... These communities are bombarded with this narrative in huge doses and on a daily basis. [It says] the West, and right now mostly the US and Israel, is single-handedly and completely responsible for all the grievances of the Arab and the Muslim worlds.'[15] Exacerbated by a 'hot' interpretation of the Islamic faith, this storyline is the prime animating force behind most extremist Islamic activity.

In the current geopolitical vacuum, these sorts of narratives, no matter how potentially destructive, are liable to continue gathering momentum because there is little friction to slow them down. Unlike in previous eras, such narratives can now develop more quickly and gain more traction thanks to the nature of the modern media, which magnify the storyline by emphasising its more polarising aspects in order to maximise ratings. Given these dynamics, it is only a matter of time before we see a major 'clash of narratives' that results in a global conflict, rather than the localised terrorist activity and conflicts that have occurred in recent years.

Yet for reasons I shall now go into, we might not receive any advance warning of such a conflict. Like the recent global financial crash, it will probably hit us like a bolt out of the blue.

A false sense of security

Earlier we looked at how difficult it can be to detect risks in a large, complex system (systemic risks). This is because on the surface everything can appear calm and smooth, while underneath the stresses can build up until they cause a catastrophic collapse. This behaviour, called 'brittleness', is a common feature of highly concentrated and interdependent networks. Unfortunately, the geopolitical system, which is really a global network, has become more and more brittle in recent years. Not that anyone would know it.

On the surface, geopolitical language is invariably polite, diplomatic and politically correct. Rarely do we see volatile exchanges between countries at the United Nations – or in any other global forum, for that matter. Countries are so interdependent today, especially economically, that they don't like to upset their major trading partners (think America and China, or 'Chinamerica'). So, as with the big banks in the lead-up to the financial crisis, they would prefer to not rock the boat by facing up to emerging problems or confronting each other over disagreements. Consider the increasingly watered-down language that countries use today when airing their differences. Even critically important resolutions by the United Nations denouncing genocide convey the robustness of a jelly pudding. But there is a price to pay for suppressing simmering tensions behind veils of diplomacy, because, like two spouses who repress their growing hostility towards each other for years, one day, one or the other may completely snap and all hell breaks loose. This is what tends to happen in polite, brittle relationships. Yet right up until the moment of conflict things can seem perfectly normal: the calm before the storm. What makes this brittleness problem so acute today, in a geopolitical sense, is that so much of our world is dependent on highly interconnected computer networks, which are vulnerable to attack.

In August 2008, a Russian military offensive on the former Soviet republic of Georgia was preceded by an Internet assault that crippled Georgian government websites as well as media, banking and transportation sites. The attack was as devastating as it was surprising. According to Tom Burling of Tulip Systems, a web-hosting firm that volunteered its Internet servers to protect Georgia's websites from malicious traffic, 'Nobody's come up with a way to prevent this from happening, even here in the US.' He says the United States is 'probably more Internet-dependent than any place in the world. So to that extent, we're more vulnerable than any place in the world to this kind of attack. So much of what we're doing [in the United States] is out there on the Internet, and all of that can be taken down at once.' [18] The same can be said for most other modern economies. Consider how difficult it would be to protect the City of London's electronic infrastructure from a small group of clever and determined computer hackers. Then consider the flow-on effect for the rest of the world if this pivotally important financial hub were incapacitated, even for a few days.

Although computer networks have been targeted by hackers for decades, large-scale cyber attacks are still a relatively new phenomenon. But they are becoming more frequent and more likely. In 2008 in the United States alone there were over fifty thousand incidents of malicious cyberactivity, and every day US computer systems are searched by millions of automated scans against foreign sources trying to find unprotected communications ports. In December 2009, US intelligence officials concluded that a mass cyber attack against thirty-three American companies was most likely the result of a coordinated espionage campaign endorsed by the Chinese government. Shortly afterwards, in January 2010, Google announced that it had uncovered widespread spying on its systems 'originating from China'.[19]

Such activities suggest that today we are at the 'reconnaissance stage' of cyber warfare, whereby most players are testing each others' resources and defences. That is, we are living in a pre-9/11 era in terms of the security and resilience of electronic information systems. It is only a matter of time, however, before we enter the next stage of cyber warfare, which is likely to be more aggressive and have more far-reaching consequences. According to an article written by Wesley Clark, the ex-supreme commander of NATO, and Peter Levin, a cyber-security expert, 'There is no form of military combat more irregular than an electronic attack: it is extremely cheap, is very fast, can be carried out anonymously, and can disrupt or deny critical services precisely at the moment of maximum peril. Everything about the subtlety, complexity, and effectiveness of the assaults already inflicted on the United States' electronic security defenses indicates that other nations have thought carefully about this form of combat.'[19]

Cyber threats represent the sharp end of asymmetric warfare where a target's strengths are used against them. In other words, the very qualities that make the Internet such a valuable tool, such as its accessibility and interconnectedness, also make it especially vulnerable to a cyber attack. And unlike a traditional military attack, which requires a considerable build-up of weapons and logistics, a cyber attack happens instantaneously – without a hint of warning. The damage inflicted can be every bit as consequential, sometimes more so, because its effects can radiate throughout the network and are not confined to just part of the infrastructure – like a bridge, say, or government building. In contrast to a military attack, a cyber attack can also incapacitate a network without causing excess collateral damage. While this may appear to be a positive development, it also enables more players to make threats as long as they have the technical know-how. Such warfare is no longer limited to the big powers. Scott Borg, director of the United States Cyber Consequences Unit, a non-profit research institute, says, 'This is such a crucial issue. At every level, our security now is dependent on computers. It's a whole new era. Political and military conflicts now will almost always have a cyber component. The chief targets will be critical infrastructure, and the attacks will emerge from within our own computer systems.'[20]

Although the Georgian conflict in 2008 was relatively minor, and ended quickly, it epitomised the type of conflict that we are bound to see more of in the future. That is, a country redefines its national story in the geopolitical 'narrative vacuum' and begins to assert its new place in the world. There is a 'clash of contexts' which threatens established relationships with other countries. For a while the growing tensions are suppressed behind a veil of diplomatic civility, until such point that they can no longer be contained. A conflict may then erupt. If this conflict involves some major powers, we can expect it to be instantaneous and devastating, because most big countries today are refining their cyber-warfare capabilities to such an extent that they will have the capacity to destroy each others' electronic infrastructure. Unlike previous conflicts, however, it would happen with little or no warning. Vital networks that seem so robust one day, would the following day crumble under the onslaught, and massive blackouts would bring major population centres to a standstill. By shutting everything down, modern cities would be forced back into the Dark Ages, stripped of even the most rudimentary utilities. Our 'assets', which consist mostly of records in bank computer systems, may be permanently erased. Incalculable amounts of vital information would be lost – eviscerated into cyberspace. The damage would not just be physical but psychological and deeply traumatic to societies that have grown so utterly dependent on modern technology.

In many respects, cyber warfare is the martial version of Big Mo. It attacks the system rather than its individual parts. It turns the strength of a network against itself, in the same way as Big Mo can turn a company's internal efficiency against itself by generating a destructive internal dynamic. This is compounded by the nature of modern military systems, which are highly integrated and automated, so once those systems are activated, they become difficult to stop. They generate a powerful forward momentum, which quickly escalates both sides of a conflict. The US secretary of defense, Robert Gates, has observed, harking back to conversations with cold warriors who thought there could be a limited nuclear war, 'Once things start, how you get control of it or keep control of it struck me as just inherently a problem.'[21]

The combination of a geopolitical vacuum, in which competing national narratives quickly develop a powerful momentum but are suppressed beneath a veil of diplomatic brittleness, together with the growing threat of cyber warfare, is fundamentally reshaping the geopolitical order. It has created an environment in which the forces of Big Mo are likely to become a lot more impactful – and lethal.

Part 4

Changing Lanes

CHAPTER 19

Avoiding the Dark Side of Momentum

At the height of the McCarthy era in America during the 1950s, when anti-communist fervour swept the nation, a remarkable film emerged, which provided a timely insight into the dangers of 'group-think' and succumbing to the flow. This film is called *12 Angry Men*. It is a low-budget, black-and-white film, which was produced during a time when free speech was under threat and, as such, has some resonance with today. The film is set in a small, smoke-filled New York jury room on a stifling, hot summer's day. Twelve white, middle-class men must decide the fate of an eighteen-year-old Hispanic kid from a poor and violent background who is accused of murdering his father with a switch-blade knife.[1]

The jury has sat through six days of evidence, in what the judge describes as a 'long and complex case of murder in the first degree'. The judge has briefed the jury: 'If there's a reasonable doubt in your minds as to the guilt of the accused, a reasonable doubt, then you must bring me a verdict of not guilty. If, however, there is no reasonable doubt, then you must in good conscience find the accused guilty. But it must be unanimous. In the event that you find the accused guilty, the bench will not entertain a recommendation for mercy. The death sentence is mandatory in this case. You are faced with a grave responsibility.'

The evidence seems compelling and overwhelming; it includes the murder weapon and an eyewitness. An open-and-shut case. The teenager seems destined to head for the electric chair. From the outset it is obvious that most of the jurors have already made up their minds and just want to get the whole thing over with. The direction and momentum have been set. The jury commence their deliberations and hold a preliminary ballot. Everyone votes for a guilty verdict, except juror number 8, played by Henry Fonda. There is a sense of puzzlement in the room. 'Do you really think he is innocent?' asked one of the others. 'I don't know,' replies Fonda's character. 'We can't decide in five minutes. Suppose we are wrong.'

'You're wasting everyone's time in here,' grumbles the man at the end of the table. 'You couldn't change my mind if you talked for a hundred years.'

But talk they do. Over the next ninety minutes, they delve deeply into the case, reconsidering each piece of evidence. Tensions rise and emotions boil over, as each man is forced to confront his own personal prejudices and character in the forensic light of the debate. The room itself becomes more claustrophobic, a perception that is magnified by the masterful close-up camera work of director Sidney Lumet. Out of this emotional crucible, and largely through one man's persistent questioning of the 'facts', the momentum of the debate begins to change from certainty to doubt. Finally, the jurors return a 'not guilty' verdict.

12 Angry Men was not a box-office success. It was a black-and-white film released during a period of widescreen colour offerings. Despite being nominated for three Academy Awards, winning the Berlin Film festival and being critically acclaimed, it did not draw the crowds.

Yet, over the past half-century, few films have resonated more deeply, topped more film critics' lists or been so influential as this classic film. It strikes a deep and perennial chord with our society. It illustrates how easy it is to follow the crowd, become over-whelmed by a system, or be persuaded by another's sheer force of personality. It reminds us of the inherent dangers of coming to conclusions too quickly. Like a cinematic circuit-breaker it says, 'Wait, just hold on a minute, maybe the crowd is not always right.'

Most significantly, the character played by Henry Fonda re-assures us that when we are being pushed in a certain direction by the crowd, we do have a choice. We can choose to listen to our innermost doubts, ask questions and make our own judgements about the best path to pursue. It may not be the easiest path, but it will be our own.

This chapter explores some of the steps we can take to unleash our own 'inner Henry Fonda' and, by doing so, avoid being swept up in negative momentum. It also offers some suggestions on how to deal with broader issues like 'systemic risks'.

Before we consider these steps, however, let's take a look at the 'rules' that appear to govern the way behavioural momentum works, based on what we have learned so far in this book. These rules could be expressed as follows:

The rules of behavioural momentum

1. The greater the degree of internal integration and alignment in an organisation, the higher the potential for negative momentum to spiral out of control. This means strong organisations can be more susceptible to Big Mo than weaker ones.
2. The subtle, immersive and cumulative nature of momentum makes it difficult to detect.
3. As networks become more integrated, interdependent and concentrated, they become more susceptible to negative momentum, which presents a 'systemic risk'. The global financial system is a classic example of this.
4. When a system is overcome by Big Mo, it does not auto-matically return to a state of equilibrium. The system may continue to spiral out of control until it collapses.
5. Once a 'storyline' has been established in the media, and gains sufficient momentum by the process of magnification, alignment and reinforcement, then any new facts – contra-dictory or otherwise – will tend to be subsumed within that

storyline. In this way, Big Mo can make an erroneous idea seem true – and persist for a long time.

6. The potential for negative momentum to occur in an organisation is inversely proportional to the level of cultural openness and diversity of viewpoints tolerated in that organisation.

7. The more modern technology insulates us from reality, the more difficult it becomes to detect systemic risks, such as a dangerous build-up of momentum.

8. Once negative momentum has gained traction, it becomes more difficult to stop as more time elapses. In an organisational setting, it will usually achieve maximum impact shortly after it is generally recognised that it is too late to stop or change direction.

9. When an individual is swept up in the flow, they will often experience a buoyant feeling, which makes it easier for them to deceive themselves about the direction in which they are heading.

10. An individual's susceptibility to the momentum effect is inversely proportional to their willingness to challenge the status quo, their curiosity, their values and, perhaps most importantly, their courage.

Given these rules of behavioural momentum, let's now look at some strategies for dealing with momentum and Big Mo in various situations.

Prevention strategies

The nature of momentum is that it tends to sneak up on us, so we often don't realise we are being swept up in the flow until it is too late. Therefore, the first step is to be vigilant for signs of a negative momentum dynamic emerging in your organisation, personal life, family, or whatever the situation. You may notice, for example, that a particular person, or group of people, has inordinate influence over a major decision, and is closing down alternative options or possibilities. You may find yourself being pushed in a particular direction that you feel uncomfortable about. Your gut feel may tell you something is wrong, even though you can't put your finger on why. The sooner you pick up on signs that a momentum trap is brewing, the easier it is to nip it in the bud.

Be honest with yourself about what you really believe is the right thing to do in a given situation. Does the proposed course of action feel right with you? Do you have doubts? What is your intuition telling you? Trust your own thoughts and feelings on the issue and come to your own conclusions.

If you work in an organisation, do what you can to encourage an open, diverse culture that supports different opinions and viewpoints. Invite colleagues to express themselves openly and challenge the status quo when necessary. A common mistake we make, especially in a group situation, is to rush to a conclusion or decision. The trouble with deciding too rapidly is that we kill off all possibilities except one.

Also consider the way you consume media, such as television and the Internet, because this has a powerful influence on the way we perceive the world and react to it. As stated in chapter 6, the frenetic pace of the modern news media creates a perceptual environment in which the world around us seems to be moving faster. This perception gradually influences the way we experience our own 'real' lives and conditions us to become more momentum-driven.

It is possible to resist these influences by being more deliberate and selective about what we watch. A helpful tip is to purchase a pre-recording device or service (such as TiVo) which enables you to pre-record the shows in which you are interested. Using such devices will enable you to reclaim some sense of control over the media, and nudge you to be more selective about your viewing habits, simply because you will have to think about them in advance. They can also save you time and money. The *New York Times* columnist Justin Wolfers did some mischievous calculations of how much time can be saved with his pre-recorder.

I watch about six hours of television programming per week. The miracle of the '30-second skip' button means that I haven't watched an advertisement in years. Consequently, six hours of programming only takes me four hours to watch, and TiVo saves me two hours per week. Let's say my hourly wage is $100, and so I value these marginal couple of hours at around $200. I'm home around 50 weeks per year, and so TiVo gives me a total of $10,000 worth of time per year. I will get to enjoy this benefit for the rest of my life, and so we should take a net present value of this benefit stream. Using a discount rate of 5 per cent, this yields a total TiVo-related bonus of $200,000 worth of leisure. Oh, and my wife Betsy loves our TiVo too, suggesting that this humble machine has improved our household's wellbeing by about $400,000, versus a cost of $200.[2]

For hard-core news junkies – the type of people who receive breaking-news updates on their BlackBerry every fifteen minutes – it may be time to ask the question, 'Do I really need to know about this now? Will my world turn upside down if I don't find out about it till later tonight?' Similar questions should be asked by individuals, such as celebrity junkies addicted to Twitter Stream: 'Do I really need to know what Angelina Jolie wore last night? Can my life continue to move forward without this knowledge?' It's a good idea to periodically calculate how many hours you spend consuming media of all sorts. You may be surprised by how much of your life is taken up by watching the world go by on a screen.

Another simple way to avoid being caught in the 'momentum stream' is to take more time out for yourself, perhaps by doing more 'grounding' activities such as physical exercise, taking a walk, yoga, meditating or spending time with your friends or family. When you do engage with people, make an attempt to go beyond the small talk and delve more deeply on subjects. This not only helps you resist the flow of the superficial but, according to a study published in the journal *Psychological Science* in March 2010, it can also lead to more happiness. Matthias Mehl, a psychologist at the University of Arizona, who conducted the study, said, 'We found this so interesting, because it could have gone the other way – it could have been, "Don't worry, be happy" – as long as you surf on the shallow level of life you're happy, and if you go into the existential depths you'll be unhappy.' But it was the exact opposite of this. Deeper discussions led to more happiness. Dr Mehl suggested the findings could be explained by people's strong need to find and create meaning in their lives.[3]

By conversing and thinking more deeply, we are less likely to float on the surface, where, as with a river, the water flows faster and we are more susceptible to being swept along like a leaf. Deeper conversations also enable us to reconnect with what's important, regain our bearings and be less reactive to the forces of momentum urging us forward.

Pushing back

If you do find yourself being pushed in a particular direction, express your concern at the earliest opportunity before the momentum gains too much traction, and encourage others to do the same. The sooner you speak up, the better chance you will have of affecting the outcome. Learn to say no when it really matters, rather than when it is too late. You don't need to be aggressive or obstinate, just polite and firm on the matter.

In chapter 10, we covered the topic of dissent, and how difficult it is, particularly in an organisational setting. Richard Haass, the senior State Department official who found himself at odds with the US administration's push for war on Iraq, reflected:

It can constitute a real dilemma for the person who disagrees. On one hand, you owe it to your conscience and your bosses to tell them what they need to hear rather than what they want to hear. Speaking truth to power is actually a form of loyalty. It is the best and at times only way to make sure that government (or any organization) lives up to its potential. On the other hand, though, no matter how good the advice, there will be times when it is resented or rejected. It may be on the merits; it may be politics or personalities. Sometimes, smart people just see things differently. [4]

Be on the look-out for momentum surfers in your organisation and try to avoid being swept up in their wave. This is difficult to do if your boss is one, but at least you can try to curb their excesses and flaws. For example, if everyone around you is getting carried away with an idea about which you have deep misgivings, you might ask, 'Excuse me if I have missed the point here, but shouldn't we also consider ... ' or, 'I am sorry but I must have blanked out during an important part of this discussion – could you please remind me exactly why we are doing this?' A little self-deprecation can go a long way when framing your challenge to the group or your boss. You could also call for more research before the final decision is made, or simply ask for 'time out' so everyone can digest the consequences of what is being planned.

If you are in a leadership position, do what you can to create an organisational culture in which your people are encouraged to speak openly and plainly, without fear of retribution. Avoid hiring or promoting yes-men or -women, and encourage employees to challenge the status quo and question orthodox thinking. The former chief executive of the chip-maker Intel, Andy Grove, often reminded his employees, 'When everyone says something is true, be very sceptical.' [5]

Sometimes a leader will have to make an unpopular change of direction, or take a stand on an issue. This can be challenging in corporate life, because management teams are under relentless pressure from the financial markets, governance requirements, shareholder activism, employee rights, diversity programmes, consumerism and the media to 'fulfil expectations'. If you, as a leader, do find yourself being pushed in a certain direction by such powerful interests, again it is better to speak up earlier rather than later. Avoid succumbing to the flow just because everyone else is heading in that direction. Think strategically not opportunistically. Consider the longer-term, bigger picture.

If you do decide to defy expectations and take a difficult stand, it can be helpful to draw inspiration from history. During the darkest days of World War II, Winston Churchill found himself surrounded by people willing to appease the Nazis, who, by this stage, seemed invincible in Europe and had developed an over-powering momentum. Yet he managed almost single-handedly to turn around the appeasers and rally them to fight the German onslaught. John Lukacs, in his book *Five Days in London: May 1940*, described Churchill as being 'like King Canute, attempting to withstand and sweep back that wave . . . This King Canute succeeded, because of his resolution.'[6] Churchill was a great leader because he was strong when it mattered; he recognised the looming threat of Germany long before his contemporaries did; he sounded the alarm early and, against seemingly insur-mountable odds, he helped turn the tide of the war – and in doing so reshaped the course of history. Interestingly, Churchill himself was driven by a kind of historical consciousness rather than political opportunism. He was the antithesis of a momentum surfer.

The management philosopher Dr Stephen Covey, who has researched and written extensively on the nature of leadership, says, 'There may be several turning points in our lives, but the most critical of all is the point at which we make the decision: "I will live by my conscience. From this time forward, I will not allow any voice – social mirror, scripting, even my own rational-lies-ing – to speak more clearly to me than the voice of conscience. And whatever the consequences, I will follow it."'[7] This is easier said than done, of course, particularly as our society becomes more conformist and momentum-driven. But leaders have an important responsibility to do just that and resist succumbing to the flow.

How to mount a challenge

Sometimes, despite all our best efforts to avoid it, we find ourselves and those around us caught up in a potentially dangerous momentum dynamic. At this point, we may need to tackle the issue more directly by mounting a challenge. This not only takes courage, it also needs to be carefully handled to ensure it doesn't backfire. Here are some tips on how to proceed:

Firstly, think the issue through. How big an issue is this? What will happen if no action is taken? What are the risks and implications? How far are you willing to take things? If you do nothing, what are the implications for your sense of self-esteem; your conscience? Could you live with that? If you do act, what are the risks to your career, your relationship, your financial situation, your family? Could you deal with that?

Next, sound out with others whether your concerns are valid and whether you are the only one who feels this way. These could be work colleagues, friends or family members, depending on the situation. You may be surprised at how many people share your concerns. But choose your sounding boards carefully. Be cautious in a work situation about approaching members of the 'inner circle' – those who advise your boss – unless you have a trusted relationship with them. Otherwise, you may find yourself prematurely alienated before you have an opportunity to make your case. If you do find that other people share your concerns, you may wish to enlist their support in mounting a challenge.

You then need to decide where and when you will mount the challenge. Will it be in a group situation, such as the next weekly staff meeting at work, at a family gathering or with a group of friends? Or will it be a one-to-one situation with your partner, friend or boss? Weigh the pros and cons. The upside of a group situation is that you can have supporters around you who bring their perspectives. It can help open up the discussion. The downside is that the decision-maker may feel ambushed and dig their heels in. The upside of a one-to-one discussion is that you can express your concerns more directly, forthrightly and emotionally if you wish, without the constraints of group dynamics getting in the way. The person in question (your boss or partner) may appreciate the fact you have approached them directly, in confidence, before discussing your concerns more widely. They may also appreciate your candour and courage for doing so. The downside is that you won't have the support of others – or a witness factor: the capacity to hold that manager to a promise – unless you go with a delegation, and if the person is particularly dominating, you may feel intimidated and less willing to express yourself.

When articulating your case, it is important to tailor your communications style to the person you are talking to, and within the context of the situation. For personal situations, such as confronting a spouse, friend or family member, you will instinctively know what style to adopt based on your relationship with them. You can often afford to be more subtle, nuanced or emotional. For work situations, there is usually less intimacy and a different power equation. You will have to be more direct, structured and responsive to the communications style of your boss. Be polite, clear and assertive. Know what you are talking about and have your facts ready.

If all goes well, and you have succeeded in persuading the relevant person (or people) to change course, then congratulations are due. If not, you will have to make a personal judgement. Do you now fall back into line, satisfied with the knowledge that at least you tried? Or, if you feel very strongly about the issue, do you continue to resist by escalating it to the next level? There are a number of ways to do this:

You can put yourself 'on the line' by making it absolutely clear that you cannot continue in the current situation or direction, given your opposition to it. If the situation is a personal one, such as a relationship conflict, you may need to threaten to end the relationship. If it is a work-related issue, then you could request a transfer to another area of the organisation. A more extreme option would be to resign in protest as a matter of principle, and as a last resort. You can raise the issue with a higher level of management – that is, go above the head of your boss. When making your case to the next level up, apply the same communication principles as outlined above: be polite, professional, clear, assertive and supported by facts. Also be aware that going above your boss's head will often damage your relationship with your boss.

If, however, these steps do not yield the results you want, you may wish to consider the most drastic step of all – which is to 'go public'. This means taking the issue to an external body that lies outside the realm of the organisation, such as a regulatory authority like the Securities Exchange Commission, a government representative such as your local MP or senator, the law-enforcement authorities, or the media. As a rule, it is best to first bring the issue to the attention of an external authority that is directly relevant to the organisation. For example, if you work in the pharmaceutical industry, you might approach the industry authority that regulates drug products, such as the Food and Drug Administration (FDA) in the United States, the Therapeutic Goods Administration (TGA) in Australia, or the Medications and Healthcare products Regulatory Agency (MHRA) in Britain.

Only ever go to the media as a last resort, because once the information is out in public, you and your organisation forfeit any control over how the story is used. And as discussed on pages 68–9, the news media are heavily influenced by ratings: they will tend to search for the most sensationalist aspect of your issue and may distort the facts. On the positive side, the media have the unique ability to draw public attention to an important issue, which can lead to quick action by the relevant authorities. You must be prepared to be interviewed by the media, which can be an unnerving experience for the uninitiated.

In recent years, attitudes towards whistleblowers have been changing, largely due to the growing recognition of their usefulness to society. Numerous threats to our security, health, financial stability and welfare have been uncovered by whistle-blowers, which have resulted in much-needed legislative change. However, as discussed below, there is often a price to pay.

Dealing with the aftermath

Hopefully, by using the strategies outlined in this book, you will have succeeded in avoiding, reducing or stopping the momentum in a way that leads to positive results, with a minimum of fuss. If your actions concerned an organisation, you may have helped to avert a problem or catastrophe. If it was about a personal issue, you may have prevented a problem getting worse, re-established an important relationship or ended a bad one, changed careers for the better or got your life back in order. By refusing to go with the flow, you improved the situation.

Sometimes, however, things don't go so smoothly and there is a difficult aftermath to deal with. If you took the most drastic step of all and became a public whistleblower, you may face ongoing enmity from the people around you. You may have also jeopardised your job prospects and been labelled a troublemaker, activist or stirrer. You may suffer ongoing financial hardship and loss. You may lose friends, if you haven't already.

Recall from chapter 10, 'The Difficulty of Dissent', the plight of Enron executive Sherron Watkins when she alerted her own chairman to accounting irregularities and was promptly demoted and threatened by the company's in-house lawyers. Consider again the fate of Kiroku Akahane, the septuagenarian Japanese meat-processing executive who blew the whistle on misleading practices by his company: he became an outcast in his local community, was shunned by relatives and friends and is being treated for depression at a psychiatric hospital. These are heavy prices to pay and represent just the tip of the iceberg in terms of what whistleblowers have to endure.

No matter what the consequences, however, there is one thing of which you can be certain. If you genuinely believe you did the right thing, you will have been true to your conscience. And in a world that often conspires against us acting on our better nature, such authenticity and integrity is no small thing.

Avoiding Systemic Risk

So far we have looked at what individuals can do to avoid or minimise the effects of dangerous momentum – and, hopefully, embolden their 'inner Henry Fonda'. Now let's turn our attention to what can be done to control momentum at the macro – or Big Mo – level, where it poses a major threat to the networks upon which our world increasingly depends. In other words, how can we prevent momentum from becoming a systemic risk? I will focus on the financial system here because it epitomises the kind of systemic problems we face at the beginning of the twenty-first century. The underlying principles are relevant to many other situations and industries.

The first step is to ensure organisations design networks so that they are less likely to generate destructive internal momentum. This means resisting the urge to concentrate and centralise networks around fewer major 'hubs' in order to make them more 'efficient'. We saw how dangerous this concentrated approach can be during the global financial crisis when a few megabanks put the entire financial system at risk. The collapse of 158-year-old Lehman Brothers – the largest bankruptcy in American history – generated such a powerful negative momentum that it almost brought down everyone else with it. It wasn't solely a matter of size – of being 'too big to fail' – but of how interconnected Lehman's was with all the other players. This interconnectivity acted as a conduit for momentum and enabled it to become self-perpetuating. In this context, the real problem with Lehman Brothers wasn't that it was allowed to fail, as is often suggested, but that it was allowed to succeed in the first place.

It would seem logical, therefore, to reduce the level of interconnectedness by reintroducing a form of Glass–Steagall legislation to create firewalls between different parts of the financial system in order to prevent them from contaminating each other.

Financial regulators should also routinely review the biggest and most connected companies in the industry and ask, 'If this institution collapsed, would it present an unacceptable risk to the entire system?' If the answer is, 'Yes', then the business must be required to be restructured or downsized in an orderly manner until it no longer presents a systemic risk. Similarly, two financial companies should not be allowed to merge if their combined size and interconnectivity present a systemic risk. Banks should be 'small enough to fail'. These reviews should also apply to the vast 'shadow-banking' system which enables non-banks to perform many of the functions of traditional banks without being subject to the same regulations.

Regulators should also consider introducing more friction into the global financial system – at the key points where and when it is needed – in order to prevent excess momentum building up. For example, a small transaction tax could be imposed on the sale or transfer of stocks, bonds and more exotic financial instruments, such as derivatives, to discourage hyperactive trading. This idea was originally proposed in 1972 by the Nobel Prize-winning Yale economist James Tobin in relation to currency speculation. It would, Tobin suggested, 'throw some sand in the well-greased wheels' of speculation. [8] His idea went nowhere at the time but deserves a second look in light of recent events. The beauty of this approach is that it would hardly impact the average individual investor, who rarely buys and sells stocks, tending to hold on to them for a reasonable time. But it would act like a 'friction brake' on the speculative traders who treat the markets like a casino and whose manic buying and selling sprees have caused so much market turmoil.

The economist Dean Baker, the co-director of the Center for Economic and Policy Research in Washington, is a strong advocate of a financial-transactions tax. He says that a tax of, say, up to 0.25 per cent would discourage speculation, while simultaneously raising much-needed revenue for governments who have funded massive bank bail-outs. 'For the typical person holding stock, who is planning to hold it for a long period of time, paying the quarter of one per cent on a trade is just not that big a deal . . . The fees would be a considerable expense for someone who is buying futures, or a stock, or any asset at two o'clock and then selling it at three. The more you trade, the more you pay.' Although the fees would be modest, they would significantly impact the big institutional investors who make millions of transactions and operate with tight margins. Such traders would think twice before buying and selling a stock within, say, an hour, if their small profit is wiped out by a transaction tax. Baker says that such a tax would tend to reduce the kind of speculation that often has little to do with productive economic output or the fundamentals of the underlying assets. 'It's a very progressive tax', he said, 'that discourages non-productive activity.'[9] Such an activity tax would also help to limit the size of the financial industry relative to the broader economy, thus reducing the damage caused by bloated financial sectors.

The issue of financial complexity must also be addressed. Does our society genuinely benefit from unbridled financial 'innovation'? What do we gain when the cream of our university graduates are being seduced by the lucrative financial industry to spend their days designing ever more complex products of dubious real-world value? It's a sobering thought that, in 2007, 47 per cent of Harvard graduates went into finance or consulting.[10]

What is the point of having a banking system that resembles a Formula One racetrack when an everyday road system would be more practical and 'fit for purpose'? Willem Buiter of the London School of Economics suggests that a far less complex financial model could provide most of what a modern economy needs. Such a basic model could deliver the core financial services more simply, with transparency and stability.[11]

It is also critical that the people charged with overseeing the financial system – the regulators – are encouraged to act independently. It is somewhat disturbing that a number of senior personnel at the US Securities Exchange Commission ended up working for the very same companies they had been policing. For example, the commission's last director of enforcement is now the general counsel at JPMorgan Chase; the enforcement boss before him became general counsel at Deutsche Bank; and one of his predecessors became a managing director for Crédit Suisse before moving on to Morgan Stanley[12.] This creates a perception of a potential conflict of interest, because if regulators perceive that their career path extends to gaining a high-paying job on Wall Street or in the City of London, they may be less likely to confront a possible future employer. To overcome this potential conflict of interest, it would make sense to impose a three-year time limit on employees leaving a regulator before they can work in the financial section in a senior capacity.

At the global level, it would seem logical that central banks should work towards the development of an international regulatory framework that is more responsive to the momentum-driven nature of the modern financial system. This could be developed in conjunction with the Financial Stability Board based in Switzerland. The current architecture was developed over fifty years ago, when the Bretton Woods Agreement established the rules for commercial and financial relations among the world's major industrial states. This mid-twentieth-century architecture was not designed to accommodate the complexities of the current environment and the huge flows of capital between countries and markets.

In designing a new framework for the global financial system, financial regulators could well benefit from lessons learned in other disciplines. For example, the mathematical biologist Lord Robert May suggests there is much to learn about managing risks in the financial system by observing how humankind relates to the natural ecosystem. He cites the example of fisheries management and explains that for the past fifty years fish stocks have been managed on a species-by-species basis that aims to maximise the 'sustainable yield' of individual fish, such as cod or herring – an approach analogous to regulatory risk analysis that focuses on individual banks. But, with the collapse of some important fishing grounds, marine scientists are coming to recognise that what really matters is the wider ecosystem and environmental context. You cannot protect cod, for example, without considering the sand eels, whiting, haddock, squid and other species on which cod feed. You have to look at the entire system.[13]

It would also make sense to establish a global systemic warning system for the financial industry. There is a precedent: the World Health Organisation (WHO), which constantly monitors the globe for early signs of an epidemic. When trouble does break out, as SARS did in 2003 and swine flu in 2009, the WHO provides information to governments, medical professionals and the general public. Similarly, the financial warning system would advise markets or specific institutions of dangerous risk, and perhaps even intervene in extreme cases. Such pre-emptive actions may rankle with the free-market ideologues, who are opposed to any form of regulation, but it is difficult to see that there is a choice. The world can scarcely afford another round of bank bail-outs on the scale of 2008–9.

Speaking of market ideology, it would seem timely for the economics profession to do some serious soul-searching. It is now patently clear that many existing economic theories and practices simply don't work, especially the neoclassical idea that markets are driven by rational choices and will find equilibrium on their own. As Michael Hirsh wrote in *Newsweek*, 'Much of the foundation of modern economics needs to be rethought because it laid the groundwork for financial recklessness and the domination of the real economy by financial markets . . . rational models don't work because there are too many unknowns to justify them. There is no real equilibrium in the real world. The models don't compute. Literally.' Hirsh argues that just as the Great Depression of the 1930s produced a wholesale rethinking of economics, including Keynes's General Theory, a similar rethinking should be occurring now.[14]

More broadly, we need to rethink our approach to designing other complex systems that underpin our world and, in particular, the idea that concentration and integration are always a good thing. For example, does it really makes sense to have the computer systems that increasingly run our infrastructure dependent on fewer, larger hubs. Surely, these vital systems should be as dispersed as possible so that if one part of the network goes down, the rest of it will survive. A dispersed network is also less vulnerable to threats from cyber attacks because it is more difficult to shut down the whole network – as the people at the US Defense Advanced Research Projects Agency (DARPA) knew all those years ago when they created the first internet. Look no further for a workable model than the immune system of our own body; it is autonomous, adaptable, distributed and diversified.

Concentrated networks are also more vulnerable to the impact of negative momentum, or Big Mo, for reasons we explored earlier (see chapter 5). And we certainly cannot count on the forces of equilibrium to restore balance to a system when things go haywire. The restorative power of equilibrium is dangerously overrated, especially when it concerns large, complex and highly interconnected systems.

We should also be wary of our growing dependence on models to minimise risks in a system. As we saw in the aftermath of the financial crisis, such models can have the unintended effect of disguising risks and making them worse. They may appear to simplify things, but as the great American cultural critic H L Mencken observed, 'There is always an easy solution to every human problem – neat, plausible and wrong.'

Finally, and perhaps most importantly, we, as a society, must take a more holistic approach to the problems we face, or at least make a more concerted effort to do so. The reality is that our world today is so highly interconnected, integrated and interdependent that it is not possible to comprehend, let alone deal with, the major challenges we face by looking at one part of the system only. It is vital to take a systemic view. Threats like Big Mo attack the whole system simultaneously. Already some fields are moving towards a more integrative and holistic view. Take medicine, for example, where there is now a realisation, albeit belatedly, that an individual's health is dependent not just on the vitality of their individual organs and systems but on how well they all work together. We must apply a similar perspective to other areas like the global financial system, climate change and computer networks.

A return to accountability

Underlying all these strategies to help us avoid the dark side of momentum there is one issue in particular that requires our special attention. This is the issue of personal accountability.

In recent years, the rise of the momentum-driven society has coincided with a precipitous decline in personal responsibility. This is no accident. When people succumb to the flow of events, their natural tendency is to surrender their own responsibility for the path undertaken. Then, if things go wrong, they can proclaim they were simply passengers along for the ride. Just victims, like everyone else.

Consider for a moment the major crises and scandals of the past decade: the global financial crisis, the Second Iraq War, the inaction on climate change, the response to Hurricane Katrina, the BP oil spill in the Gulf of Mexico, the revelations of widespread abuse of children by the Catholic Church. In each case, no one in a position of authority has been personally held accountable for these failures. It is as if they happened all by themselves, with no human involvement.

According to Frank Rich, writing in the *New York Times*, 'We live in a culture where accountability and responsibility are forgotten values. When "mistakes are made" they are always made by someone else.' The days when powerful executives would proclaim: 'The buck stops here, with me,' seem long gone. Rich cites the example of Alan Greenspan, who, as chairman of the Federal Reserve was one of the most powerful men in the world, yet recently appears to have washed his hands of his responsibility for the financial crisis. 'In his rewriting of history,' Rich says, 'Greenspan claimed his clout in Washington was so slight that he was ineffectual at "influencing the Congress", and that "Everybody missed it [the impending bubble] – academia, the Federal Reserve, all regulators."' These sentiments were echoed by the former Citigroup guru Robert Rubin, who described Wall Street's meltdown as 'a crisis that virtually nobody saw coming', citing regulators, auditors, analysts and commentators. Rubin said that even though he was chairman of Citigroup's executive committee – and was paid over $100 million while he was there – he had no significant operational responsibility.[15]

Similarly, not a single member of the Bush administration has taken responsibility for their part in the debacle of the Second Iraq War. Everyone chants the same alibi: 'We were misled by faulty intelligence ... there was nothing we could do ... it was just one of those things that *happened*.'

This lack of accountability is not just a symptom of our increasingly momentum-driven world, it is also a prime cause, because it is much easier for people to become swept up in the flow of events when they know they won't be held accountable for the direction taken. If, however, they know they will be held personally responsible for the consequences, they will tend to think and act more prudently.

The damage caused by the widespread lack of accountability in our society today is far-reaching. When people see their leaders and those around them constantly shirking their responsibilities, particularly for failures, they eventually lose faith in the viability of their community and the institutions within it. A society can only be as accountable as its individual members. According to Howard Fineman, writing in *Newsweek*, 'Never in modern times have Americans been more bitterly skeptical of their political and business leaders – in other words, the people in charge. Nearly four in five don't trust the federal government, according to Pew (public opinion poll). A recent Bloomberg poll shows that most Americans have a negative view of Wall Street, big banks, and insurance companies. Approval ratings for Congress are the lowest on record.'[16]

This is why it is critical to re-instil a strong sense of personal accountability, particularly at the individual level. In his inaugural address, in January 2009, Barack Obama called for 'a new era of responsibility'. Some months later, after he mishandled the appointment of a key cabinet minister – Tom Daschle – he walked the talk and said, 'I'm here on television saying I screwed up and that's part of the era of responsibility.' Obama has subsequently admitted responsibility for other mess-ups.

While these presidential mea culpas are welcome, and set a good example, what really matters is how we take more personal accountability in our own everyday lives, in terms of the roles we fulfil.

Specifically this means being willing to accept responsibility for the course of action we are taking – even when it feels like we have no choice and everyone around us is heading in the same direction. Because we do have a choice – and that is whether to accept responsibility for the part that we play, no matter how big or small that part is.

Also, if the path we have taken turns out to be wrong and ends in failure, then it is better to own up to that failure. Otherwise how can we learn from it? By reclaiming more responsibility for our actions we will be less vulnerable to becoming swept up in the waves of Big Mo that now drive much of our world. We will be in a better position to chart our own course.

CHAPTER 20

Constructive Momentum

Much of the focus of this book has been on the negative or dark side of momentum and its increasing influence in our world. But momentum is a two-edged sword. The very same forces that can wreak havoc can be harnessed to achieve constructive outcomes.

Momentum can help create the impetus necessary to achieve difficult goals. It can galvanise people in pursuit of a worthy cause and generate a groundswell of support. It can accelerate the speed at which positive action is taken. It can be a force for good.

This constructive potential of momentum has long been recognised, particularly in fields where dynamic activity – in other words, movement – is of paramount importance. In sports, for example, momentum can have a decisive impact on the outcome of a competition between two evenly matched teams. The score may be neck and neck almost up until the final whistle, when suddenly the momentum shifts in favour of one team, who begin to play as if they can do no wrong. They become 'hot'. Every move they make appears to be perfectly synchronised. They have entered the zone. In sports lingo, this magical phenomenon is sometimes referred to as Big Mo. But as every sports coach knows, positive momentum is a frustratingly elusive power to tap into. You can create the conditions for it to occur – by training a team to the highest possible level and optimising game strategy, for instance – but there is no guarantee that Big Mo will be on your side on the day of the match.

It's the same for other competitive fields, like marketing, the media, film-making, music and politics. Everyone wants to get momentum on their side, but it can be notoriously fickle. Consider, for example, the film-making business, which often has huge resources at its disposal and some of the shrewdest marketing brains around. A movie studio can spend over $200 million on a film, employ the most bankable A-list stars, conduct exhaustive premarket testing on every aspect of the film, squeeze every possible distribution advantage – and the movie can still be a flop. Why? Because the film didn't achieve sufficient momentum at the box office, especially during the critical first week. Big Mo didn't turn up.

Some years ago, I asked George Miller, the Academy Award-winning director of box-office blockbusters like *Happy Feet*, *Mad Max* and *Babe*, why cinematic success can be so elusive, given the resources often available to production companies? He explained: 'You can create all the marketing hype in the world, but if the central story and the lead character or hero don't work together to offer an authentic experience, then the movie will not gain traction with audiences. Successful films are more than the sum of their parts. Everything has to work together for the magic to happen.' Bill Miller, who has co-produced these features, adds that creatively original, financially successful movies somehow tap into or help shape the zeitgeist. 'Follow-on or copycat movies that try to catch a ride on the wave of success generated by a box-office hit almost always fail.'[1]

So why can't we simply switch on positive momentum when it is needed?

Probably for the same reasons that we find it so difficult to control negative momentum: because there are mysterious forces at work here, about which we have little understanding, and can only speculate on. In chapter 8 we explored the parallels with quantum physics and how momentum seems to generate a powerful energetic field, or coherent domain, that influences everything within it. This field appears capable of aligning a range of disparate forces in a particular direction, magnifying their power and accelerating their impact. Once this process gets under way, it can be self-perpetuating, and difficult to change direction. As we have seen throughout *The Big Mo*, even the most adept momentum surfer has trouble riding the momentum wave, let alone directing it. Big Mo typically cannot be controlled and is notoriously fickle.

Given the mysterious and elusive nature of momentum, how can we at least optimise our chances of making it work for us and not against us?

The first step is to be clear about what the momentum is to be used for. People, and particularly organisations, get into trouble when they try to generate momentum as an end in itself, rather than using it as a means to an end. Consider, for example, what happened to the bankers who became swept up in the global financial crisis because they didn't really care where the market momentum took them, as long as they kept moving forward – even when it meant going over a cliff. Consider also the effect of the Bush administration's inability to define what success would look like in the Second Iraq War. This lack of clarity helped unleash a torrent of escalating forces; without an endgame in sight, there is no end.

Establishing clear goals, however, is just the first step in trying to tame the Big Mo.

Lessons from the front line

When Fiona Courtenay-Evans headed up UBS Bank's Tsunami Relief programme in 2005, following the devastating tsunami that struck the Indian Ocean at the end of 2004, her team was initially overwhelmed by the sheer scale of activity going on around them. She told me, 'There was so much positive momentum for the relief effort that resources flowed into the affected areas in an uncoordinated way. People rushed in from everywhere. Different relief organisations were treading on each others' toes, and there was a wasteful duplication of effort.' After a few months, however, she observed that the problem had reversed. 'We went from having too much uncontrolled momentum to potentially having too little. The media spotlight was starting to move away from the tsunami story, and we know that many relief efforts fail when the public loses interest. So we had to work very hard to keep the media focused on what we were doing to maintain the public support.'[2]

Even the largest global relief efforts tend to run out of steam. After Sir Bob Geldof launched the Band Aid and Live Aid concerts in July 1985, which raised over £150 million in aid for famine-stricken Ethiopia, he and fellow activists like Bono have found it a constant challenge to keep public attention focused on Africa's dire plight. 'You have to keep the momentum going,' said Bono. Twenty years after the original Live Aid concerts, in July 2005, Geldof launched the Live 8 concerts, which helped to reduce the crippling debt owed by Third-World countries, and provided a much-needed momentum boost. But it is a constant struggle.

People also have short memories. Growing up in Australia, as I did, you come to expect that every few years there will be a devastating bushfire that results in a tragic loss of life and property. Sometimes entire towns are wiped out, as happened in February 2009 during the huge fires in the state of Victoria. Such events invariably prompt a public outcry for stringent fire-prevention measures to be introduced. But once this momentum for change fades away, which it inevitably does, the enthusiasm for new regulations diminishes too, and people often rebuild their houses in exactly the same spots as before with few precautions. It is difficult to maintain constructive momentum when a threat recedes.

Similarly, with climate change, it only takes a few mild summers or winters and the long-term threat of climate change rapidly drops down the priority list of public concerns. Recall from chapter 16, 'Enviro Mo', how difficult it was to raise public awareness of climate change a few years ago. It took the combined efforts of the Stern Report, Al Gore's film, the IPAAC papers and numerous other initiatives – all working simultaneously – to effect a shift in sentiment. And even this shift turned out to be relatively short-lived.

Consider another example of how difficult it can be to maintain constructive momentum. On Christmas Day 2009, less than a decade after the attacks of 9/11 in New York, a twenty-three-year-old Nigerian man was able to board Northwest Airlines flight 253 in Europe, bound for Detroit with three hundred other passengers, while laden with enough explosives to bring the plane down. This happened because the airport scanners were too old to detect the explosives, and the security agencies on both sides of the Atlantic had not coordinated their information, despite knowing the young man was a threat. The intelligence failure was so acute that you could be forgiven for thinking 9/11 had never happened. President Obama was furious over the incident. 'A systemic failure has occurred, and I consider that totally unacceptable . . . The system that has been in place for years now is not sufficiently up to date to take full advantage of the information we collect and the knowledge we have.'[3] It wasn't just a systemic failure, though, it was also a failure to maintain the momentum needed to keep the systems up to date.

Overcoming inertia is a big challenge. When Kim McKay, the co-founder of the United Nations Environment Programme-supported Clean Up the World campaign, first began her project in 1992, she was up against a lot of entrenched inertia. 'Governments and industry would pay lip service to keeping their local environment clean, and many resisted real change until concerted community action forced them to change,' she told me. 'Fortunately, we had already demonstrated that a major community environmental clean-up programme could work through our successful "Clean Up Australia" programme.' One of the big lessons of this programme, explained McKay, was that 'you really have to keep at it – year in, year out – to build the momentum over time. After a while this starts to change the collective mindset and the behaviour. But it's a long hard slog and you have to keep reinventing the appeal of the message year in year out to keep people motivated.'[4]

This is why for the really big issues like climate change, financial reform and extreme poverty it is so important to relentlessly keep at it. Constructive momentum does respond to tenacity, as demonstrated over many years by people like Al Gore, Bob Geldof and Bono. The other lesson is to make the most of any constructive momentum generated and not waste it. This is why it is critical to capitalise on the momentum generated by the shock of the global financial crisis to make any necessary changes to the financial system, because once the momentum fades, as it already has, regulators will face an uphill battle.

Reflecting on the tsunami project some years later, Courtenay-Evans observed that the relief programme was really an exercise in large-scale momentum management – how to generate it, direct it and maintain it – in order to help the victims of the tragedy. 'One of the things we learned was that you have to work very hard to maintain positive momentum, whereas negative momentum seems to get worse without any effort at all. Problems just seem to magnify and reinforce each other if left unchecked.' Courtenay-Evans suggests that momentum 'is a twin-edged sword, you have to recognise its dual nature and handle it with care. But in the right hands it can make a powerful and positive difference. When you do manage to get momentum on your side, you can accomplish remarkable things against the greatest of odds.'[5]

CHAPTER 21

The Big Mo

There is an argument that human behaviour has been, and always will be, motivated by the innate drives of ambition, love, fame, compassion, lust, greed, power and fear – and that these immutable primal forces are what really propels our society.

This argument is self-evident and hard to refute. We also know, however, that at certain times in our history the environment changes in such a way that some human traits are more likely to manifest themselves than others and have a greater impact on the world. Outbreaks of plague or war, for example, tend to bring out different behaviours from stretches of prosperity and peace, as do periods of great technical innovation or creativity. Over time, the combination of the environment and our human behaviours produces a particular dynamic, which crystallises the spirit of the era. Various cultures have different names for this dynamic: the Germans, for example, refer to it as the *Zeitgeist*.

This book proposes that our zeitgeist is 'momentum'.

The idea that momentum influences our world is hardly a revelation. The ancient Persians recognised its latent power, as have all subsequent civilisations. But what is fundamentally different today is the scale and consequences of the momentum we are dealing with and the rise of momentum to a colossal global level. This has been brought about through the rapid and unprecedented integration of technology, the media, communications and markets, which accelerates and magnifies the impact of events, often with catastrophic results. Our world has become ultra-efficient and automated, with little friction to slow the ever-increasing momentum. As citizens, we are less able to resist the forces of alignment that propel us forward in a particular direction, like leaves in a fast-flowing stream. It is becoming more and more difficult for us to step out of the flow, or change direction, no matter how ominous the warning signs are. What's more, we are barely aware of the currents stirring deep beneath us, because we are distracted and engulfed by so much fast-flowing information.

The examples throughout this book illustrate how pervasive the phenomenon has become and how it affects so many aspects of our world, both big and small. Momentum has a tendency to exacerbate negative aspects of human nature by encouraging us to behave opportunistically and selfishly, with scant regard for the longer-term consequences of our actions. It can bring out the worst in us. I hasten to add that not for one minute am I suggesting that individuals should be absolved for making bad judgements based on greed or ignorance, or that their actions are simply a product of 'social physics'. Each of us is ultimately accountable for our own actions. But when trying to understand what causes errant behaviour, let's recognise there is often another culprit involved by adding momentum to the list of usual suspects.

It's not just individuals that are affected. Large, powerful organisations are vulnerable too because momentum feeds on their internal efficiency and integration to accelerate and magnify its power. Indeed, a strong organisation can be just as susceptible to the momentum effect as a weaker one, often more so. Just as, paradoxically, strong and intelligent individuals can also be surprisingly susceptible to momentum – because they are able to self-rationalise quickly and convince themselves to follow a certain path. Their heightened sense of certainty makes them unwilling to entertain doubts or change course. They become locked into the flow.

We have also looked at some of the positive aspects of momentum, and how it can be harnessed towards constructive ends. But this is easier said than done. For there is a mystery about momentum, and its behaviour can be unpredictable. As any sports coach knows, no matter how hard you prepare, Big Mo might not be on your side when it counts.

No one really knows how or why momentum exerts such power over human affairs. Like the astrophysicists dealing with the conundrum of an accelerating universe, we have entered uncharted territory in terms of our understanding of momentum and its impact on collective human behaviour. Let's recognise this fact, and not pretend it will be business as usual. This requires that we have the intellectual courage to challenge some of our core societal assumptions, such as our persistent belief in the power of 'equilibrium' to restore balance, or the idea that bigger is better, or that 'efficiency' is always a good thing. The recent global financial crisis has illustrated how dangerous such erroneous beliefs can be. It showed what happens when a system becomes unfathomably complex and self-perpetuating: it reaches an inflection point where the system itself begins to drive things – and the people who thought they were in charge suddenly find themselves to be passengers along for the ride. The real driver becomes Big Mo, as we saw in the financial crisis and the Second Iraq War – and no doubt will see over and over again as our world becomes ever more integrated and efficient. In the meantime, it may be necessary to rethink some of the central tenets of the Western capitalist system in order to constrain its excesses and imbalances in a 'post-equilibrium' world.

Another issue to come to terms with is the paradox of the modern media and the Internet, which offer so much information but so few genuinely different points of view and which play such pivotal roles in the creation of a momentum-driven society. To cope with this information overload, many people resort to skimming the surface of the media, and gleaning the fragments of data that seem most relevant to what they are looking for. But what to do? There are limits to how much fast-flowing information that we, as a society, can digest. The historical record suggests that our *collective* learning tends to be rather slow, and for good reason. New information must be rigorously tested against reality, over long periods of time in different circumstances, before it is digested and assimilated into the collective psyche. According to Professor David W Orr, information must go through a maturation process to become useful to society.

> We have scarcely begun to fathom the full meaning of Ghandi's ideas about nonviolence or that of Aldo Leopold's 'Land ethic'. Nearly a century and a half after *The Origin of the Species*, we are still struggling to comprehend the full implications of evolution. And several millennia after Moses, Jesus, and Buddha, we are about as spiritually inept as ever. The problem is that the rate at which we collectively learn and assimilate new ideas has little to do with the speed of our communications technology or with the volume of information available to us, but it has everything to do with human limitations and those of our social, economic, and political institutions.[1]

Consider the implications: the speed of the Information Age actually thwarts humanity's maturation process by preventing the information from sinking in long enough to be properly digested. So information flows around us rather than through us. Like wearing a wetsuit in the shower, we don't truly feel or experience the water, although we can see it and to all intents and purposes are immersed in it. What we do experience is a 'media-cracy' in which the trivial trumps the truth: priorities are distorted, and celebrity gossip is consumed as news, rather than as entertainment. Journalism, meanwhile, is becoming more partisan and polarising, particularly on the Internet, where bloggers' 'news reports' are more likely to be veiled attacks on their ideological opponents. Facts are used as ammunition, not as the stuff of understanding, and all information is spun and hyped. We have entered a post-journalistic world.

Meanwhile, the forces of technological momentum and convergence (Techno Mo) propel us forward, mesmerising us with terabytes of data pumped through our smart phones, computers and flat-screen TVs. Many of us spend our days dealing intermittently with an endless stream of texts and emails, each one seemingly important or urgent, while being drip-fed Twitter updates.

It appears that an ever-increasing number of us has an insatiable need to be plugged in to the fast-moving current. We have come to equate progress and civilisation with speed, as if our evolutionary survival depends on getting somewhere faster than everyone else. It doesn't matter where, just as long as it's faster. But is speed the hallmark of civilisation? Or is it, as John Ralston Saul suggests, 'consideration'? 'Any animal can rush around a corral four times a day. Only a human being can consciously oblige himself to go slowly in order to consider whether he is doing the right thing, doing it the right way, or ought in fact to be doing something else . . . Speed and efficiency are not in themselves signs of intelligence or capability or correctness.'[2]

Quite the opposite, in fact. Some would argue that what really matters over the long run is 'patience'. According to Andrew Haldane, executive director for financial stability at the Bank of England, the virtues of patience and delayed gratification have, for centuries, been critical to building sustainable financial, social and economic systems. But now people expect their needs to be met almost immediately. We are becoming a more impatient society. 'Impatience is socially, as well as technologically, contagious,' he warns, citing the example of the investment trading business that has recently undergone a quantum leap in terms of speed. 'A decade ago, the execution interval for a high-frequency trade (HFT) was seconds. Advances in technology mean today's HFT's operate in milli- or micro-seconds. Tomorrow's may operate in nano-seconds.' This hyper speed is compounded by the behaviour of traders who tend to 'harbour the impatience gene,' he says. 'Often, they harbour little else.' Investors too are becoming more impatient. Between 1940 and the mid-1970s, a typical stock in the US was held for around seven years. This fell to two years by 1987; one year by 2000 and now it is around six months. 'Impatience is mounting,' laments Haldane.[3]

A more impatient outlook generates more momentum, which in turn creates more impatience. It is a destructive self-reinforcing dynamic. Moreover, when we are caught in this fast-flowing current, we are much less inclined to question the direction we are heading in, or why we are so addicted to the Big Mo.

The bigger picture

At this point it may be constructive to ask ourselves what is the ultimate purpose of momentum in the broader scheme of things? Why does this potentially destructive force exist? After all, we have a fairly good idea why other forces exist. Take gravity: it helps keep things stable and orderly and our feet firmly planted on the ground. But what role does Big Mo play, particularly in the realm of human affairs? Perhaps if we could appreciate its purpose, or even speculate about it, we might come to a clearer understanding of how to manage this mysterious and elusive force.

Let's start with what we do know. We know that momentum tends to accelerate things and rapidly align a range of forces in a particular direction. We have seen how this process can spiral out of control and cause all sorts of problems, particularly for large, complex systems and organisations. It feeds on their heightened levels of efficiency, integration and scale – to propel them forward until they reach an unsustainable level before collapsing. So, in effect, momentum can bring things to a head much more quickly than if events had simply progressed at an incremental, non-exponential rate.

Perhaps herein lies its value to our world. For in an evolutionary sense, momentum – particularly Big Mo – ensures the rapid and continued evolution of our society by ensuring that we don't become bogged down in models that don't work. It brings such models to their natural conclusion by accelerating their development, magnifying their consequences and revealing for all to see their inherent inadequacies.

Consider, for a moment, if there had been no Big Mo effect

in the context of the recent global financial crisis. The world's banking system would have continued to grow each year at an incremental pace, until it accounted for an ever-greater share of the world's gross domestic product (GDP). By 2007, finance and insurance activities already accounted for 8 per cent of US GDP, more than twice its share in the 1960s. It also accounted for a whopping 41 per cent of corporate profits, up from 16 per cent in the mid-1980s.[4] This increasing share of GDP and profits, however, would not represent real economic output, but would be largely the result of speculative shuffling of paper assets between banks and companies – or 'socially useless' activity, as the chairman of the UK's Financial Services Authority, Adair Turner, described it.[5] Meanwhile, the bankers would be rewarded for this ultimately unproductive activity by having their salaries soar further beyond their current stratospheric levels. Eventually, this 'instrumentalism' would probably help usher in a new age of economic feudalism, whereby a few ultra-rich corporations and individuals controlled an inordinate share of wealth. It would also destabilise the rest of the economy because, according to the influential economist the late Hyman Minsky, an oversized financial sector tends to magnify fluctuations in prices and outputs.[6] A financial system should be the servant of an economy, not its master.

Yet, the public would barely be aware of this dangerous bloating of the financial sector, because it would emulate the 'boiling frog' syndrome, whereby if someone puts a frog in water and gradually raises the temperature, the frog will not realise it has reached boiling point until it is too late. Momentum circumvents this incrementalist process by bringing things to boiling point very quickly, so that people see the danger and react with a sense of urgency. It puts the 'fear of God' into the situation. Perhaps this is what the chief executive of Goldman Sachs, Lloyd Blankfein, meant (as a Freudian slip) when he told an interviewer that he was 'doing God's work' in the lead-up to the financial crisis.[7] For some of Goldman Sachs' actions certainly exacerbated the level of Big Mo in the system.

Does this mean that we should just let Big Mo take its course?

Certainly not. Many of the global challenges humankind now faces are of such magnitude and consequence that we simply cannot afford to let things come to a head, whether they be issues of climate change, nuclear proliferation, technological convergence, financial collapse or geopolitical conflicts. The stakes are too high, and the world is not as resilient as we may like to believe. And we certainly cannot count on 'equilibrium' to restore any imbalances in the system.

What I am suggesting, however, is that we pay closer attention to momentum, and particularly Big Mo, in its early stages – and use it as a warning sign that things may spiral out of control if we continue in a particular direction. For example, in the lead-up to the global financial crisis, there were numerous signs that the US subprime property markets were shaky and required urgent intervention. But these signs were ignored. Big Mo was allowed, even encouraged, to escalate to such a point that it almost drove the world's financial system to complete collapse. Similarly today, there are clear warning signs of imminent threats to our natural environment, our computer networks, nuclear proliferation safety and public health. These are large systemic threats that cannot be solved by the equivalent of bank bail-outs. They must be addressed early, before they fall prey to Big Mo.

The other important lesson we can take from recent events is that when a Big Mo crisis does reveal the folly of our actions, as it did with the global financial crisis, we must use this opportunity to make the necessary changes to the system. So the pain is not wasted.

It is disturbing that in the aftermath of the financial crash, the global financial system continues to operate, for the most part, as it did before. The relatively few reforms that have been made have focused on the scale – 'too big to fail' – issue, while ignoring the other half of the equation, which is the sheer speed, or velocity, at which money flows through the system. Speculative capital flows just as freely and rapidly between markets, and stocks and derivatives are traded on a massive scale in milliseconds by automated computer systems that operate with little oversight and periodically fail. Although banks are now required to hold more capital in reserve through the Basel 3 Accord, this is like increasing the size of a car's airbags in the event of a crash, while doing nothing to limit the speed – which is the real danger. Indeed, the global regulatory environment resembles a giant 'lubrication' system, with no braking capacity. In this frictionless world, bank executives are still encouraged to take excessive risks through extremely generous bonus payments that bear little relation to their company's long-term performance, let alone their contribution to society. The gap between Wall Street and the rest of America has never been greater,' observed former deputy Treasury secretary, Roger Altman. More broadly, the entire global system is still dominated – and dependent on – a handful of institutions that are so big they represent an unacceptable 'systemic risk'. Meanwhile, many advanced countries remain at the mercy of oversized, bloated financial industries that threaten to destabilise their local economies.

Some might argue that this 'back to business as usual' scenario merely shows the resilience of the global financial system. The truth is, however, that the only reason the system survived was the massive injection of trillions of dollars that the taxpayers will be paying off for generations to come. As Paul Krugman observed, 'What happens when you lose a vast amount of other people's money? You get a big gift from the government.'[7] According to the IMF's 2009 World Economic Outlook, the outlay of advanced economies on capital injections, asset purchases, guarantees and liquidity provision amounts to a massive 30 per cent of their combined gross domestic product – that's $15 trillion. Mervyn King, governor of the Bank of England, aptly summed up the situation: 'To paraphrase a great wartime leader [Churchill], never in the field of financial endeavour has so much money been owed by so few to so many. And, one might add, so far with little real reform.'[8]

There is also the issue of fairness. Under the current system, the gains of financial innovation are privatised, but the losses are socialised. That is, bankers make millions by speculative dealing but when things go bust, it is the public that pays. It's hardly what Adam Smith and the forefathers of modern capitalism had in mind when they spoke of the inherent fairness and morality of the system. Rather, it is more like crony capitalism.

Moreover, if the global financial system does spin out of control again in the near future (which is a distinct possibility), there simply won't be enough money in the government coffers to bail out the banks again. They may just be left to fail. This would cause a run on the banks globally as depositors rushed to withdraw their savings, the impact of which would make the last financial crisis seem mild indeed. According to a report released in March 2010 by the non-partisan Roosevelt Institute, whose authors included leading economists such as Nobel Laureate Joseph Stiglitz, financiers and former federal regulators, 'Another crisis – a bigger crisis that weakens both our financial sector and our larger economy – is more than predictable, it is inevitable . . . In 2008–9, we came remarkably close to another Great Depression. Next time we may not be so "lucky" . . . What will happen when the next shock hits? We may be nearing the stage where the answer will be – just as it was in the Great Depression – a calamitous global collapse.'[9]

For reasons that I have attempted to outline in this book, there is a pronounced reluctance to recognise that in our desire to create a more efficient, stable and certain world we have created the opposite. We have created a 'brittle' world that appears on the surface to be slick and strong, like carbon composite, but is more likely to crack catastrophically under pressure – without warning. Ours is a world of sophisticated models and formulae that enable people to be wrong with infinite precision. Attempts by central banks and governments to smooth out the business cycle, by making it less volatile, have the opposite effect, by accelerating and magnifying the boom/bust cycle. So really big busts, like the one we experienced recently, happen more frequently. There used to be a gap of a few decades between financial crashes, as was the case between the 1929, 1966 and 1987 crashes, and the dot.com crash of 2000. But the recent global financial crash happened just eight years after the previous one, and it was a lot bigger. Things are speeding up. As Lawrence Summers, President Barack Obama's principal economic adviser, has warned, every few years 'for the last generation a financial system that was intended to manage, distribute, and control risk has, in fact, been the source of risk – with devastating consequences for workers, consumers, and taxpayers.'[10]

But can we absorb the lessons? The Nobel Prize-winning economist Vernon Smith conducted an experiment whereby some traders were asked to trade an imaginary stock among themselves. They soon bid up the price of the stock way beyond its real value until it became a speculative bubble and finally burst. The traders were then asked to start over and trade the same stock again, knowing full well what had happened last time. The result? They did exactly the same thing again, but this time the velocity at which the bubble was created was much greater. 'We think we can beat the crowd,' says Smith. 'But we are the crowd.'[11] The implications of this experiment for our momentum-driven environment are as obvious as they are disturbing, and are borne out by recent experience.

Martin Wolf, the chief economic commentator at the *Financial Times*, summed up the dilemma:

Trying to make financial systems safer has made them more perilous. Today, as a result, neither market discipline nor regulation is effective. There is a danger, therefore, that this rescue will lead to still greater risk-taking and an even worse crisis at some point in the not too distant future. Either we impose a credible threat of bankruptcy, or institutions we have to support are made safer, or, better, we have both of these. Open-ended insurance of weakly regulated institutions that take complex gambles is intolerable. We dare not return to business as usual. It is as simple – and brutal – as that.[12]

The post-equilibrium world

In highlighting these issues, my intention is not to question the legitimacy of capitalism, which has helped raise standards of living for billions of people. Nor am I suggesting we take a second look at the Soviets' Gosplan – their ill-fated attempt to control the economy through a central committee. But, to paraphrase Winston Churchill's observation about democracy, I do believe that 'capitalism is the worst economic system, except for all the others'.[13] The system has its flaws, and the biggest one, I would argue, is its vulnerability to destructive momentum. This is why capitalism should not be allowed to operate in such a highly deregulated (frictionless) vacuum in the hope that the forces of equilibrium will keep it in balance. We have seen where this thinking leads us. Similarly, with many other big issues we face, such as climate change, cyber warfare or nuclear proliferation, we cannot afford to allow destructive momentum to spin out of control in the belief that somehow things will automatically return to a state of equilibrium. In the words of Wendell Berry, a prominent American author, poet and cultural critic, 'There is a kind of idiocy inherent in the belief "that we can first set demons at large, and then, somehow, become smart enough to control them.' [14] We must acknowledge the reality that we live in a post-equilibrium world that will often require our pre-emptive intervention to ensure balance. For our civilisation is as fragile as glass.

It has also become clear that the discipline of economics, if it is to remain relevant in the twenty-first century, must evolve beyond its reliance on complex models that have little to do with actual human behaviour. It's time to put to rest that creature *Homo economicus*, whose fabled existence skewed so much of economic theory by perpetuating the myth that people are inviolably rational beings. The deepest truths about economics are to be found in history, psychology and literature, rather than in the acridly dry science of econometrics. Such truths are also influenced by morality, as Keynes wrote many years ago, when he described economics as a 'moral science' that deals with 'motives, expectations, psychological uncertainties'.[15] It is towards these humanist dimensions that economists must turn their attention.

More broadly, we should consider the impact of increasing centralisation and concentration. Every recent crisis – whether it be the global financial meltdown, intelligence failures, the Greek euro debacle, or environmental disasters – has resulted in greater concentration of power by the very elites who caused the crisis in the first place. So the banking system becomes even more concentrated, and the national security agencies become more integrated, and so on. But by centralising our systems, we make them more vulnerable to the power of negative momentum, or Big Mo, which feeds on such centralisation. Ross Douthat, writing in the *New York Times*, explained the problem this way. 'Taken case by case, many of these policy choices (i.e. centralisation) are perfectly defensible. Taken as a whole, they suggest a system that only knows how to move in one direction. If consolidation creates a crisis, the answer is further consolidation. If economic centralisation has unintended consequences, then you need political centralisation to clean up the mess. If a government conspicuously fails to prevent a terrorist attack or a real-estate bubble, then obviously it needs to be given more powers to prevent the next one, or the one after that . . . But (these) fixes tend to make the system even more complex and centralised, and more vulnerable to the next national-security surprise, the next natural disaster, the next economic crisis . . . This isn't the end of the "too big to fail" era. It's the beginning.'[16]

Finally, we could learn a lot from the older, more experienced people in our community and move beyond the youth-culture syndrome that has permeated society for the past fifty years, particularly in the West. It is no coincidence that one of the few people to predict the global financial meltdown was seventy-seven-year-old Warren Buffet, the billionaire investor and philanthropist. As early as 2003 he said that financial derivatives were weapons of mass destruction and would lead to a collapse.[17] The octogenarian George Soros also warned, for many years, of an impending financial meltdown. [18] There is no shortcut to wisdom and experience; it comes from a lifetime of observing what's important and what's not, and from separating reality from delusion.

According to Dr Lynn Hasher, a professor of psychology at the University of Toronto, recent studies suggest that older people have a wider focus of attention and retain a lot more information, which they can transfer from one situation to another.[19] 'A broad attention span may enable older adults to ultimately know more about a situation and the indirect message of what's going on than their younger peers.' Older people are also less susceptible to becoming swept up in fads and following the crowd. They are more likely to make up their own minds about an issue and act on it accordingly, even if it goes against the status quo. Whatever the reasons, we would do well to reacquaint ourselves with the ancient idea of 'councils of tribal elders', groups of experienced men and women who, through their unique perspective, can offer valuable advice about important issues – and steer us away from the short-term perspective that plagues so much of our contemporary thinking and behaviour.

Fortunately, as human beings, we always have a choice about our behaviour and direction. We also have a responsibility to ensure that this direction is the right one, for ourselves and our civilisation. We need to develop a wisdom that is commensurate with our power and impact on the world. An important step in this direction is for us to develop greater awareness of the nature of the momentum that is reshaping our world.

This book is an invitation to pull ourselves out of the current and stand on the riverbank for a while, to observe the mighty river that has been propelling us swiftly forwards. By doing so, let's hope that we may develop a greater awareness of the Zeitgeist of our era and learn to avoid the perils of surrendering to the flow.

Afterword

KEEPING QUIET

Now we will count to twelve
and we will all keep still.

This one time upon the earth,
let's not speak any language,
let's stop for one second,
and not move our arms so much.

It would be a delicious moment,
without hurry, without locomotives,
all of us would be together
in a sudden uneasiness.

The fishermen in the cold sea
would do no harm to the whales
and the peasant gathering salt
would look at his torn hands.

Those who prepare green wars,
wars of gas, wars of fire,
victories without survivors,
would put on clean clothing
and would walk alongside their brothers
in the shade, without doing a thing.

What I want shouldn't be confused
with final inactivity:
life alone is what matters,
I want nothing to do with death.
If we weren't unanimous
about keeping our lives so much in motion,

if we could do nothing for once,
perhaps a great silence would
interrupt this sadness,
this never understanding ourselves
and threatening ourselves with death,
perhaps the earth is teaching us
when everything seems to be dead
and then everything is alive.

Now I will count to twelve
and you keep quiet and I'll go.

Pablo Neruda

Acknowledgements

This book would not have been possible without the support of many people.

In particular I would like to thank my agent in London, Andrew Gordon, for his invaluable guidance, insights and support throughout the process. I am also most grateful to Ed Faulkner at Virgin Books who has been a great champion of *The Big Mo* and brought the book to the UK and European markets. Also to Davina Russell and Clare Wallis, whose mastery with words has helped the book enormously, as has the rest of the great team at Virgin Books. And special thanks to the brilliant Lyn Tranter in Sydney, for believing in the book from the start and making it all happen.

I am especially grateful to Lottie Horsman for being such a wonderful partner throughout the insular process of writing. And to Sue Stafford for being such a great and loving mum to Orlando. Many thanks too to Tom and Lizi Hill, whose ongoing support and guidance was invaluable, and to Fiona Blaszkowski for her insights and infectious enthusiasm.

I am indebted to many current and former colleagues at UBS for their candour and support for this project, and who have been generous with their time and observations.

Many others too, have contributed to this work either directly or indirectly, including my parents Joanne and Reuben Mendick, Clarence Roeder, Fareed Zakaria, Max Fulcher, David Hale and

Lyric Hale, Lord and Lady Leitch (Sandy and Noelle), Professor Paul Marsh, Barney Greer, Jon Kabat-Zinn, Janine Bavin, Professor Ray Norris, Shannon Bell, Wallace Dobbin, Jeff Beyer, Dr Adrian Cohen, Dr Carolyn Sein, Maggi Eckardt, Brian Bona, Kim McKay, Bill Miller, Lucinda Maguire, Rosalyn Maguire, Linda and Christoph von Graffenried, Rina Canonica, Nick Wright, Geraldine Paul, Caroline Denton, Surinda and DK Matai, Fiona Courtenay-Evans, Simon Bunce, Ruth Liley, Gabi Kueng, Beni Eggli, Tim Binnington, Denise Shaw, Tom York, Diana Hannes, Steven and Elizabeth Kennedy, Bob Stafford, John Dawson, Michael Roberts, Andrea Carla Baer, Michael Darling, Diana Hannes, Caroline Stewart, Lucia and Henry Wolanski, Nikola Sekalic, Lucy Messervy, Frank Fowler, Helen Corner, Kris Vail, Charles Dalrymple-Hay, Lynton Barber, Jenny O'Meara, Derryn Heilbuth, Peter Harris, Dr David Beales, Andrea and Jeffrey Mendick, Holly and Nick Saunders, Brent Roeder, Phyllis Roeder, Ken and Mary Betty Roeder, Beverley and Tim Fowler, John Barter and my family.

Notes

Introduction: A Mystery

1. Elroy Dimson, Paul Marsh & Mike Staunton, *108 Years of Momentum Profits*, research conducted on behalf of ABN Amro by the London Business School, February 2008. See also Steve Johnson, 'Ignore Momentum at Your Peril', FT.com, viewed 18 February 2008; Tom Stevenson, 'Momentum Buying Can Beat the Stock Market', *Daily Telegraph*, 19 February 2008; 'Grab the Moment Not the Momentum', *Financial Times*, 22 February 2008.
2. Elroy Dimson, Paul Marsh & Mike Staunton, *108 Years of Momentum Profits*.
3. Paul Krugman, 'Innovating Our Way to Financial Crisis', *New York Times*, 3 December 2007.
4. Steven Erlanger and Jack Ewing, 'Air Travel Crisis Deepens as Europe Fears Wider Impact,' *New York Times*, 17 April 2010.
5. *Forbes*, Global 2000 survey, 'The Biggest Companies in the World', 17 April 2006. www.woopidoo.com/reviews/news/companies-2006.htm

Part 1: The Flow

1. THE THRILLS AND PERILS OF THE FLOW

1. UBS annual and quarterly financial reports, 2005–7.

2. Interview with Hans Jurgen Schmolke, managing director of Metrinomics, on 21 April 2010. See also article by Steve Johnson, 'UBS Came off Worst in Crisis', *Financial Times*, 25 October 2009.

3. Claude Baumann, 'Retreat in Instalments: Banking', *Die Weltwoche* (in German), 3 September 2008.

4. Uta Harnischchfeger & David Jolly, 'UBS Vows Errant Unit Will Get Tighter Rein', *New York Times*, 24 April 2008.

5. http://news.bbc.co.uk/2/hi/business/7046152.stm. *IMF World Economic Outlook*. 'The Global Economy Continues to Grow Strongly', 25 July 2007. http://www.imf.org/external/pubs/ft/web/2007/update/01/index.htm.

6. Interview with investment bank trader, London, August 2008.

7. Graham Bowley, 'Origin of Wall Street's Plunge Continues to Elude Officials', *New York Times*, 7 May 2010.

8. *Prospects: The Quarterly Review of Comparative Education*, Paris, UNESCO: International Bureau of Education, vol. XXIII, no. 1/2, 1993, pp. 53–69. See also Karen Armstrong, *Islam: A Short History*, Phoenix, 2001; Maurice Lobard & Jane Hathaway, *The Golden Age of Islam*, Markus Wiener Publishing, 2004.

9. Sir Isaac Newton, *Philosophiae Naturalis Principia Mathematica*, Richardson, 2009; James Gleik, *Isaac Newton*, HarperPerennial, June 2004; www.grc.nasa.gov/WWW/K-12/airplane/newton.html. See also www.lightandmatter.com/html_books/1np/ch04/ch04.html

10. Quentin Skinner, *Reason and Rhetoric in the Philosophy of Hobbes*, Cambridge University Press, Cambridge, 1996; A P. Martinch, *Hobbes: A Biography*, Cambridge University Press, Cambridge, 1999; Auguste Comte, *Positive Philosophy of Auguste Comte*, Part I (1855), trans. Harriet Martineau, Kessinger Publishing, 2003; John Stuart Mill, *A System of Logic*, University Press of the Pacific, Honolulu, 2002.

11. James Surowiecki, *The Wisdom of Crowds: Why the Many Are Smarter Than the Few and How Collective Wisdom*

Shapes Business, Economies, Societies and Nations, Little, Brown, New York, 2004; Malcolm Gladwell, *The Tipping Point: How Little Things Can Make a Big Difference*, Little Brown, London, 2000; Philip Ball, *Critical Mass: How One Thing Leads to Another*, Farrar, Straus & Giroux, New York, May 2006.

2. THE EQUILIBRIUM DELUSION

The introductory analogy of the Millennium Bridge has been used before in John Cassidy's excellent book *How Markets Fail: The Logic of Economic Calamities*, but my own application of it was purely serendipitous as I lived adjacent to the bridge and its stark symbolism had long been apparent to me.

1. Editorial: 'Greenspan Ignores Warnings: A Crisis Long Foretold', *New York Times*, 19 December 2007.
2. George Soros, *The New Paradigm for Financial Markets: The Credit Crisis of 2008 and What It Means*, Perseus Books Group, 2008, pp. 16, 48, 57.
3. Alan H Guth, 'Inflation and the New Era of High-Precision Cosmology', web.mit.edu/physics/alumniandfriends/physicsjournal_fall_02_cosmology.pdf; Kathy Sawyer, 'Expansion of the Universe Is Accelerating, Data Suggests', *Washington Post*, 27 February 1998.
4. Alan H Guth, 'Forecasting the Fate of Mysteries', special report, *Newsweek*, 14 October 2008, www.newsweek.com/id/157518/page/3
5. Interview, Ray Norris, Sydney, April 2010.
6. *The Tech*, MIT newsletter online edition, 27 February 1998.
7. Clive Cookson, Gillian Tett & Chris Cook, quoting Lord May in 'Organic Mechanics', *Financial Times*, 26 November 2009.
8. Bob Herbert, 'Safety News for the Rich', *New York Times*, 19 October 2009.

9. Lucian Bebchuk & Yaniv Grinstein, 'The Growth of Executive Pay', *Oxford Review of Economic Policy*, 2005 21(2): 283–303. See also http://papers.ssrn.com/so13/papers.cfm?abstract_id=648682; Lucian A Bebchuk, Martijn Cremers & Urs Peyer, *The CEO Pay Slice*, http://oxrep.oxfordjournals.org/cgi/content/abstract/21/2/283

10. John Cassidy, *How Markets Fail: The Logic of Economic Calamities*, Allen Lane, London, 2009, p. 289.

11. Lucian Bebchuk & Yaniv Grinstein, 'The Growth of Executive Pay'. See also http://papers.ssrn.com/so13/papers.cfm?abstract_id=648682

12. www.neweconomics.org/press-releases/hospital-cleaners-worth-more-society-city-bankers-says-new-nef-research

13. Jason Zweig, 'Inefficient Markets Are Still Hard to Beat', *Wall Street Journal*, The Intelligent Investor, 9 January 2010. http://online.wsj.com/article/SB10001424052748703535104574646530815302374.html

14. Stephen Mihm, 'Why Capitalism Fails; The Man Who Saw The Meltdown Coming Had Another Troubling Insight: It Will Happen Again', Levy Economics Institute of Bard College, September 2009www.levyinstitute.org/publications/?docid=1190

15. www.csun.edu/~hfspc002/baud/;http://plato.stanford.edu/entries/baudrillard/

16. Herbert R Lottman, *Albert Camus: A Biography*, Ginko Press, April 1997; http://quotationsbook.com/quote/19059/

3. Non-Friction

1. Alan Greenspan, *The Age of Turbulence: Adventures in a New World*, Allen Lane, September 2007.

2. John Cassidy, *How Markets Fail: The Logic of Economic Calamities*, Allen Lane (Penguin), London, 2009, p. 82.

3. Ibid, p. 26.

4. Stephen Labaton, 'Agency's 04 Rule Let Banks Pile Up New Debt', *New York Times*, 3 October 2008.

5. Gordon Brown, 16 June 2004, speech at Mansion House, London, www.hm-treasury.gov.uk/speech_chex_160604.htm

6. George Monbiot, 'One Financial Meltdown, it Seems, is Just Not Enough for Gordon Brown', *Guardian*, 7 September 2009.

7. Andrew G Haldane, 'Rethinking the Financial Network', April 2009. www.bankofengland.co.uk/publications/speeches/2009/speech386.pdf

8. George Cooper, *The Origin of Financial Crises: Central Banks, Credit Bubbles and the Efficient Market Fallacy*, Vintage, October 2008.

9. 'The Financial Crisis: A Crash Course', *The Week*, 27 September 2008.

10. Thomas L Friedman, 'All Fall Down', *New York Times*, 26 November 2008.

11. Paul Krugman, 'The Market Mystique', *New York Times*, 26 March 2009.

12. James Pressley, 'Use Printing Presses to Pay Off Outstanding Debt', *Sydney Morning Herald*, 19 December 2008.

13. Thomas L Friedman, 'All Fall Down', *New York Times*, 26 November 2008.

14. Roger Lowenstein, 'Triple-A Failure: The Ratings Game', *New York Times*, 27 April 2008; Wachovia securities report, 4 June 2007. See also Sam Jones, Gillian Tett & Paul J Davies, 'CPDOs expose ratings flaw at Moody's', *Financial Times*, 20 May 2008.

15. Steve Lohr, 'In Modelling Risk, the Human Factor Was Left Out', *New York Times*, 5 November 2009.

16. *The Economist*, 'A Special Report on the Future of Finance', 22 January 2009.

17. Gillian Tett, *Fool's Gold*, Little, Brown, 2009, p. 162.

18. Ibid, p. 161.

19. Clive Cookson, Gillian Tett & Chris Cook, 'Organic Mechanics', *Financial Times*, 26 November 2009.

20. Albert Einstein (1879–1955), *Ideas and Opinions*, Bonanza Books, 1988.

21. David W Orr, 'Speed', *Conservation Biology*, vol. 12, no. 1 (Feb. 1998), pp. 4–7: www.jstor.org/stable/2387456
22. Sewell Chan, 'Global Crisis Leads IMF Experts to Rethink Long-Held Ideas', *New York Times*, 22 February 2010.

4. GORILLAS ON SPEED

1. Bank of International Settlements (BIS): www.bis.org/. See also New York Stock Exchange figures: www.nyse.com/
2. Linda Davies, *Into the Fire*, Twenty First Century Publishers, 2007.
3. Clive Cookson, Gillian Tett & Chris Cook, 'Organic Mechanics', *Financial Times*, 26 November 2009.
4. On LTCM near collapse, see Federal Reserve Bank of New York, www.newyorkfed.org/
5. 2002 Berkshire Hathaway Annual Report: www.berkshire hathaway.com/2002ar/2002ar.pdf
6. Ibid.
7. Ibid.
8. Tom Wolfe, *Portfolio* magazine, May 2007.
9. David Cho, 'Hedge Funds Mystify Markets, Regulators', *Washington Post*, 4 July 2007.
10. Paul Farrell, 'Derivatives, the New Ticking Time Bomb', *Marketwatch*, 10 March 2008.
11. Louise Story and Nelson D Schwartz, 'Pay of Hedge Fund Managers Roars Back', *New York Times*, 31 March 2010. See also story by Jenny Anderson & Julie Creswell, 'Top Hedge Fund Managers Earn Over $240 Million', *New York Times*, 24 April 2007. See also Louis Armistead, 'Hedge Fund Titans', *Sunday Times*, 1 July 2007.
12. Interview with David Hale, global economist, August 2009.
13. Nicholas Ferguson, quoted in 'Kill the Competition', timesonline, 5 June 2007.
14. Niall Ferguson, quoted at London Business School event on 2 July 2007. Source: Daniel Mackie, 'The Business of Making

Money: Private Equity's Strengths and its Increasingly Apparent Weaknesses', 5 July 2007.

15. Roger Cohen, 'The Filthy Rich are Different from You and Me', *International Herald Tribune*, 1 July 2007.

16. EADS purchase: Zawya, Middle East Business information. 5 July 2007. See also article by Thomas Landon Jr, 'Cash-Rich, Publicity-Shy, Abu Dhabi Fund Draws Scrutiny', *New York Times*, 28 February 2008.

17. Lawrence Summers, 'Funds That Shake Capitalist Logic', *Financial Times*, 29 July 2007. See also article by Lee Teslik, 'Sovereign Wealth Funds', Council on Foreign Relations, 18 January 2008.

5. THE PARADOX OF THE STRONG

1. Cheryl Pellerin, 'US Researchers Discovering What Makes Flu Viruses Lethal: Mouse studies offer clues about virulence of 1918 flu pandemic', 2 October 2006: www.america.gov/st/washfile-english/2006/October/20061002112409lcnirellep0.6752283.html

2. Report by Subir Lall, Roberto Cardarelli & Selim Elekdag, published in *IMF World Economic Outlook*, October 2008.

3. Albert-Laszlo Barabasi, Jennifer Frangos, *Linked: The New Science of Networks*, Perseus Books, 2003.

4. Robert Peston, BBC News, 15 September 2009.

5. Simon Johnson, 'Big Is Bad Again,' *New York Times*, 8 October 2009.

6. Tom Vasich, 'Epilepsy Marked by Neural "Hub" Network', 25 March 2008: www.universityofcalifornia.edu/news/article/17532. See also www.sciencecentric.com/news/article.php?q=08032552

7. Phillip Blond, 'Rise of the Red Tories', *Prospect* magazine, 28 February 2009.

8. Ibid.

9. Peter Cohan, 'Boeing's 787 Dreamliner Faces Another

Nightmare Engineering Delay', *Daily Finance*, 13 November 2009. See also Cohan's book, *You Can't Order Change: Lessons from Jim McNerney's Turnaround at Boeing*, Portfolio, December 2008.

10. Arnold Reiner, 'Pilots on Autopilot', *New York Times*, 17 December 2009.

11. Ibid.

12. Ibid.

13. Ken Bensinger & Ralph Vartabedian, 'Data Point to Toyota's Throttles, Not Floor Mats', *Los Angeles Times*, 29 November 2009.

14. Stevenson Jacobs and Bernard Condon, 'Wall Street Plunge: Cause Still Unclear To Regulators, Computer Trading Eyed', *Huffington Post*, 7 May 2010.

15. Bernard Donefer, 'Algos Gone Wild, Risk in the World of Automated Trading Strategies', *The Journal of Trading*, Spring 2010, Vol. 5, No 2: p. 31–34.

6. SYSTEMIC RISK

1. Duncan Watts, 'Too Complex to Exist', *Boston Globe*, 14 June 2009.

2. Steven Strogatz, 'Like Water for Money', *New York Times*, 2 June 2009. See also www.nzier.org.nz/Site/about/NZIER_Moniac.aspx

3. Duncan Graham-Rowe, 'Mapping the Internet', *MIT Technology Review*, 19 June 2007.

4. Wesley Clark & Peter Levin, 'Securing the Information Superhighway', *Foreign Affairs*, December 2009.

5. Marian Wilkinson, 'Crisis of Climate-Change Confidence', *Sydney Morning Herald*, 13 February 2010.

6. Intergovernmental Panel on Climate Change, 'Climate Change 2007', the Fourth IPCC Assessment Report.

7. David Brooks, 'Drilling for Certainty', *New York Times*, 27 May 2010.

7. Perpetual Prime Time

1. Alfred Rappaport, *Creating Shareholder Value: The New Standard for Business Performance*, Free Press, 1986.
2. Al Gore, *The Assault on Reason*, Bloomsbury Publishing, London, 2007, p. 17.
3. Gary Small (UCLA neuroscientist), *iBrain: Surviving the Technological Alteration of the Modern Mind*, Collins Living, 2008. See also Sharon Begley, *Train Your Mind: Change Your Brain*, Ballantine Books, 2007.
4. Americans spend eight hours a day on screens, according to Breitbart.com, 27 March 2009. See also Al Gore's book, *The Assault on Reason*, p. 6.
5. Paul Krugman, 'Decade at Bernie's', *New York Times*, 16 February 2009.
6. Frank Rich, *New York Times*, 22 February 2009.
7. Ibid.
8. President Participates in Social Security Conversation in New York: www.whitehouse.gov/news/releases/2005/05/20050524-3.html
9. Steven Pinker, lecture on the 'History of Violence' at UCSB's SAGE Center for the Study of the Mind, 15 January 2009.
10. Fareed Zakaria, *The Post-American World*, W W Norton & Company, 2008.
11. Roy Morgan Research, 'Journalists Strongly Oppose Government's Media Laws' (press release, 10 August 2006): www.roymorgan.com/news/press-releases/2006/541/>; viewed 24 June 2007. See also Margaret Simons, *The Content Makers: Understanding the Media in Australia*, Penguin Books, 2007.
12. Margaret Simons, *The Content Makers: Understanding the Media in Australia*, p. 326.
13. 'Views of Press Values and Performance: 1985–2007', Pew Research Center for the people and the press, 9 August 2007.
14. Media Reform Information Centre: www.corporations.org/media/; 'The State of the News Media', 2007, annual report

on American journalism: www.journalism.org. See also www.mediauk.com/

15. Interview with Errol Morris in 'Making Sense of Ambiguous Evidence', *Harvard Business Review*, September 2008, p. 53.

16. David Bauder, 'Jon Stewart Puts Spotlight on CNBC and Meltdown', Associated Press, *Washington Post*, 14 March 2009. See also article by Dave Smith, 'America Cheers as Satirist Delivers Knockout Blow to TV Finance Gurus, *Guardian*, 15 March 2009.

17. David Bauder, 'Jon Stewart Puts Spotlight on CNBC and Meltdown'.

18. Rachel Smolkin, 'What the Mainstream Media Can Learn from Jon Stewart', *American Journalism Review*, June/July issue.

19. Geoffrey Baym, '"The Daily Show" and the Reinvention of Political Journalism', 1 September 2004. See also Michiko Kakutani, '"Fake" Anchor Becomes Trusted Journalist in US', *International Herald Tribune*, 19 August 2008.

20. Rachel Smolkin, 'What the Mainstream Media Can Learn from Jon Stewart'.

21. Analysis provided by Advertising Age and Nielsen Online: www.stateofthemedia.org/2009/narrative_online_ownership.php ?media=5&cat=5#OnOwnTopSites2. See also Nate Anderson, 'Online Oligarchy Dominates Net News Coverage', 17 March 2008: http://arstechnica.com/news.ars/post/20080317; Who Owns the Media? www.pbs.org/independentlens/democracyon deadline/mediaownership.html

22. Rachel Smolkin, 'What the Mainstream Media Can Learn from Jon Stewart'.

23. William Falk, 'Should Old Articles Be Forgot?', *New York Times*, 28 December 2009.

24. Nicholas Carr, 'Is Google Making Us Stupid?', *Atlantic*, July/August 2008. See also Nicholas Carr's *The Big Switch: Rewiring the World, From Edison to Google*, W W Norton & Company, January 2008.

25. Nicholas Carr, 'Is Google Making Us Stupid?'

26. Richard Foreman commentary in *Edge: The Third Culture*, August 2005. www.edge.org/3rd_culture/foreman05/foreman05_index.html

27. www.pnas.org/content/early/2009/08/21/0903620106.full.pdf+html

28. John Tierney, 'The Madness of Crowds and an Internet Delusion', *New York Times*, 11 January 2010.

29. Paul Kedrosky, 'The First Disaster of the Internet Age', *Newsweek*, 27 October 2008.

30. Ibid.

31. Nicholas D Kristof, quoting Nicholas Negroponte, 'The Daily Me', *New York Times*, 19 March 2009.

32. Bill Bishop, *The Big Sort: Why the Clustering of Like-Minded America is Tearing Us Apart*, Houghton Mifflin Harcourt, May 2009.

33. Nassim Nicholas Taleb, *The Black Swan: The Impact of the Highly Improbable*, Random House, April 2007.

34. Marshall Van Alstyne & Erik Brynjolfsson, *Electronic Communities: Global Village or Cyber Balkans*, MIT Sloan School, March 1997.

35. Herbert Marshall McLuhan (1911–80) was a Canadian educator, philosopher and scholar; Marshall McLuhan & Lewis Lapham, *Understanding Media: The Extensions of Man*, Critical Edition, MIT Press, 1994.

Part 2: Behavioural momentum

8. The Coherent Domain

1. Jon Kabat-Zinn, *Wherever You Go, There You Are*, Hyperion, 1994.

2. The Goethe Society USA: www.goethesociety.org/pages/quotescom.html

3. Michael Kent, *Oxford Dictionary of Sports Science and Medicine*, Oxford University Press, 3rd edn, 2006.

4. J A Nevin, C Mandell & J R Atak, 'The Analysis of

Behavioral Momentum', *Journal of the Experimental Analysis of Behavior*, 39 (1983), 49–59: www.ncbi.nlm.nih.gov/pmc/articles/PMC1347882/pdf/jeabehav00066-0050.pdf

5. Research conducted on behavioural momentum by Bell, 1999; Grace, Schwendimann & Nevin, 1998; Podlesnik, Jimenez-Gomez, Ward, & Shahan, 2006; Podlesnik & Shahan, 2008.

6. Lynn McTaggart, *The Field*, HarperCollins, 2001, p. 180.

7. Paul Bloom, 'First Person Plural', *Atlantic*, November 2008.

8. Richard Thaler & Cass Sunstein, *Nudge: Improving Decisions About Health, Wealth and Happiness*, Yale University Press, 2008.

9. David Hume, *A Treatise on Human Nature*: http://davidhume.org/texts/?text=thn1

10. Walt Whitman: www.whitmanarchive.org/biography/walt_whitman/index.html

11. Paul Bloom, 'First Person Plural'.

12. Thomas Blass, 'The Man Who Shocked the World', *Psychology Today*, March 2002: www.psychologytoday.com/articles/200203/the-man-who-shocked-the-world. See also CNN article, Elizabeth Landau, December 2008:http://edition.cnn.com/2008/HEALTH/12/19/milgram.experiment.obedience/

13. Philipp Meyer, 'American Excess: A Wall Street Trader Tells All', *Independent*, 27 April 2009.

14. Tom Wolfe, *Bonfire of the Vanities*, Picador, August 1990.

15. Evan Thomas & Mark Hosenball, 'Cracking the Vault', *Newsweek*, 23 March 2009; Nelson D Schwartz, 'Bedrock of Swiss Banking Fractures', *International Herald Tribune*, 5 March 2009; 'US Fight Against UBS Intensifies', 5 March 2009: Swissinfo.ch; Haig Simonian, 'Diamonds in Toothpaste As Bankers Sought to Help', *Financial Times*, 22 February 2009.

16. Nelson D Schwartz, 'For Swiss Banks, an Uncomfortable Spotlight', *New York Times*, 3 March 2009.

17. David Segal, 'Wall St: A Financial Epithet Stirs Outrage', *New York Times*, 2 February 2009.
18. UBS Annual Shareholder Meeting, April 2008; Uta Harnischchfeger & David Jolly, 'UBS Vows Errant Unit Will Get Tighter Rein', *New York Times*, 24 April 2008.

9. THE RISE OF THE MOMENTUM SURFER

1. Joseph Heller, *Good as Gold*, Prentice Hall & IBD, November 1997.
2. 'A Week in the Markets', *Euroweek*, 22 February 2002, pp. 10–12.
3. Stephanie Baker-Said & Elena Logutenkova, 'The Mess at UBS', *Bloomberg Markets*, July 2008. See also Dirk Schütz's biography of Marcel Ospel, *The Master of UBS*, 2007.
4. *Forbes*, Global 2000 survey, 'The Biggest Companies in the World', 17 April 2006: www.woopidoo.com/reviews/news/companies-2006.htm
5. Camilla Cavendish, 'Disasters, not Masters, of the Universe', timesonline, 30 August 2007.
6. John Gapper, 'Wall Street's Bruising Musical Chairs', *Financial Times*, 15 November 2007.
7. Peter F Drucker, *The Essential Drucker*, Butterworth-Heinemann Ltd, 2007, p. 203.
8. Dr Janine Wedel, *Shadow Elite: How the World's New Power Brokers Undermine Democracy, Government, and the Free Market*, Basic Books, New York, 2009.
9. Tom Redburn, *A Rallying Cry to Claw Back Bonuses*, New York Times Dealbook, 28 January 2009.
10. David Segal, 'Wall St: A Financial Epithet Stirs Outrage', *New York Times*, 2 February 2009.
11. Carl Hulse, 'Candidates Put Premium on Momentum', *New York Times*, 17 January 2004.
12. Nicholas D Kristof, 'Earning A's in People Skills at Andover', *New York Times*, 10 June 2000.

13. 'Project for the New American Century': www.newamerican century.org/RebuildingAmericasDefenses.pdf

14. 'Project for the New American Century': www.newamerican century.org/iraqclintonletter.htm

15. Cullen Murphy, Todd S Purdum & Philippe Sands, 'Farewell To All That. An Oral History of the Bush White House', *Vanity Fair*, February, 2009, p. 68.

16. Bob Woodward, *State of Denial*, Simon & Schuster, 2006, p. 260.

17. Ibid. p. 455.

18. Richard Haass, 'Two Bushes, Two Iraq Wars: An Insider's View from an Advisor who Served in Both Administrations', *Newsweek*, 18 May 2009.

19. Interview with Richard Haass by Philippe Gohier, *Maclean's* magazine, 19 May 2009.

20. 'Mission Accomplished': www.whitehouse.gov/news/releases/2003/05/20030501-15.html

21. Bob Woodward, 'Doubt, Distrust, Delay: The Inside Story of How Bush's Team Dealt with its Failing Iraq Strategy', *Washington Post*, 7 September 2008.

22. Michiko Kakutani, 'A Leader Beyond Denial, as War Plans Flounder', *New York Times*, 7 September 2008.

23. Richard Haass, *War of Necessity, War of Choice: A Memoir of Two Iraq Wars*, Simon & Schuster, May 2009.

24. Scott McClellan, *What Happened: Inside the Bush White House and Washington's Culture of Deception*, Public Affairs, 2008.

25. Ron Suskind, 'Faith, Certainty and the Presidency of George W Bush', *New York Times* Magazine, 17 October 2004.

26. Paul Krugman, 'All the President's Enablers', *New York Times*, 20 July 2007.

27. Christopher Beam, 'Talk Good Now', *Slate*, 21 October 2009: www.slate.com/id/2233177/

10. The Difficulty of Dissent

1. Laura Sessions, 'Just Saying "No" is Not Easy for Some', *Washington Post*, 9 January 2008. Stanley Greenspan, Washington University Medical School. See curriculum vitae at www.stanleygreenspan.com/biography.html

2. UN News Center, 'Powell Presents US Case to Security Council of Iraq's Failure to Disarm', 5 February 2003.

3. Sarah Baxter, 'Powell Tried to Talk Bush Out of War', *Sunday Times*, 8 July 2007.

4. Cullen Murphy, Todd S Purdum & Philippe Sands, 'Farewell to All That: An Oral History of the Bush White House', *Vanity Fair*, February 2009, p. 121.

5. Ian Drury, 'Blair and a Deal Signed in Blood', *Mail* online, 27 November 2009: www.dailymail.co.uk/news/article-1231126/Iraq-inquiry-told-U-S-mentioned-link-Saddam-Hussein-hours-9-11-attacks.html

6. Tom Baldwin, Philip Webster, 'US State Department Official: Relationship Is One-Sided', timesonline, 30 November 2006.

7. 'Mandela Condemns US Stance on Iraq', BBC, 30 January 2003; http://news.bbc.co.uk/2/hi/africa/2710181.stm

8. Nick Assinder, 'Blair Battles "Poodle" Jibes', BBC, 3 February 2003.

9. Michiko Kakutani, 'An Ex-CIA Chief on Iraq and the Slam Dunk That Wasn't', *New York Times*, 28 April 2007; George Tenet, *At the Center of the Storm: My Years at the CIA*, HarperCollins, 2007.

10. Maureen Dowd, 'Better Never than Late', *New York Times*, 2 May 2007.

11. Jeffrey Goldberg, 'Woodward vs. Tenet: The New Intelligence War', *New Yorker*, 21 May 2007. See also Bob Woodward's review of Tenet's book in the *Washington Post*, 6 May 2007.

12. CBS *60 Minutes* interview with George Tenet: www.cbsnews.com/stories/2007/04/25/60minutes/main2728375.shtml

13. Mark Leibovich, 'George Tenet's "Slam Dunk" into the History Books', *Washington Post*, 4 June 2004.

14. Senate Intelligence Committee Report: http://intelligence. senate.gov/phaseiiaccuracy.pdf

15. Gene Healy, 'Why Saddam Did Not Give Weapons to Al Qaeda', Cato Institute, 5 March 2003: www.cato.org/ pub_display.php?pub_id=3017

16. Bob Woodward, *State of Denial*, Simon & Schuster, 2006, p. 280.

17. Press conference with Colin Powell aboard plane en route to Egypt, 23 February 2001: www.fas.org/news/iraq/2001/ 02/iraq-010224zsb.htm

18. Paul Krugman, 'Lifting the Shroud', *New York Times*, 23 March 2004. http://www.nytimes.com/2004/03/23opinion /23KRUG.htm

19. Al Gore, *The Assault on Reason*, Bloomsbury Publishing, 2007, p. 126.

20. Ibid.

21. Matthew Engel, 'US Media Cowed by Patriotic Fever, Says CBS Star', *Guardian*, 17 May 2002.

22. Walter Pincus, 'Prosecution of Journalists is Possible in NSA Leaks', *Washington Post*, 22 May 2006: www.washington post.com/wp-dyn/content/article/2006/05/21/AR2006 052100348.html

23. Gilbert Cruz, 'What Happened: Scott McClellan's What Happened', *Time*, 28 May 2008.

24. Richard N Haass, commencement address at Oberlin College, 2009: http://new.oberlin.edu/events-activities/commence ment/haass-speech-2009remarks.dot

25. 'Whistleblowers Honoured By Time: Magazine Names 3 Women "Persons Of The Year"', 22 December 2002: www. cbsnews.com/stories/2002/12/22/national/main534019.shtml

26. Martin Fackler, 'In Shift for Japan, Salarymen Blow the Whistle', *New York Times Global Edition*, 7–8 June 2008.

27. Stephanie Saul, 'Doctor Says Drug Maker Tried to Quash His Criticism of Avandia', *New York Times*, 2 June 2007: www.nytimes.com/2007/06/02/business/02drug.html. Note: in a follow-up statement Dr John B Buse set out to clarify his

current position on the matter. Refer *New York Times* article 2 June 2007: www.nytimes.com/2007/06/02/business/02statement.html

28. 'Time Names Whistleblowers as Persons of Year', 23 December 2002: http://edition.cnn.com/2002/US/12/23/time.persons.of.year/

29. Tom Nugent, 'Witness for the Whistleblowers: Soeken '64 Heals Those Who Fight for Right', *Valpo* magazine, Spring 2003: www.soeken.lawsonline.net/articles/witness.html

11. A New Age of Conformity

1. Solomon Asch experiments on conformity: www.experiment-resources.com/asch-experiment.html; www.simplypsychology.pwp.blueyonder.co.uk/ asch-conformity.html. See also Solomon Asch Centre www.brynmawr.edu/aschcenter/about/solomon.htm

2. Richard Thaler & Cass Sunstein, *Nudge: Improving Decisions about Health, Wealth and Happiness*, Yale University Press, 2008.

3. David Brooks, 'Greed and Stupidity', *New York Times*, 3 April 2009.

4. John Cassidy, *How Markets Fail: The Logic of Economic Calamities*, Allen Lane, 2009, p. 178.

5. Laura Sessions Stepp, 'Why Is It Hard for Adults to Say "NO"?', *Washington Post*, 11 December 2007.

6. A special report on financial risk, 'Why Some Banks Did Much Better than Others', *The Economist*, 11 February 2010.

7. Elizabeth Bumiller, 'We Have Met the Enemy and he is PowerPoint', *New York Times*, 26 April 2010.

8. David Sapsted, 'Failed at School? No, It was Merely a "Deferred Success"', *Telegraph*, UK, 20 July 2005: www.telegraph.co.uk/news/uknews/1494409/Failed-at-school-No-it-was-merely-a-deferred-success.html

9. Rebecca Camber, 'We're Living in a Land of Ghettos Bedevilled by Political Correctness, Warns P D James': www.dailymail.

co.uk/news/article-563346/Were-living-land-ghettos-bedevilled-political-correctness-warns-PD-James.html. See also *Independent* article: www.independent.co.uk/news/uk/ crime/ pd-james-criticises-political-correctness-in-policing-speech-819720.html

10. Ben Leach, 'Dame Kelly Holmes: Medals for All Culture Risks Generation of Bad Losers', *Daily Telegraph*, 22 July 2009.

11. Diane Ravitch, *The Language Police: How Pressure Groups Restrict What Students Learn*, Knopf, New York, 2003. See also www.foxnews.com/story/0,2933,85594,00.html

12. Scott Shane & James Dao, 'Investigators Study Tangle of Clues on Fort Hood Suspect', *New York Times*, 14 November 2009. See also Thomas L Friedman, 'America vs. The Narrative', *New York Times*, 28 November 2009: www.nytimes.com/2009/11/29/opinion/29friedman.html

Part 3: The Faces of Big Mo

12. THE MOMENTUM-DRIVEN COMPANY

This chapter draws heavily on a number of sources, and in particular, Malcolm Gladwell's essay 'The Talent Myth', published in the *New Yorker* on 22 July 2002. See also R Hogan, R Raskin & D Fazzini, 'The Dark Side of Charisma' (1990), in K E Clark & M B Clark (eds), *Measures of Leadership*, Center for Creative Leadership, Greensboro, NC; Ed Michaels, Helen Handfield-Jones & Beth Axelrod, *The War for Talent*, Harvard Business School Press, 2001; Keith Naughton et al., 'Who Killed Enron?', *Newsweek*, 21 January 2002.

1. Interview with London analyst, London, December 2009.
2. Geoff Gibbs, 'Enron Suffers Biggest Collapse in Corporate History', *Guardian*, 30 November 2001.
3. Robert Bryce, *Pipe Dreams: Greed, Ego, and the Death of Enron*, Public Affairs, 2004.

4. Jason Nissa, 'The Thing Is: Enron's "Smart" Guy Goes Head to Fed', *Independent*, 22 February 2004.

5. Robert Bryce, *Pipe Dreams*.

6. *Enron: The Smartest Guys in the Room*, written and directed by Alex Gibney, Magnolia Pictures. An HDNet Films Production.

7. Robert Bryce, *Pipe Dreams*.

8. Ibid.

9. *Fortune*, company ranking survey, 2000.

10. Keith Naughton et al., 'Who Killed Enron?', *Newsweek*, 21 January 2002.

11. Paul Maidment, 'How the Media Missed Enron', *Forbes* online, 30 January 2006 (quoting FT editor Richard Lambert on Enron).

12. Alexander Dyck & Luigi Zingales, 'The Bubble and the Media', essay featured in *Corporate Governance and Capital Flows in a Global Economy*, P Cornelius & B Kogut (eds), Oxford University Press, New York, 2002.

13. Malcolm Gladwell, 'Open Secrets: Enron, Intelligence, and the Perils of Too Much Information', *New Yorker*, 8 January 2007.

13. CELEBRITY MO

1. Ben Sisaro, 'Susan Boyle, Top Seller, Shakes Up CD Trends', *New York Times*, 2 December 2009.

2. Antonio Vargas, 'How a Villager Became the Queen of All Media', *Washington Post*, 20 April 2009.

3. The line orginally appeared in a catalogue for Warhol's exhibition at the Moderna Museet in Stockholm from February to March of 1968. It was reiterated by Warhol in 1975.

4. Frank Rich, 'In Defense of the "Balloon Boy" Dad', *New York Times*, 24 October 2009.

5. *The Lancet* on dangers of celebrity endorsements, 14 November 2003: http://news.bbc.co.uk/2/hi/health/3266829.stm

6. Jo Chandler, 'The Darkness of Truth's Heart', *Sydney Morning Herald* and *The Age*, 27 December 2008.

7. Nick Cullen, 'Sir Michael Parkinson: "Jade Goody Was a Wretched Role Model"', timesonline, 7 April 2009: http://entertainment.timesonline.co.uk/tol/arts_and_entertainment/tv_and_radio/article6048656.ece

8. Brandon Griggs & John D Sutter, 'Oprah, Ashton Kutcher mark Twitter "Turning Point"', CNN, 18 April 2009.

9. Bill Moyers on journalism and democracy: http://findarticles.com/p/articles/mi_m1058/is_8_124/ai_n19328405/pg_3/

14. Techno Mo

1. Global phone use facts and figures from GSM World: www.gsmworld.com/news/statistics/index.shtml

2. Environmental Protection Agency (EPA) United States, 'Pesticide Health Risks': www.epa.gov/opp00001/health/human.htm1. See also 'BlackBerry Service Problems', CNN Money, 18 April 2007.

3. NRDC Report, 'Poisoning the Well', August 2009: www.nrdc.org/health/atrazine/files/fatrazine.pdf

4. Geoffrey Lean, 'Danger on the Airwaves: Is the Wi-Fi Revolution a Health Time Bomb?', *Independent*, Health & Wellbeing, 22 April 2007.

5. Federal Communications Commission (FCC), 'Comparison of Specific Absorption Rate Levels in Mobile Phones': www.fcc.gov/cgb/sar/; Federal Communications Commission (FCC) 'Policy on Human Exposure to Radiofrequency Electromagnetic Fields': www.fcc.gov/oet/rfsafety/. See also report in AskMen: http://uk.askmen.com/sports/health_150/187_mens_health.html. See also SARS discussion paper: www.ofta.gov.hk/en/ad-comm/rsac/paper/rsac2-2002.pdf

6. Institute of Science in Society, 'Influence of Herman Schwan's Work on Mobile Phone Safety Limits': www.i-sis.org.uk/FOI3.php

7. Transcript from Dr George Carlo's Health, Social Services and Housing Sub-Panel: Telephone Mast Review, 26 February 2007: www.jerseymastconcern.co.uk/drcarlotranscript.html.

See also detailed analysis by Michael Bevington, 'Attitudes to the Health Dangers of Non-Thermal EMFs', January 2008: www.es-uk.info/docs/20080117_bevington_emfs.pdf; Institute of Science in Society, 'Non-Thermal Effects of Electromagnetic Radiation': www.i-sis.org.uk/FOI3.php

8. Larry King interview on CNN with Dr Devra Davis, director of the Center for Environmental Oncology at the University of Pittsburgh's Cancer Institute, Dr Keith Black, chairman of the Department of Neurosurgery and director of the Maxine Dunitz Neurosurgical Institute in Cedars-Sinai in LA, and Dr Paul Song, radiation oncologist. Aired 29 July 2008.

9. Precautionary memo on mobile phone cancer from Ronald B Herberman, MD University of Pittsburgh Cancer Institute: www.upci.upmc.edu/news/upci_news/072308_celladvisory.cfm. See also *International Herald Tribune* article, 24 July 2008: www.iht.com/articles/2008/07/24/business/cellphone.php

10. Geoffrey Lean (environment editor), 'Mobile Phone Radiation Wrecks Your Sleep. Phone Makers' Own Scientists Discover that Bedtime Use Can Lead to Headaches, Confusion and Depression', *Independent*, 20 January 2008. See also Karolinska Institute home page: http://ki.se/?l=en; B Arnetz et al., 'The Effects of 884MHz GSM Wireless Communication Signals on Self-reported Symptoms and Sleep: An Experimental Provocation Study'.

11. The Belgian school children report was a study conducted by Jan Van den Bulck, PhD, of the Leuven School for Mass Communication Research at Katholieke Universiteit, Leuven, in Belgium, which focused on 1,656 school children with an average age of 13.7 years in the youngest group and 16.9 years in the oldest group. Findings released 2008. Also see 'Teenagers' Use of Cell Phones After Bedtime Contributes to Poor Sleep', *ScienceDaily*, viewed 16 October 2008: www.science daily.com/releases/2007/09/070901073641.htm

12. Geoffrey Lean, 'Mobile Phone Radiation Wrecks Your Sleep'.

13. Dr Siegal Sadetzki, Tel Aviv University study, '"Cancer Link"

to Heavy Mobile Use', BBC, 18 February 2008. See also, 'Cellular Phone Use and Risk of Benign and Malignant Parotid Gland Tumors: A Nationwide Case-Control Study', *Am. J. Epidemiol.*, 15 February 2008, 167: 457–67; 'Heavy Cell Phone Use Linked To Cancer, Study Suggests', *ScienceDaily*, 15 February 2008: www.sciencedaily.com

14. Report by Dr Kjell Hansson Mild et al., 'Occupational Environmental Medicine' (2007) 64:626–32, published online first: 4 April 2007. See also article by Geoffrey Lean, 'Public Health: The Hidden Menace of Mobile Phones', *Independent*, 7 October 2007.

15. 'Mobile Phone Addiction in Teenagers May Cause Severe Psychological Disorders', 27 February 2007: News-Medical.Net. www.news-medical.net/?id=22245

16. '6473 Tests a Month. But at What Cost?', *Washington Post*, 21 February 2009.

17. Jerald J Block, MD, 'Issues for DSM-V: Internet Addiction', *American Journal of Psychiatry*, March 2008: http://ajp.psychiatryonline.org/cgi/content/full/165/3/306

18. A Pew Internet & American Life Project study, April 2010.

19. David W Orr, *The Nature of Design: Economy, Culture and Human Intention*, Oxford University Press, New York, October 2004.

20. Federal Communications Commission, Wireless Auctions Process: wireless.fcc.gov/auctions/default.htm?job=auctions_home

21. Report by Dr George L Carlo, chairman of Science and Public Policy Institute, to Eileen O'Connor, EM Radiation Research Trust, 14 October 2006.

22. Interphone Project: www.mmfai.org/public/interphone.cfm.

23. Market Wire and TMC, 17 May 2010: http://www.tmcnet.com/usubmit/-institute-health-the-environment-university albany-rensselaer-new-/2010/05/17/4791566.htm. See also University of Albany Press Release: http://www.healthand environment.org/wg_emf_news/7495

24. Richard Alleyne, 'Mobile Phone Study Reveals Cancer "Concerns" Over Heavy Users', *Daily Telegraph*, 17 May 2010: http://www.telegraph.co.uk/health/healthnews/7733586/Mobile-phone-study-reveals-cancer-concerns-over-heavy users.html

25. Clare Murphy, 'No Proof of Mobile Cancer Risk, Major Study Concludes', BBC News, 17 May 2010.

26. Tara Parker-Pope, 'Questions about Cellphones and Brain Tumours', *New York Times*, 18 May 2010.

27. Maureen Dowd, 'Are Cells the New Cigarettes?', *New York Times*, 25 June 2010.

28. WHO, European Commission, Luxembourg, 'Application of the Precautionary Principle to EMF': www.who.int/peh-emf/meetings/Lux_PP_Feb2003/en/

29. Eleanor Abaya & Fred Gilbert, 'University of Lakehead says "No to WiFi"', university magazine, Spring/Summer 2008: http://magazine.lakeheadu.ca/page.php?p=81&i=10

30. Geoffrey Lean, 'Germany Warns Citizens to Avoid Using Wi-Fi: Environment Ministry's Verdict on the Health Risks from Wireless Technology Puts the British Government to Shame', *Independent*, 9 September 2007: www.independent.co.uk/environment/green-living/germany-warns-citizens-to-avoid using-wifi-401845.html

31. Ecologistas, 'Wifi Technology and Its Risks': www.ecol ogistasenaccion.org/spip.php?article11598

32. Glastonbury 'Why WiFi?' campaign: http://glastonbury naturalhealth.co.uk/WhyWi-Fi.html. See also 'Mast Taken Down', BBC online; 'Mast Group Claiming Small Victory', 7 July 2006.

33. Associated Press, 'A Federal Appeals Court Reinstates Five Class Action Lawsuits Against Mobile Phone Companies. Phones May Pose a Risk for Kids', 21 March 2005: www.foxnews.com/story/0,2933,151017,00.html. See also article by Amanda Brown, 'Cell Phones Invisible Hazards of the Wireless Age', Common Ground, December 2006.

Further information about research into the potential health effects of wireless technologies:

'Heavy Cell Phone Use Linked To Cancer, Study Suggests', *ScienceDaily*.

Ashok Agarwa et al., 'Effect of Cell Phone Usage on Semen Analysis in Men Attending Infertility Clinic: An Observational Study', *Fertility and Sterility*, V. 89, issue 1, January 2008, pp. 124–8.

Anu Karinen et al., 'Mobile Phone Radiation Might Alter Protein Expression in Human Skin', web journal of BMC Genomics, 11 February 2008.

Iddo Genuth, Tomer Yaffe, 'Cell-Phone Radiation Can Cause Visual Damage', 25 July 2005: IsraCast.com

Douglas Fields, 'Mind Control by Cell Phone', *Scientific American*, 7 May 2008.

Rob Harrill, 'Wake-Up Call', *University of Washington Alumni Magazine*, March 2005.

Wireless Technology Research project (WTR) headed by Dr George Carlo, 1993–9, International Association of the Wireless Communications Industry (CTIA). See also 'Can Cell Phone Usage Lead to Cancer?', CBC News, 25 November 2003; Chris Oaks, 'Cell Study: Hazards are Real', *Wired*, June 1999.

Michelle McDonagh, 'Mobile phone safety guidelines "outdated"', *Irish Times*, 26 February 2008.

Dr Mae-Wan Ho and Prof. Peter Saunders, 'Confirmed: Mobile Phones Break DNA and Scramble Genomes', *Institute of Science in Society*, 17 January 2005. See also *Powerwatch* online magazine: www.powerwatch.org.uk/science/emhealth.asp

15. When Big Mo Finds God

This chapter draws extensively on a special report on faith and politics, 'The New Wars of Religion', *The Economist*, 3–9 November 2007.

1. Cover story, 'Is God Dead?', *Time*, 8 April 2006: www.time.com/time/covers/0,16641,19660408,00.html;

2. 'The New Wars of Religion', *The Economist*.

3. Titus Lucretius Carus (*c.99–c.55* BCE), *De Rerum Natura* ('Of the Nature of Things'), ed. E J Kenney, Cambridge University Press, 1977.

4. 'The New Wars of Religion', *The Economist*.

5. This idea of 'sacrifice of the intellect to God' ('*Dei sacrificium intellectus*', in Latin) is believed to have come from 'Suscipe' ('Offering of Oneself'), a prayer by St Ignatius Loyola. See: www.secondexodus.com/html/prayers/suscipe.htm

6. 'Muslims in Europe', country guide, BBC, 23 December 2005.

7. Timothy Samuel Shah, 'Born Again in the USA', *Foreign Affairs*, September/October 2009.

8. Report prepared for Rep. Henry A Waxman in 2004, 'The Content of Federally Funded Abstinence-Only Education Programs'. See also paper by Diane di Mauro & Carole Joffe, 'The Religious Right and the Reshaping of Sexual Policy: An Examination of Reproductive Rights and Sexuality Education', *Sexuality Research & Social Policy*: www.longviewinstitute.org/research/joffe/religiousrightand-sexuality

9. James Wagoner, president, Advocates for Youth, James Wagoner's blog, 1 November 2007: www.advocatesfor youth.org. See also articles in *New York Times*, 'Experts in Sex Field Say Conservatives Interfere With Health and Research', by Mireya Navarro, 11 July 2004; 'PUBLIC LIVES: An Advocate for the Sexual Health of the Nation's Youth', by Diana Jean Schemo, 20 August 2001; 'Critics Say Government Deleted Sexual Material From Web Sites to Push Abstinence', by Adam Clymer, 26 November 2002.

10. Nick Carey, 'Some Christians Keep Tithing Even As They Face Foreclosure', *USA Today* and Reuters, 24 September 2008.

11. Hanna Rosin, 'Did Christianity Cause the Crash?', *Atlantic*, December 2009.

12. Richard Dawkins, *The God Delusion*, Bantam Press, 2006, p. 344.

13. Griff Witte, Jerry Markon & Shaiq Hussain, 'Terrorist Recruiters Leverage the Web', *Washington Post*, 13 December 2009: www.washingtonpost.com/wp-dyn/content/article/2009/12/12/AR2009121201598.html

14. Maajid Nawaz, 'Why I Joined the British Jihad – and Why I Rejected It', *Sunday Times*, 16 September 2007.

15. Nasra Hassan, 'An Arsenal of Believers: Talking to the "Human Bombs"', *New Yorker*, 19 November 2001.

16. 'The New Wars of Religion', *The Economist*.

17. Christopher Hitchens, *God is Not Great*, Atlantic Books, 2007, p. 19.

18. Sigmund Freud, *The Future of an Illusion*, W W Norton & Company, 1989.

19. *The Economist* projections, 3 November 2007.

20. 'The New Wars of Religion', *The Economist*. See also Philip Jenkins, *The Lost History of Christianity*, HarperCollins, 2008. Also, Pew Forum on Religion and Public Life, held 14 May 2007, 'Global Schism: Is the Anglican Divide the First Stage in a Wider Christian Split?': http://pewresearch.org/pubs/484/anglican-split

21. Oscar Wilde, *The Critic as Artist*, 1891. See also Mark Lilla's book, *The Stillborn God: Religion, Politics, and the Modern West*, Knopf Publishing, 2007.

16. Enviro Mo

1. 'Fewer Americans See Solid Evidence of Global Warming', Pew Research Center, 22 October 2009: http://people-press.org/report/556/global-warming Zogby. See also www.zogby.com/news/ReadNews.cfm?ID=1783

2. Report on ExxonMobil Corporation, *Business Insight Zone*, 5 October 2007.

3. Jonathan M Samet, MD, MS & Thomas A Burke, PhD, MPH, 'Turning Science Into Junk: The Tobacco Industry and Passive

Smoking', *American Journal of Public Health*, November 2001: www.ajph.org/cgi/content/full/91/11/1742; Ken Silverstone, 'Smoke and Mirrors: The Tobacco Industry's Influence on the Phony "Grassroots" Campaign for Liability Limits', 19 March 1996.

4. David McKnight, 'Who Is Behind the Climate Deniers?' *WA Today*, 2 August 2008; Union of Concerned Scientists, 'Scientists' Report Documents ExxonMobil's Tobacco-like Disinformation Campaign on Global Warming: Science Oil Company Spent Nearly $16 Million to Fund Skeptic Groups, Create Confusion', press release, 3 January 2007: www.ucsusa.org/news/press_release/ExxonMobil-GlobalWarming-tobacco.html; David Michaels, *Doubt Is Their Product: How Industry's Assault on Science Threatens Your Health*, Oxford University Press, 2008; 'Former Tobacco Spin Doctor Supports Anti-Climate Change Groups': www.desmogblog.com/former-tobacco-spin-doctor-plays-cruel-climate-change-hoax

5. David McKnight, 'Who Is Behind the Climate Deniers?'.

6. The Global Climate Change Lobby, 'A 2009 report by the International Consortium of Investigative Journalists for the Center for Public Integrity': www.publicintegrity.org

7. A C Grayling, *Descartes: The Life of René Descartes and Its Place in His Times*, Free Press, 2005.

8. David Bohm, *Unfolding Meaning: A Weekend of Dialogue with David Bohm*, Routledge, 1996.

9. Interview with Kim McKay in Sydney, Australia, January 2009.

10. David Michaels, *Doubt Is Their Product: How Industry's Assault on Science Threatens Your Health*.

11. Paul Krugman, 'The Fire Next Time', *New York Times*, 16 April 2010.

12. Lester Brown, 'Global Temperature Near Record for 2002: Takes Toll in Deadly Heat Waves, Withered Harvests, and Melting Ice', Earth Policy Institute: www.earthpolicy.org/Updates/Update20.htm; Global temperature graph: www.global-greenhouse-warming.com/global-temperature.html;

Breitbart, 'Global Warming: Rise of 4.5°C if Pollution
Doubles': www.breitbart.com/article.php?id=070130144355
.3d4dht2o&show_article=1
13. European Project for Ice Coring in Antarctica (EPICA),
European Science Foundation: www.esf.org/index.php?
id=855x. See also Department for Environment, Food and
Rural Affairs DEFRA (UK), 'About Climate Change: Global
Facts and Figures': www.defra.gov.uk/environment/climate
change/about/g-gases.htm
14. Sir Nicholas Stern, *The Stern Report*, 2006.
15. Intergovernmental Panel on Climate Change, 'Climate Change
2007', the Fourth IPCC Assessment Report.
16. John Vidal, Allegra Stratton & Suzanne Goldenberg, 'Low
Targets, Goals Dropped: Copenhagen Ends in Failure',
Guardian, 19 December 2009. See also George Monbiot, 'US
is Culprit for Copenhagen Failure but Shifts Blame to China',
The Age, 24 December 2009.
17. Richard Gray & Ben Leach, 'New Errors in IPCC Climate
Change Report', *Daily Telegraph*, 6 February 2010. See also
'IPCC Errors: Facts and Spin', *Guardian*, 15 February 2010:
www.guardian.co.uk/environment/2010/feb/15/ipcc-errors-
facts-spin
18. John M Broder, 'Why Washington Can't Get Much Done',
New York Times, 10 June 2007: www.nytimes.com/
2007/06/10/weekinreview/10broder.html. See also article by
Felicity Barringer & Andrew Revkin, 'Gore Warns of
Planetary Emergency', *New York Times*, 22 March 2007.

17. POLITICAL MO

1. 'Historic Moment as Obama Sworn In', BBC, 20 January
2009: http://news.bbc.co.uk/2/hi/americas/obama_inaugura
tion/7839229.stm
2. Carl Hulse, 'As Voting Nears, Candidates Put Premium on
Momentum', *New York Times*, 17 January 2004:
www.nytimes.com/2004/01/17/us/2004-campaign-political

-memo-voting-nears-candidates-put-premium-momentum.html?pagewanted=1

3. Paul Vitello, 'Campaign Smears Reach a New Level: Warp Speed', Letter from America, *New York Times Global Edition*, 18 August 2008.

4. Arianna Huffington, 'OffTheBus: HuffPost's Citizen Journalism Project Gets a Name, and Gets Rolling', *Huffington Post*, 19 June 2007.

5. Ryan Lizza, 'Battle Plans: How Obama Won', *New Yorker*, 17 November 2008.

6. Kenneth T Walsh Interview, 'Obama Reaches Out to Critics and Republicans', *US News*, 13 February 2008.

7. John Rentoul, 'Defining Moment as Blair Wins Backing for Clause IV', *Independent*, 14 March 1995.

8. John Darnton, 'British Labor Party Sheds Marx for Middle Class', *New York Times*, 5 October 1994: www.nytimes.com/1994/10/05/world/british-labor-party-sheds-marx-for-middle-class.html?pagewanted=1

9. Scott McClellan, *What Happened: Inside the Bush White House and Washington's Culture of Deception*, Public Affairs, 2008.

10. Interview by Bill Moyers with Jon Stewart, PBS, aired on 11 July 2003.

11. Churchill speech: www.historyplace.com/speeches/churchill.htm

12. For full quote, view website of the Marshall McLuhan Centre of Global Communications: www.mcluhanmedia.com/m_mcl_centercomm.html

18. GEOPOLITICAL MOMENTUM

1. World Economic Forum: www.weforum.org/en/index.htm

2. 'The Global Realignment: The End of a US-centric world', *Washington Post*: www.secure-x-001.net/Secure-X.asp?Direction=Emerging.htm&Site=109&Portal=100&Inline=True&hidetop=true; See also Robert D Kaplan's article 'A Gentler Hegemony', in the *Washington Post*, 17 December

2008. See also Pew Research: http://people-press.org/report/569/americas-place-in-the-world. See also FareedZakaria, 'How Long Will America Lead the World?', Fareed Zakaraia.com, 12 June 2006. See also Global Powerhouse Barometer (GPB) published by *Washington Post* and *Newsweek*, 19 September 2007: http://blog.washington post.com/postglobal/drg/index.html

3. Newsweek global country rankings 2010: http://www.newsweek.com/2010/08/16/best-countries-in-the-world.html

4. Richard Haass, 'The Age of Nonpolarity: What will follow US dominance?', *Foreign Affairs*, May/June 2008: www.foreignaffairs.com/articles/63397/richard-n-haass/the-age-of-nonpolarity

5. Niall Ferguson, 'Complexity and Collapse: Empires on the Edge of Chaos', *Foreign Affairs*, March/April 2010.

6. Bob Herbert, 'When Greatness Slips Away', *New York Times*, 21 June 2010.

7. Niall Ferguson, *The Ascent of Money*, Allen Lane, October 2008.

8. Richard Haass, 'The Age of Nonpolarity: What will follow US dominance?'

9. Fareed Zakaria, *The Post-American World*, W W Norton & Company, 2008.

10. Gideon Rachman, 'America is Losing the Free World', *Financial Times*, 4 January 2010: www.ft.com/cms/s/0/3ef8f012-f969-11de-8085-00144feab49a.html

11. Voltaire (1694–1778) was a French author, humanist, rationalist and satirist: www.lucidcafe.com/library/95nov/voltaire.html

12. Francis Fukuyama, 'The Fall of America Inc.', *Newsweek*, 4 October 2008.

13. Katrinz Bennhold, 'As China Rises, Conflict With West Rises Too', *New York Times* and *International Herald Tribune*, 26 January 2010.

14. Clive Cookson, 'China Set for Global Lead in Scientific Research', *Financial Times*, 26 January 2010.

15. Gideon Rachman, 'Why America and China Will Clash', *Financial Times*, 18 January 2010.

16. Thomas L Friedman, 'America vs. The Narrative', *New York Times*, 28 November 2009.
17. Brandon Griggs, 'US at Risk of Cyberattacks, Experts Say', CNN.com, 18 August 2008.
18. 'Hillary Clinton Calls on China to Probe Google Attack', BBC, 21 January 2010.
19. Wesley Clark & Peter Levin, 'Securing the Information Superhighway', *Foreign Affairs*, December 2009.
20. Brandon Griggs, 'US at Risk of Cyberattacks, Experts Say'.
21. Maureen Dowd, 'Doubts about Certitude', *New York Times*, 15 December 2009.

Part 4: Changing Lanes

19. AVOIDING THE DARK SIDE OF MOMENTUM

1. Film synopsis: www.filmsite.org/twelve.html
2. Justin Wolfers, 'TiVo Economics', Freakonomics column, *New York Times*, 26 November 2008.
3. Roni Caryn Rabin, 'Talk Deeply, Be Happy?', *New York Times*, 17 March 2010.
4. Richard N Haass, commencement address at Oberlin College, 2009: http://new.oberlin.edu/events-activities/commencement/haass-speech-2009remarks.dot
5. G Pascal Zachary, 'Genius and Misfit Aren't Synonyms, or Are They?', *New York Times*, 3 June 2007.
6. John Lukacs, *Five Days in London: May 1940*, Yale University Press, 2001, pp. 217–18.
7. Dr Stephen Covey; A Roger & Rebecca Merrill, *First Things First*, Franklin Covey Co., p. 302. See also *The Habits of Highly Effective People*. See also *The 8th Habit*, www.stephencovey.com
8. Paul Krugman, 'Taxing the Speculators', *New York Times*, 26 November 2009.
9. Bob Herbert, 'Where the Money Is', *New York Times*, 13 January 2009.

10. David Brooks, 'The Power Elite', *New York Times*, 19 February 2010. www.query.nytimes.com/gst/fullpage.html? res=9506EFDE1031F93AA25751C0A9669D8B63

11. 'Wild Animal Spirits', special report in *The Economist*, 24 January 2009.

12. Michael Lewis and David Einhorn, 'The End of the Financial World as We Know It', *New York Times*, 4 January 2009.

13. Clive Cookson, Gillian Tett & Chris Cook, 'Organic Mechanics', *Financial Times*, 26 November 2009.

14. Michael Hirsh, 'Blame the Economists', *Newsweek,* 13 April 2010.

15. Frank Rich, 'No One Is to Blame for Anything', *New York Times*, 11 April 2010.

16. Howard Fineman, 'Eight Reasons America Is On Edge', *Newsweek*, 20 April 2010.

20. CONSTRUCTIVE MOMENTUM

1. Conversation with George Miller and Bill Miller, London, December 2006. Follow-up discussion with Bill Miller in April 2010.

2. Interview with Fiona Courtenay-Evans, London, July 2008.

3. Phillip Elliot, 'Obama: Systemic Failure in Detroit Incident', *Washington Times*, 29 December 2009.

4. Interview with Kim McKay, Sydney, April 2010.

5. Interview with Fiona Courtenay-Evans, London, July 2008.

21. THE BIG MO

1. David W Orr, *The Nature of Design: Economy, Culture and Human Intention*, Oxford University Press, New York, October 2004.

2. Ibid.

3. Presentation by Andrew G Haldane, titled 'Patience and Finance' delivered to the Oxford China Business Forum, Beijing, on 9 September 2010.

3. Paul Krugman, 'The Market Mystique', *New York Times*, 27 March 2009.

4. Phillip Inman, 'Financial Services Authority Chairman Backs Tax on "Socially Useless" Banks', *Guardian*, 27 August 2009.

5. Stephen Mihm, 'Why Capitalism Fails; The Man Who Saw the Meltdown Coming Had Another Troubling Insight: It Will Happen Again', Levy Economics Institute of Bard College, September 2009. www.levyinstitute.org/public ations/?docid=1190

6. John Arlidge, "I'm doing God's work". Meet Mr Goldman Sachs', *Sunday Times*, 8 November 2009.

7. Paul Krugman, 'Bailouts for Bunglers', *New York Times*, 1 February 2009.

8. Martin Wolf, 'How To Manage the Gigantic Financial Cuckoo in Our Nest', *Financial Times*, 20 October 2009.

9. Matthew Jaffe, 'Economists Warn Another Financial Crisis on the Way', *ABC News*, 2 March 2010.

10. Lawrence H Summers, 'Why American Families and Businesses Need Financial Reform', The White House Blog, 15 October 2009, www.whitehouse.gov/blog/Why-American-Families-and-Businesses-Need-Financial-Reform/

11. Rana Foroohar, 'Boom and Gloom', *Newsweek*, 9 November 2009. See also research by Reshmaan N Hussam, David Porter and Vernon L Smith, 'Thar She Blows: Can Bubbles Be Rekindled with Experienced Subjects?' *American Economic Review*, vol. 98, no. 3, June 2008: www.aeaweb.org/articles. php?doi=10.1257/aer.98.3.924

12. Martin Wolf, 'How to Manage the Gigantic Financial Cuckoo in Our Nest'.

13. Eric Hobsbawm and Jacques Attali, 'The New Statesman Essay – Democracy Can Be Bad For You', *New Statesman*, 5 March 2001.

14. David W Orr, *The Nature of Design: Economy, Culture and Human Intention*. See also www.poets.org/poet.php/prm PID/675

15. Letter dated 10 July 1938 from John Maynard Keynes to

R F Harrod and later republished in *Keynes's Collected Writings*. See also article by Robert Skidelsky, 'The Crisis of Capitalism: Keynes Versus Marx', *Indian Journal of Industrial Relations*, vol. 45, no. 3, pp. 321–35, January 2010.

16. Ross Douthat, 'The Great Consolidation', *New York Times*, 16 May 2010.

17. Berkshire Hathaway 2002 Annual Report.

18. Simon Carswell, 'The Age of Soros', *Irish Times*, 5 March 2010.

19. Sara Reistad-Long, 'Older Brain Really May Be a Wiser Brain', *New York Times*, 20 May 2008.

Selected Bibliography

Ball, Philip, *Critical Mass: How One Thing Leads to Another*, Farrar, Straus & Giroux, New York, May 2006.

Begley, Sharon, *Train Your Mind, Change Your Brain*, Ballantine Books, New York, 2007.

Bryce, Robert, *Pipe Dreams: Greed, Ego, and the Death of Enron*, Public Affairs, New York, January 2004.

Cassidy, John, *How Markets Fail: The Logic of Economic Calamities*, Allen Lane, London, 2009.

Damon, William, *Noble Purpose*, Templeton Foundation Press, Philadelphia and London, 2003.

Davies, Linda, *Into the Fire*, Twenty First Century Publishers, London, 2007.

Dawkins, Richard, *The God Delusion*, Mariner Books, New York, January 2008.

Soto, Hernando de, *The Mystery of Capital: Why Capitalism Triumphs in the West and Fails Everywhere Else*, Perseus Books Group, New York, 2000.

Derman, Emanuel, *My Life as a Quant*, John Wiley & Sons, Hoboken, New Jersey, 2004.

Eichenwald, Kurt, *Conspiracy of Fools: A True Story*, Broadway Books, New York, 2005.

Emerson, Ralph Waldo, *Selected Essays, Lectures and Poems*, Bantam Books, New York, 1990.

Flannery, Tim, *The Weather Makers: The History and Future Impact of Climate Change*, Text Publishing, Melbourne, 2005.

Gardner, Howard, *Five Minds for the Future*, Harvard Business School Press, Boston, Massachusetts, 2006.

Gladwell, Malcolm, *The Tipping Point: How Little Things Can Make a Big Difference*, Little Brown, London, 2000.

Gore, Al, *The Assault on Reason*, Bloomsbury Publishing, London, 2007.

Greenspan, Miriam, *Healing Through the Dark Emotions*, Shambhala Publications, Boston, Massachusetts, 2003.

Hamburger, Joseph, 'Intellectuals in Politics: John Stewart Mill and the Philosophical Radicals', *Yale Studies in Political Science*, no. 14, 1965.

Jacoby, Susan, *The Age of American Unreason*, Vintage Books, New York, 2009.

Kabat-Zinn, Jon, *Wherever You Go There You Are*, Hyperion, New York, 1994.

Kabat-Zinn, Jon *Coming to Our Senses*, Hyperion, New York, 2005.

Kindleberger, Charles, & Aliber, Robert, *Manias, Panics and Crashes*, John Wiley & Sons, Hoboken, New Jersey, 2005.

Kolbert, Elizabeth, *Field Notes from a Catastrophe*, Bloomsbury, London, 2006.

Larreche, J C, *The Momentum Effect*, Wharton School Publishing, Philadelphia, 2008.

Lukacs, John, *Five Days in London: May 1940*, Yale University Press, London, 2001.

McClellan, Scott, *What Happened: Inside the Bush White House and Washington's Culture of Deception*, Public Affairs, New York, 2008.

McConnell, Mike, 'Overhauling Intelligence', *Foreign Affairs*, July–August 2008, p. 49.

MacKay, Charles, *Extraordinary Delusions and the Madness of*

Crowds (1st edn 1841), John Wiley & Sons, New York, 1996.

McLean, Bethany, & Elkind, Peter, *The Smartest Guys in the Room: The Amazing Rise and Scandalous Fall of Enron*, Portfolio, New York, 2004.

McLuhan, Marshall, & Lapham, Lewis, *Understanding Media: The Extensions of Man: Critical Edition*, MIT Press, Boston, 1994.

McTaggart, Lynne, *The Field* (updated edition), HarperCollins, New York, 2008.

Mailer, Norman, *The Spooky Art*, Random House, New York, 2003.

Michaels, David, *Doubt Is Their Product: How Industry's Assault on Science Threatens Your Health*, Oxford University Press, New York, 2008.

Monbiot, George, *Heat: How to Stop the Planet Burning*, Allen Lane, London, 2006.

Orr, David W, *The Nature of Design: Economy, Culture and Human Intention*, Oxford University Press, New York, October 2004.

Rimmington, Stella, *Open Secret: The Autobiography of the Former Director-General of MI5*, Arrow Books, London, 2001.

Sheldrake, Rupert, *The Sense of Being Stared at and Other Aspects of the Extended Mind*, Arrow Books, London, 2004.

Soros, George, *The Crash of 2008 and What it Means: The New Paradigm for Financial Markets*, Public Affairs Books, New York, 2008.

'State of the News Media, 2007, The,' annual report on American journalism, www.journalism.org

Surowiecki, James, *The Wisdom of Crowds: Why the Many Are Smarter Than the Few and How Collective Wisdom Shapes Business, Economies, Societies and Nations*, Little, Brown, New York, 2004.

Thaler, Richard, & Sunstein, Cass, *Nudge: Improving Decisions About Health, Wealth and Happiness* (updated version), Penguin Books, London, 2009.

Woodward, Bob, *Bush at War; Part III: State of Denial*, Simon & Schuster, New York, 2006.

Zakaria, Fareed, *The Future of Freedom: Liberal Democracy at Home and Abroad*, WW Norton & Company, New York, 2003.

Zakaria, Fareed, *The Post-American World*, WW Norton & Company, New York, 2008.

Index